Reviewers' Comments

Carol L. Stimmel casts a wide net to explore innovation, collaboration, and performance across natural and human-constructed systems. She pulls together useful and usable examples to encourage businesses to look beyond the current ways of thinking about product-focused organizational structures, roles, and processes. It is important for business leaders and product teams to consider her call to look beyond the ways everyone thinks innovation happens to be open to the sometimes messy, imprecise, and unexpected results of openness and flexibility. Loosening the grip of metrics and trendy methodologies can make us uncomfortable but creates possibilities that might be missed when rigidity rules.

— Lyn Bain
UX Strategy, Research, and Design
Chili Interactive, LLC

Carol L. Stimmel's OpenXFORM model incorporates natural systems (bio-empathy, animal form and function, diversity) and human-centric design processes (shared responsibility, interdependence) for achieving meaningful innovation in future tech. The framework anticipates organizational success while valuing individual dignity and worker satisfaction. Stimmel brilliantly derives her schema from Martin Luther King, Jr.'s exhortation to civil rights activists to persevere and maintain forward momentum. She incorporates elements from diverse fields (biology, anthropology, sustainability, law and intellectual property, economics, industrial and organizational psychology) to develop this new paradigm. OpenXFORM can serve as a framework for progress in design, engineering, business, manufacturing, entrepreneurship. This model is flexible and could easily be adopted by noncommercial organizations seeking to effect change: government agencies, educational institutions, and nonprofits.

— Sarah E. McCleskey, MA, MSLS
Head of Resource and Collection Services, Hofstra University Library

Until corporate leadership is ready to get out of their own shorts, the term "innovation" will remain a useless buzzword thrown around in Board Reports and advertising. True innovation requires abandoning fear. The fear of being wrong. The fear of giving up control. The fear of being uncomfortable in front of shareholders, Board members, and employees. That's not something most leadership is prepared to do. But that's exactly what's required. And that's exactly why massive industries continue to get disrupted. In *Evolving Innovative Ecosystems,* Carol lays out a detailed view into both the psychology and process required to escape that fear, understand the pain that drives true innovation, and create a leadership that embraces the primal energy that true innovation unleashes.

— David Mandell
Founder and CEO, Pivot Desk

Carol Stimmel applies exhaustive thought and research into her writing. I know after completing one of her works—whether a research paper, brief, or book— that I will walk away having learned something concrete I can apply to my own work. When I learned her latest would be on innovation—a word that has permeated our dialogue so much that it means everything and nothing at the same time—I knew it would be an important read. For any executive wanting to not only explore the role innovation can play in their organization, but learn how to harness it, I highly recommend Carol's latest.

— Brad Langley
Director of Marketing, Tendril

If you've ever spoken with Carol Stimmel, she made you think, made you challenge every assumption you had. It was not a confrontational challenge but neither was it placid.

This book is clearly Carol's: it makes you think. A simmering tension underpins nearly every paragraph: the tension of openness and innovation with corporate objectives and self-perpetuation. Even this book itself is in tension. When Carol writes, "Our digitally enabled society is faced with the colliding traditions of property ownership and the use of incentives for efficiency to increase profits," I think of her intellectual property within and wonder if she has written *Steal This Book* for the 21st century.

But tension it is. This book is a travel guide for the tightrope walkers of future tech. Free flowing information is indispensable for innovation, especially in multi-stakeholder undertakings such as smart cities. But what of the companies such as utilities that have invested billions of dollars building the infrastructure whence comes that data? Tightropes abound. And tightropes imply an appetite for risk.

My favorite sentence in the book is: "It is invaluable to be proven wrong." Is that counterintuitive? Certainly I like to know as soon as possible when I've turned onto the wrong Interstate. And what of rejoicing at being proven wrong? Can our results-oriented culture tolerate such humility?

Tension.

Carol faces head-on that innovation is often hands-on dirty work. Ideas are nice but solutions matter. This book includes a route map from idea to solution. Not an etched-in-stone path. Just as your phone gives you a detour when an accident occurs, the path to an innovation requires your willingness to *pivot*. To change routes when half-way there. To change destination if a better opportunity presents itself.

Finally, this book reminds us that innovation can be incremental, not always in grand scale. A series of incremental innovations has in one generation reduced AIDS from a death sentence to a chronic illness. Who made that happen? Countless mostly anonymous heroes. The fight against AIDS is far from over but the increments, in aggregate, are stunning.

Innovation isn't just cool. It's required of a world that produces enough food to feed all its inhabitants but has no idea how to get the food to those who are starving. It's required of a world where decreasing the digital divide implies energy consumption on a scale never imagined. Those and other challenges will not be met by extrapolating the past.

Here is a route planner to the future.

— *Bob Lockhart*
Vice President of Cybersecurity, Technology, and Research
Utilities Technology Council

Evolving Innovation Ecosystems

A Guide to Open Idea Transformation
in the Age of Future Tech

Evolving Innovation Ecosystems

A Guide to Open Idea Transformation
in the Age of Future Tech

Carol L. Stimmel

CRC Press
Taylor & Francis Group
Boca Raton London New York

CRC Press is an imprint of the
Taylor & Francis Group, an **informa** business

AN AUERBACH BOOK

CRC Press
Taylor & Francis Group
6000 Broken Sound Parkway NW, Suite 300
Boca Raton, FL 33487-2742

First issued in paperback 2022

© 2017 by Taylor & Francis Group, LLC
CRC Press is an imprint of Taylor & Francis Group, an Informa business

No claim to original U.S. Government works

ISBN 13: 978-1-03-247678-0 (pbk)
ISBN 13: 978-1-4987-6279-3 (hbk)

DOI: 10.1201/9781315153391

Visit the Taylor & Francis Web site at
http://www.taylorandfrancis.com

and the CRC Press Web site at
http://www.crcpress.com

Dedication

This book is dedicated to Rabbi Deborah Ruth Bronstein, a teacher of great compassion and an inspiration to many in her work for social justice. As my teacher, she taught me to set aside an attachment to rational explanation in exchange for enjoyment of the mysteries found in a single moment of contemplation that requires no justification.

Kol hakavod v'rav b'rachot

Epigraph

The Investigator who, in the name of scientific objectivity, transforms the organic into something inorganic, what is becoming into what is, life into death, is a person who fears change . . . in seeing change as a sign of death and in making people the passive objects of investigation in order to arrive at rigid models, one betrays their own character as a killer of life.

— Paulo Friere in *Pedagogy of the Oppressed*

Contents

Foreword

The word *innovation* has been so emptied of meaning that it now sits forlornly in the same pile of once-rich terms such as *paradigm, synergy leverage, disruptive,* and even *agile.* Once it becomes essential for everyone to at least pretend to understand the concept behind such a word, it soon enters the lexicon as required in every communiqué, memo, advertisement, corporate rah-rah speech, and résumé. Within months, if not weeks, it becomes nothing but punctuation—noticeable if it missing and essential to the organization of the words around it, but carrying no meaning at all itself. When everything is awesome, then awesomeness is reduced to the required minimum utterance to signal nothing more than a response. A grunt is just as useful. A new breakfast sandwich is declared innovative, and I suppose if your team spent two years designing its marketing, it is. But it's still just a sandwich.

So, more's the pity when an important discussion of innovation breaks the surface of all the noise below, because how does one talk about it without having to use the word? Indeed, put "innovate" in the title of a book or an article, and it might as well carry the subtitle, *TL;DR*[1]—*skim only.* For an author writing about innovation—and let me emphasize that it remains an *essential* concern across our civilization—the evisceration of the word demands a compelling and useful argument on *how* to innovate—not conceptually, but in concrete terms and stepwise directions.

The many benefits of capitalism obscure the often-damaging hunger of capitalism. To sustain the society that modern methods of production have given us requires continuously more efficient use of resources, capital, means of production, and, yes, innovation. And the continuing improvements in efficiencies of production perversely render the entire edifice of capitalism increasingly

---

[1] "Too long; didn't read"

more fragile, in turn demanding even more innovation for efficiency as well as new products and services.

In the technical world—and it's difficult to determine anything not affected by technology these days—efficiencies can be very elusive because measurement of innovation in thinking, in bringing new ideas and methods into utility for companies, is notoriously hard. How do you capture the rate of an idea catching fire? How do you quantify the effort of invention in virtual worlds? In future tech, how does one tell a good egg from a bad egg, and how does one accelerate incubation to get the thing hatched and into the pipeline of innovation?

Carol Stimmel and I have known each other a long time. Our experiences together—and here comes one of those damned words—have a synergy that, for my part at least, brings out the very best in my thinking. She is a challenger to settled thought—not just as a disruptive force, but as one that is creative, always planting seeds in what are often burned-over fields of old and accepted, um, paradigms. There is an energy to her approach to discourse about technology that is infectious and inspiring, and it is grounded and presented with sound and practical advice for application. She is not content with theoretical detachment. If what we're talking about can't find its way into praxis, then it won't attract the attention of anyone who is actually making things happen.

So, here's the book that makes things happen. In a lot of tech companies in my experience, innovation was typically used as a cover term for the infinite monkey cage trying to generate *King Lear,* rather than a directed activity that continually pruned and shaped ideas into useful practices and products. *Evolving Innovative Ecosystems* teaches innovators (and I am not using this term ironically) how to map the process and also how to make the compass or GPS or whatever is needed to navigate it—how to recognize waypoints, how to correct errors, how to invest the landmarks, and how to harvest from the new lands conquered. It's based on hard experience, learned research, and expert sources, well-seasoned with humor, anecdotes, and facts, and laid out as a linear path so that complexity builds in a logical and learnable manner.

You probably want to survive the future tech unknown that marches always slightly ahead, daring to starve out the laggards, dullards, and stragglers, not by sheer effort or size or capital or luck, but by methodical application of sound practices. That is precisely why you are reading this book.

But there are other reasons to be reading this book—moral reasons.

Innovation often springs from need, of course, but absent the necessity for some improvement, it can also come about by accident, or unintentional results, or serendipity. For example, the drug Prazosin, used to treat high blood pressure, was found to also help curb the symptoms of post-traumatic stress disorder in combat veterans. Treated for hypertension with the drug, veterans soon began to report in their therapy groups that nightmares occurred less frequently and that they felt calmer than they had in a long time. And how often have you or I repurposed some object in our household in a repair to save one more trip to the hardware store?

But for future tech, I think that perhaps too much motivation for innovation is driven by fear—the propulsive fear that drives capitalism in general—missing the market window. Sometimes this drive creates new products absent an actual demand, and so demand must be created through marketing to convince potential consumers that they *need* this new innovative thing. Certainly, our lives are better for having yielded to effective marketing—light bulbs are better than whale-oil lamps both for us and for Moby Dick's species—but often they are diminished when our impulses can't be curbed for things like UFO detectors or self-adhesive emergency moustaches or—my all-time favorite—an electrically controlled license plate that flips up to say "thank you" to automated toll booths as you drive away.

Would I characterize such "innovation" as immoral? I suppose context matters, and we all like to have a little frivolous fun now and then, but at some point those who wish to thrive in future tech markets are obligated to have some moral authority to not only do what they do, but in how they do it.

The best writing professor I ever had always posed this question about new work: is what you write *adding to the conversation?* If it's not, then what's the point? Implicit in this question is that whatever one produces, it should expand the discourse in a way that is beneficial to the art and to the participants, whether raising consciousness or adding knowledge or even just providing good entertainment. I think Carol's book asks and answers that question in terms of the innovative urge: will this add to, and benefit, the discourse that we call civilization?

Of course, business survival wraps all this artsy-fartsy notional discussion in a more brutal context. If we don't make money, then the "conversation" will soon be over, no matter how high the moral ground on which we stand. But this book at least adds morality to the conversation, whether we choose to examine it or not, and that's a rare, innovative, and, I hope, new direction for texts on innovation to start heading. This book puts forth the dialectic:

Q: What is to be done?

A: Innovate!

Q: For whose benefit?

A: (Your answer here)

Q: To what purpose?

A: (Your answer here)

Q: At what expense and to whom?

A: (Your answer here)

Q: How?

A: (Your answer here)

This is a book that will confront and subvert your thinking simultaneously. If you want to study it hard, you will learn and benefit. If you skim and dip, you will learn and benefit. Either way, this text will add to the conversation, *your* conversation.

So, get on with it. There is much to be done.

— Don Sherwood Olson
20 February 2017

Acknowledgments

This work, focused on innovation and collaboration in the field of future tech, began when I read Dr. Frances M. Magee's dissertation, *How Faculty at Undergraduate Institutions Incorporate Undergraduate Research in Their Work Lives* (Teachers College, Columbia University, New York, NY, 2014.) We hadn't seen each other for decades, and given my absolute ignorance and constant criticisms of higher education, I asked to read it. Why she consented, I have no idea. But I became hooked on the way she explored the topic because I could relate my own professional experiences to the phenomena she was examining.

One of the intriguing issues in her study on the nature of innovative practice in undergraduate institutions was that it focused *not* on the student beneficiaries, but instead on those faculty who facilitate it. While I confess I don't appreciate the nuances of the academy, I do understand how brilliant and important it is to turn entrenched ideas on their head, especially when it comes to the question of why and how people collaborate, share, and enjoin others to succeed even when they aren't compelled to do so. Francy's research gave me the inspiration to explore human-sense approaches to successful innovation in the sphere of future tech, where the complex forces of market economics and the corporate proprietary impulse too often frustrate the yearning of those who wish to create.

And Francy herself, now my wife, continues to encourage me every day with her sweet nature, persistence, and dedication to her life's work.

Finally, to this work itself, I owe a debt of gratitude to Don S. Olson. Don is an indescribably fine friend, in myriad ways that I would largely be embarrassed to fully portray. Suffice it to say, he has stress-tested my ideas over the years, tolerates my indiscriminate flights of fantasy, and never wavers in his dedication to me as a person and an author.

About the Author

Carol L. Stimmel is the author of several books, including three standard texts; syndicated research producer; analyst; and frequent speaker. She is the founder of Manifest Mind, LLC, which works to ensure that companies and investors have the information they need to make enduring investment decisions in the complex world of cleantech and sustainability. She is recognized chiefly for her two most recent publications, *Building Smart Cities: Analytics, ICT, and Design Thinking* and *Big Data Analytics Strategies for the Smart Grid*, and now *Evolving Innovation Ecosystems: A Guide to Open Idea Transformation in the Age of Future Tech.*

Since 2004, she has been exclusively developing, researching, and speaking on energy and cleantech topics, as a subject-matter expert on behavioral home energy management, the smart grid, home orchestration, data analytics, sustainability, and smart cities. She has participated in new ventures for most of her career, including engineering, designing new products, and providing market intelligence and analysis to new media and energy industry stakeholders. In 1991, years before "big data analytics" ever became buzzword compliant, Stimmel began working with massive streams of experimental flight data, hacking code and modeling 3D systems for meteorological and aviation research.

Carol has owned and operated a digital forensics company, worked with cutting-edge entrepreneurial teams, and authored many industry publications. Among other positions, she has served as Chief Advisor to Engerati, Vice President of New Ventures at Gartner, Vice President of Research at E Source, software and hardware product designer at Tendril, and Director of the Smart Utilities Practice at Navigant Research.

She holds a BA in philosophy from Randolph-Macon Woman's College and has satiated her curiosity by continuing coursework in various disciplines, including anthropology at the University of Virginia, professional studies at

Stanford in energy systems, and leadership at the Daniels School of Business. In early 2016, Carol received a merit fellowship from Clark University to attend the Master's program in International Development and Social Change, to finish in 2018. She is on the board of directors for Sangsangai, an organization dedicated to redeveloping villages in various parts of Nepal using a holistic approach that considers the needs for housing reconstruction, infrastructure, economic development, and environmental sustainability.

She has participated in many presentations and panels for private industry, international conferences, government interests, and public interest groups. She has also written for, provided background on, been interviewed and referenced by major media and industry outlets, including the BBC and the *Washington Post*.

Stimmel is known for her optimism, integrity, years of experience and personal scholarship, independent spirit, and ability to provide coherent and trusted insight into developing human economies, the built environment, and natural ecosystems.

Introduction

Conceptualizing Technology and Its Development: Where Innovation Begins

By its nature, technological process has always helped us get more of what we desire, and advanced technology has created an abundance of many goods—including books, music, 3D printers that can generate amazing creations, and virtual reality—as well as digitally enabled disintermediation, boxes of food, unregistered driving services, and instantaneous room reservations in a stranger's house across the ocean. By nearly any definition, innovation matters.

From an economic perspective, innovation is described as a new idea, process, or method that brings value to a firm and is seen as a driving force for growth. Yet the innovation process itself, especially within the digitally enabled knowledge economy, is fraught with peril. It doesn't help that a lack of consensus for how to measure and analyze innovation as the economy becomes more entwined with the forces of highly available (and often free) information limits those who wish to extract coherent principles to guide innovation investments.

But let's stick with the economic drivers of innovation for a moment: if we believe that technology innovation reduces scarcity and that economic opportunity is part and parcel the result of the monetization of scarce commodities, then we have a problem. We must admit that, in the long run within this classic model, the future's technological innovation may actually reduce—not enhance—economic opportunity. In thinking about technological progress, then, we must seek to understand if there are more coherent methodologies for measuring the relationship of innovation to growth in a manner that avoids a conflict of goals. There are two concepts in particular that must be examined in this regard: technical emergence and trajectory.

Technical Emergence

Technical emergence is a way of describing technological development. Academic researchers describe technical emergence as a framework from which we might examine how to extract certain characteristics of innovation that will help clarify technological development from the perspectives of change and progress. Assuming that today's technology processes are by definition more complex than they were during the industrial revolution, we are offered a view of technology innovation as a system that includes all the interactions among the elements of that system. Technical emergence could then be viewed as a cluster of synergistic agents. In particular, we can envision an environmental construct that might allow economists to identify macro indicators that would help them understand technological emergence properties scientifically. As mentioned previously, without a new understanding of the mechanisms of technical change, it is an impossible task to rationally understand the technology market, let alone forecast against it.

These same researchers have run into limits, though, because despite their theses that understanding emergent behaviors holds important clues for establishing a new way to measure technological change, they curiously and explicitly stop short of really grappling with emergence itself. It can sometimes be hard even to find a consensus definition. However, there are several important observations that will help in understanding how OpenXFORM was conceived, including that emergent phenomena cannot exist outside of its system (this is a marked difference from the typical view of many software engineers who employ generative modeling approaches in their designs). This underscores the remarkable problem of innovation measurability. In that spirit, researchers Alexander et al., in their work on emergent technology published by the IEEE, insist that, " . . . emergent phenomena cannot be isolated from the system—if one were to remove the agents exhibiting emergent behavior from their surrounding system, that behavior would change or would cease altogether."[1]

---

[1] Alexander, Jeffrey, Chase, John, Newman, Nils, Porter, Alan, and Roessner, J. David (2012, July). "Emergence as a Conceptual Framework for Understanding Scientific and Technological Progress." *Proceedings of PICMET'12: Technology Management for Emerging Technologies*. IEEE, pp. 1286–1292.

Perhaps this firm position is necessary to begin to make a beginning in developing new approaches to analyzing technology innovation, although as a result, we may only draw general conclusions. Admittedly, I do not feel that there has been sufficient guidance in this area, even if we do have the opportunity to navel gaze that an evolutionary perspective from biological sciences could somehow be helpful for economists to get "un-stuck" in our conflict.

If it indeed ultimately ends up that technology innovation does hold to something like genetic determinism, as Alexander and his research team asserted, then technology emergence might well be likened to speciation. As both an undergraduate who studied biological systems and as a sustainability and clean technologies researcher and analyst, I personally find the concept of speciation quite intriguing, as in the case of specific examples of ecological speciation, where reproductive barriers occur between members of a single species, ultimately resulting in an adaptive divergence. *In a world in which there are abundant resources of information, data, and content, innovations will emerge that claim the use of identical resources, but in wholly unrelated ways.* I spent many hours while writing *Building Smart Cities: Analytics, ICT, and Design Thinking*[2] wondering about this sort of problem; for example, with the exact same body of traffic flow data in NYC, I can chart the quickest route to the hospital between two points; or variously, I may use the data to tune the city's traffic lights for dynamic traffic flow mitigation. How do we share, use, manage, and engender new forms of value collaboratively?

Stan Metcalfe, Emeritus Professor at the University of Manchester, might agree with my thinking, as he so succinctly states in his discussions of human agency, technology, and the economy, "That a group of individuals may be party to the same information flow does not imply that they will experience the same changes in their personal knowledge."[3] Same resource, different technological trajectory.

Technical Trajectory

Technological trajectory is classically described by the innovation economist Giovanni Dosi as a way of capturing the phenomenon of cumulativeness within a particular cluster of innovations that represent a direction of advancement. This is one way, Dosi asserts, to begin to make sense of the difficulties of econo-

---

[2] Stimmel, Carol (2015). *Building Smart Cities: Analytics, ICT, and Design Thinking.* Boca Raton, FL: Auerbach Publications. ISBN-13: 978-1498702768.
[3] Metcalfe, J. Stan (2010). "Technology and Economic Theory." *Cambridge Journal of Economics,* vol. 34, pp. 153–171.

mists who seek to measure innovative activity on the basis of market demand, believing that those market dynamics themselves drive direct "innovative activity and technical changes."[4] With this concept of technical trajectory, Dosi sought to build some sort of bridge between two entrenched perspectives of technological change.

The first concept is that there must be some way to know not only what the market wants from technology but how to measure that a specific technology has met its demand (called *demand pulling*). The implication of this position is clear to any junior economist; if a firm ignores these market conditions, they aren't serving their market. They will likely fail. Or secondly, that there is a sort of "technology-push" reality in which, while economic facts may shape the innovative process, the linkages to innovative output are amorphous and uncertain. This is because the innovation process is so complex and intertwined that it is, in the end, autonomous from market changes. This is obviously unacceptable to an economist and, frankly, is perhaps why I find it so worthy of investigation. In large part, it is this idea that is the seed for what became OpenXFORM, the notion described in this book, sometimes negligently as a model, a framework, a concept, or just an idea.

Dosi is an optimist like me; I've often felt challenged by his work to think of a particular technology innovation with a limited set of possibilities, resting on the idea that there is an identifiable and select set of problems that exist within a field of enquiry (for example, smart cars, wind turbines, or mobile technology). Given the known drivers within a field, it should be possible to understand the direction or trajectory that a technology could take (and, based on the demands of the market, perhaps should take). In this way, it then becomes possible to extract some objective criteria of an economic dimension from understanding the trajectory itself. Furthermore, these trajectories imply that the emergence of a new technology will extend based on a known sequence, even if is disruptive.

In the end, my thirty years of work in the field of open-source engineering, engineering management, startups, large companies that overtly eschewed open concepts, boutique consultancies with aggressive marketing strategies, agile product management (and subsequent C-suite abuse), and a ceaseless study of theory have never offered me an explicit framework that specifically addresses how innovation can be well managed in the age of highly available, replicable ideas, data, and content abundance. **In my mind, it is absolutely clear that technological innovation must be viewed more holistically.** In the case that economists cling to the economic concepts of market demand being pulled

---

[4] Dosi, Giovani (1982). "Technological Paradigms and Technological Trajectories: A Suggested Interpretation of the Determinants and Directions of Technical Change," *Research Policy*, vol. 11, pp. 147–162.

around on the leash of scarcity, innovation output will remain largely unexplained by economic indicators, and breakthrough thinking (and its beneficiaries) will be the ultimate loser.

When traditional measures such as intellectual property and patents are used to measure innovation, we are all banking on an artificial scarcity that not only wastes knowledge, but is notoriously ineffective. Many are in search of a fresh and useful framework to measure new investment and record success. Therefore, the idea of defining clusters of innovations as within a system that shares characteristics with natural systems—such as the adaptive process of ecological speciation—not only holds special promise as a useful analogy, but may also already bring systems of measurement that will prove useful to those who wish to enhance their efforts for technological advancement.

And that is what I offer to you: OpenXFORM.

Section One

OpenXFORM: Evolutionary Model for Innovation

Chapter One

Reconsidering Information Freedom

Nelson Mandela burns his pass in 1960[1]

*For to be free is not merely to cast off one's chains, but to live in a way
that respects and enhances the freedom of others.*

— Nelson Mandela in *The Long Walk to Freedom*[2]

---

[1] Unknown. [1], Public Domain, https://commons.wikimedia.org/w/index.php?curid=
18560868, via Wikimedia Commons.
[2] Nelson Mandela (1995). "Nelson Mandela." Retrieved from https://en.wikiquote.
org/wiki/Nelson_Mandela.

1.1 Chapter Theme

Emerging innovations in the realm of future tech are not only changing the world, they are creating jobs for inventors and designers; and as they become accessible and affordable, we need people to build, distribute, sell, and service these products. They expand opportunities for many, including investors and companies that seek more adaptable forms of economic value and growth than offered by the tired tradition of invention that defines profitability by the height of a stack of inert dollar bills. Open data, content, and information may indeed be the key to mass innovation for future technologies, although they bring difficult challenges to private industry business models that depend on the established ideas of intellectual property.

1.1.1 The Costs of Tradition

Traditions can sometimes be hard to understand; they seem to carry a divine authority, although often the meaning behind the symbolism as well as the special significance can be lost as they are transmitted from generation to generation. They are passed down from our families and through our societies, with some imbued significance, although often we don't know exactly what; and even the most peculiar traditions are difficult for a society to leave behind. In Rome, for generations, they would feed the dead by pouring honey and wine into the grave of the deceased through a pipe; some cultures have intense body modification rituals designed to enhance beauty and mark status, such as neck stretching and other mutilations; athletes will provide Gatorade showers to their coaches to celebrate championship wins; while other societies have deeply entrenched caste or racial separation traditions. Some are quirky and hilarious, some are painful, and some may be dangerous, but perhaps none are as deeply-rooted as the tradition of "grandma's cooking."

The tale goes like this (in some variation): A newlywed is making her first big meal and decides to try her mother's brisket recipe. With great attention and care, she cuts off the ends of the roast and places the meat in the oven. The meal is a grand success, although her curious, but perhaps foolish, husband says, "What a wonderful meal, Blanche, but why do you cut off the ends of the roast? That is the very best part." "Because," she says, "that's the way my mother and her mother did it, and for generations my family cooks the brisket this way. And it is good, isn't it?" She provides further insight, "It must help the tough meat cook evenly, while keeping the moisture. Delicious, no?" The very next week, they are at her grandmother's house, where the elderly doyenne offers the young family the delectable brisket meal with the ends cut off. While the groom is accepting of the abridged meat, the young bride follows her grandmother into the kitchen and asks, "Nana, your meal was delicious, but why is it so good to cut the ends off? Is it because it helps it cook evenly?" Somewhat perplexed, Nana holds the bride's hand gently and points to the roasting pan drying next to the sink, "Darling, I could not fit it in the pan if I didn't cut the ends off."

Often unquestioned and blindly accepted, tradition can be a natural evolution of the desire to pass some value or special concept down through the generations, and it may even help societies remain bound together through songs and other practices. These practices might also be deliberately made up to create a system that promulgates some interest, be it national, personal, or political. The British Marxist historian E. J. Hobsbawm called this manifestation "the invention of tradition."[3] Invented traditions may be intended simply to help sell greeting cards on Ferris Wheel Day, or they may be used as political devices to assist in establishing legitimacy. In a modern day example, the first American Thanksgiving in 1621 most assuredly did not occur on a blanket somewhere in the northeast over a bowl of "traditional" gelled cranberry sauce from a can. In any case, invented traditions do provide an opportunity for the sweet bonds of common experience, but they may also distort the truth, even create disharmony or exaggerate and promote a bias toward a particular point of view.

There is no question that, for good or ill, the role of tradition is to reinforce a particular collection of values that provide the cohesion that creates continuity, identity, and solidarity within a community. We also have many traditions when it comes to creating prosperity in the world, including extensive ideas about the notion of *productive* or *wage* labor. Specifically, people work for dollars, and it is of key importance that their labor be as efficient as possible so that it can be measured positively as "productivity."

Largely, this efficiency has been judged in the tradition of "economies of scale," which divides what people do for their wages into smaller (as small as possible) units of productivity. Unfortunately, this approach also lowers the value of any individual worker, in terms of both their developed skills and their earnings potential. For example, one summer I worked on a lobster trawler. It was my job, and my only job, to band the claws of the captured stalk-eyed crustaceans and throw them in a bucket of water. I may have helped tie up the boat once or twice, or haul a trap, but even though I did this job for three months, one could hardly call me a lobster fisherman. Why? I never learned to navigate the fishing grounds or bait the traps (not my job), and I certainly didn't negotiate the state

---

[3] Hobsbawm, Eric J. and Ranger, Terrance, Eds. (1983). *The Invention of Tradition.* Cambridge, UK: Cambridge University Press.

and federal laws required to sell the capture. I may have worked a nauseating and smelly job, but I was just doing a job, I wasn't developing a skill. I was productive, but I was also a commodity.

Under a pure system of capitalism, advantage justifies the consequences of actions taken to gain that advantage, even if it means environmental damage, employee exploitation, nefarious contracts and agreements, and deception of its very customers. There is an aspect of capitalism that allows the divorce of production and distribution of goods from the humanity of the people that do the work, instead treating them as "units" of work completely independent of flesh and blood—more specifically, that a company is primarily an economic entity, not a social or human one, and thus the issues of companies are abstracted and isolated as purely about economic functionality. Avoiding the pitfalls of a discussion about capitalism as a framework, it is undeniable that capitalism requires us to treat the world as rational, predictable, and even mechanical. Otherwise, there is absolutely no reason for the stock market or the talking heads on Bloomberg TV. We use these economic calculations to direct our future investments, for one thing; and our societal traditions in a capitalist society dictate that we protect the idea of "economic growth" without end, and—unless we're gamblers—we must work to pay for our mortgages, the cars we drive, and the promotion of materialism to keep the economic engine running (that's why we have so many indices that reflect consumer spending).

1.1.2 Unconstrained Traditions

However, this book is not designed to discuss capitalism, other than to assume that we will exist in a capitalist economy for the foreseeable future, that the free exchange of goods and services will continue in some manner, and that this system requires rules for how we acquire resources. We can all, at least emotionally, agree that the marauding, unconstrained activity of the bankers who dealt the world the blow of the credit crisis of 2008 have done much to damage the capitalist system and opened it up to rules, regulations, and agreements that, like all rules, are made to be broken. But still, if untrammeled capitalism is noxious in many ways, it is the model that we rely upon to create prosperity, even if it is no longer considered legitimate by enlightened society to exploit employees, foster customer ignorance, and use lies and exaggeration to create value. More so, there is widespread and rapidly emerging recognition that society *does* care about how value is created and who or what is degraded in the process. But still, the fundamentals of capitalism remain unshaken—that the free exchange of goods is completely dependent on the principle that one party owns something someone else wants, and that they will acquire these goods through the rules of private property and ownership.

And thus, we finally come to the crux of the problem that this book hopes to address. It is not only to question the colliding traditions of property ownership and the use of incentives for efficiency to increase profit, but also to suggest a new way of thinking about how to mitigate the stresses brought about by our current system of production and distribution, which has been rocked by the exploding availability of information and knowledge in the connected world. The threat is real for any orthodox corporate entity that cannot face the fact that there is no need for the occupations of capitalist trade in a world where we can simply take what we want. Furthermore, if we persist in our traditional thinking that we achieve power through our information resources, our ability to rapidly innovate will diminish.

While we have been trained to believe that, to avoid market failure and collapse, it is an absolute condition for corporate survival that we hold private as many and as much of the assets that drive our business as possible, this does not make sense in a world of information abundance, in which it is cheap, if not free, and certainly not limited. After all, once this book is stored in digital form, it can be shared without end for zero further production costs and potentially near-zero distribution costs. It is quite possible that you acquired this work by pointing your browser to a site outside of a copyright regulated zone and downloaded it with no interference from an interface, upsell, or withdrawal from your bank account. In such a failing model, the writer or the producer of this work got zilch when you conveniently grabbed the book from your favorite free website, but that piracy did drive up the cost of the book without enhanced return to the creator or publisher. The truth, especially in industries that rely on information-based innovation for growth and survival, is simple; while many may strive to extract business value from intellectual property, the value can be diminished easily, or worse, lost in obscurity as other companies learn to become richly abundant in a post-information-scarcity world.

But let's be clear—for most of us, this isn't about dishonesty and stealing. Evidence, in fact, exists that piracy doesn't reflect a dishonest person or a propensity for online shoplifting. But the response from the industries that sell information resources directly don't map to the behavioral realities. Many companies use systems for digital rights management (DRM) that are designed to prevent the unauthorized redistribution of content by restricting the ways that consumers can consume it. In cultural observer Cory Doctorow's assessment of the strange state of copyright law, called *Information Doesn't Want to Be Free,* he describes how most consumers become illegal downloaders not to freeload, but because of frustration with digital locking schemes that can change their behavior in a sustained manner.[4]

---

[4] Doctorow, Cory (2015). *Information Doesn't Want to Be Free: Laws for the Internet Age.* San Francisco, CA: McSweeney's, pp. 32–33.

Doctorow recounts a Carnegie Mellon University (CMU) paper that reveals the impacts of contract disputes between Apple's iTunes and NBC that kept users from downloading DRM-protected NBC content from the iTunes portal. Not surprisingly, NBC content was downloaded with vigor from piracy sites. But most interesting, after the NBC content was again available through iTunes, the piracy rates stayed higher than they had been before the dispute. Among several conclusions about human behavior, a little nugget emerged that showed that once customers run into frustration with DRM schemes, they learn how to rip off the entire segment. Specifically, once they learned how to easily access and download the content they wanted, which they had previously been buying legitimately, they developed habits that persisted after the end of the blackout period.

From the authors of the study itself (with my emphasis):

> *[Our study found] that NBC's decision to remove its content from iTunes in December 2007 is causally associated with an 11.2% increase in the demand for pirated content. This is roughly equivalent to an increase of 49,000 downloads a day for NBC's content and **is approximately twice as large as the total legal purchases on iTunes for the same content in the period preceding the removal.***[5]

Furthermore, the study found that there was a statistically insignificant decrease in piracy when the content was restored to iTunes just nine months later. Well, they are still stealing, you might say. Technically, that is true, but the story isn't shared to judge iTunes users, but to demonstrate something entirely different about the unintended consequences of making money by controlling how and when customers can access content: that managing customer access and, by extension, DRM, doesn't do anything to reduce piracy once customers learn that they can avoid intermediaries to directly retrieve what they want. In fact, this study, at least, shows that it actually drove people to the exact opposite behavior. There is significant evidence not only that people are willing to pay for what they desire from artists, but that when it is made difficult or annoying to procure content, the exactly equivalent byte-for-byte, non-subtractable, same quality content is just a click away.

So why are companies cutting off the ends of their roasts when their pans are big enough to accommodate the whole? Because there is a traditional and

---

[5] Danaher, Brett, Dhanasobhon, Samita, Smith, Michael D., and Telang, Rahul (March 3, 2010). "Converting Pirates Without Cannibalizing Purchasers: The Impact of Digital Distribution on Physical Sales and Internet Piracy." Retrieved May 7, 2016, from http://ssrn.com/abstract=1381827 or http://dx.doi.org/10.2139/ssrn.1381827.

persistent belief among information-property-rights advocates that if they share their knowledge, data, or content, it will be depleted in some way that will destroy their business, if not collapse the entire capitalist system.

1.2 When the Herd Gets Hungry

The Tragedy of the Commons is a theoretical economic problem that describes how individuals will sooner or later exploit a shared resource to the extent that the resource will be exhausted, washed out, or completely destroyed, and hence unavailable for the whole. Essentially, it's an argument against sharing. This theory first emerged when an evolutionary biologist, Garrett Hardin, wrote a paper of the same name, "The Tragedy of the Commons," in the journal *Science* in 1968.[6] Specifically, Hardin was addressing the issue of overpopulation by discussing the adverse effects of overpopulation on public grazing land. The theory is in no way bizarre or outlandish on the face of it; in fact, it feels completely intuitive—if the population of grazing animals increases past the point that the grazing lands can produce food, the system collapses. There are countless examples of human self-interest producing this tragic outcome—overfishing, carbon pollution, and the dead zone in the Gulf of Mexico, which was created by run-off from over-farming along the fertile Mississippi River.[7]

So, let's allow Hardin to recap our rush to collective ruin: "Ruin is the destination toward which all men rush, each pursuing his own best interest in a society that believes in the freedom of the commons. Freedom in a commons brings ruin to all."

Of course, if it is true that people can be compared usefully to a grazing herd, then surely if too many people want the same thing, and there is only so much of that thing to go around, then without proper management that thing will run out, and the "herd" (the people) will starve. And that is indeed a tragedy. This story fits our traditional viewpoint that, in the face of chronic scarcity and contention, as Hobbes insisted, "the life of man [would be] solitary, poor, nasty, brutish, and short."[8] To prevent the tragedy, we must privatize or regulate the resource. One thing, though—should we decide that Hardin's model is correct, then rather than just shake our heads and quote curmudgeons from the mid-1600s, we must also accept that people will always act only in their

---

[6] Hardin, Garrett (1968). "The Tragedy of the Commons." *Science,* vol. 162, issue 3859, pp. 1243–1248.

[7] Tragedy of the Commons Definition (n.d.). Retrieved May 17, 2016, from http://www.investopedia.com/terms/t/tragedy-of-the-commons.asp.

[8] Hobbes, Thomas (1651). *Leviathan.* eBook available from Project Gutenberg https://www.gutenberg.org/files/3207/3207-h/3207-h.htm#link2H_4_0080.

immediate self-interest and are unlikely, to any great extent, to consider the collective benefits or impacts of their behavior. In other words, that life is indeed a zero-sum game. And if we are trapped, we might just as well go on enclosing, privatizing, patenting, slapping digital locks on all of our media, constructing gates and, for heaven's sake, give up the irrational unicorn-*cum*-socialist dream of building systems of trust and reciprocity upon which to re-form our capitalist markets to accelerate innovation.

But Hardin's tragic model just doesn't pass the herdsman's smell test. His theory and even his solutions make sense under some conditions, but as a lever with which to model more complex arenas of innovation—especially when such a tradition thwarts technological or medical advancements at the risk of human and environmental health—then something has gone very, very wrong. Believing that the resources of information, data, and knowledge just simply cannot be managed creates a false obstacle to managing for robust innovation in an increasingly complex and interconnected world. Charlotte Hess and Elinor Ostrom remark on the failure of Hardin's model (and others) in their very well-studied and evidenced edited work on advancing the *knowledge commons,* the term describing information, data, and content that is collectively owned and managed by a particular community of users. They write, "There may be situations where this model can be applied, but many groups can effectively manage and sustain common resources if they have suitable conditions, such as appropriate rules, good conflict-resolution mechanisms, and well-defined group boundaries."[9] This statement is as clearly true as it is liberal, and even more difficult to translate into a practice that demands measurable performance, as every profit-driven company must.

1.2.1 The Uncertain Relationship Between Collaboration and Scarcity

Indeed, there are innumerable examples of human collaboration in the face of resource scarcity, and in technology circles we frequently point to the successes of open source—the towering success of Linux, the Android operating system, the Firefox browser, the Apache HTTP server, and MySQL, among others. But what we don't like to talk about are the failures, and most open-source efforts fail. In 2011, Schweik and English, two researchers at the University of Massachusetts, measured the open-source projects hosted on SourceForge, the largest and oldest open-source repository, with the result that, "Among the

---

[9] Hess, Charlotte and Ostrom, Elinor (2006). "Understanding Knowledge as a Commons," p. 11. Retrieved May 6, 2016, from https://mitpress.mit.edu/sites/default/files/titles/content/9780262083577_sch_0001.pdf.

174,333 projects they reviewed, Schweik and English found they could assess success or abandonment for 145,475. Of that total, only one in six—17 percent—were successful. Almost half the projects (46 percent) were abandoned in the initiation stage—before the first software release. More than a third (37 percent) were abandoned after the initial release."[10] Although the researchers attempted to capture some of the common characteristics for the successful projects, what we don't know is why the others failed to thrive.

The serious researcher is forced to admit that what we do know about open source (and, where open source is a reasonable framework of success, open information and collaboration) is largely anecdotal, because there are few studies that actually question the relationship of conflict or collaboration and scarcity. Instead, collaboration is usually viewed as only one of many factors that influence how a community responds in certain conditions. As we will discuss, the sense that collaboration is just a side effect of some process may be a misperception.

If you are investor or a company leader, and this whole concept of the commons is making you nervous, please don't worry. It is not the *commons* that should be keeping you up at night, it's really the *"anticommons"* that should give you pause. The anticommons is a term used by Michael A. Heller when referring to "too many owners [who] are each endowed with the right to exclude others from a scarce resource, and no one has an effective privilege of use"—truly a tragedy, because imposing such scarcity impedes others from building upon important ideas.[11] Rajni Bakshi, Gandhi peace fellow, in her 2013 Gateway House piece, further discusses the uneasy relationship between the knowledge commons and capitalism, averring that the "excessive privatization of knowledge is stifling the quest for critical inventions and discoveries."[12] But Bakshi makes an even more important point in her exploration: if the principals and stewards of the capitalist model themselves—which is every entity that exists, thanks to free trade and profit—cannot find new ways to truly foster innovation, then capitalism itself will stagnate and fail.

---

[10] Gordon, Rich (2013). "Six Things to Know About Successful Open-Source Software," Northwestern University Knight Lab. Retrieved July 23, 2013, from http://knightlab.northwestern.edu/2013/07/24/six-lessons-on-success-and-failure-for-open-source-software/.

[11] Heller, Michael A. (1998). "The Tragedy of the Anticommons: Property in the Transition from Marx to Markets," *Harvard Law Review*, vol. 111, issue 3, pp. 621–688. Retrieved from http://repository.law.umich.edu/articles.

[12] Bakshi, Rajni (2013). "Knowledge Commons and the Future of Capitalism." Gateway House. Retrieved May 17, 2016, from http://www.gatewayhouse.in/knowledge-commons-and-the-future-of-capitalism/.

1.3 Transforming Anti-Innovation

In the interconnected world of knowledge and information, the potential for rapid growth is becoming inextricably linked to the fulfillment of human potential through technology, and the creative process is the economic engine that drives a growing and increasingly powerful social agenda to create jobs in a sustainable way. Innovation can transform the comic book dreams of future technology—complicated and expensive—into products from which many (the commoners) can benefit. And innovation is becoming easier and easier, as we learn to collaborate and create over a global network and share open technologies, data learnings, wisdom, and understanding. The testimony is there: two decades after Linus Torvalds started his Linux "hobby," and with the help of enthusiasts across the world sharing ideas and code, ninety-five percent of the top 500 most powerful computers in the world (not to mention many other computers, possibly including the mobile phone hooked to your belt) run Linux.[13]

Advanced cancer therapies, the credit card-sized computers that are running many of the sensors that make up the Internet of Things (see Raspberry Pi at http://www.raspberrypi.org/), and projects that are helping us understand the principles of physics at a subatomic level are changing the face of innovation from a smiling headshot of the VP of a research and development division of your favorite private company to one of the masses who contribute to massive collaborative projects built on a cultural framework first defined by the open-source movement. Emerging innovation in the realm of future tech is not only changing the world, it is creating jobs at a rapid clip for inventors and designers. Further, as new ideas become broadly accessible and affordable products, we need people to build, distribute, sell, and service them. Innovation of this nature can expand opportunities for all, including investors and companies that seek real economic value and growth.

1.3.1 Shared Knowledge Is Power

> *The day before something is a breakthrough, it's a crazy idea.*
>
> — Peter Diamandis[14]

The age-old adage often attributed to Frances Bacon, *"scienta potentia est,"* or "knowledge is power," says a lot about the advantages of not sharing what you

---

[13] List Statistics (n.d.). "TOP500 Supercomputer Sites." Retrieved May 16, 2016, from http://www.top500.org/statistics/list/.

[14] Socrates (2011). "Peter Diamandis' Laws: The Creed of the Persistent and Passionate Mind." Retrieved May 17, 2016, from https://www.singularityweblog.com/peter-diamandis-laws-the-creed-of-the-persistent-and-passionate-mind/.

know, especially in an infocentric society. Perhaps an even more pointed statement to this effect is the earliest documented version of this phrase, appearing in Imam Ali's 10th-century book, *Nahj Al Balagha,* in which he wrote, "Knowledge is power and it can command obedience. A man of knowledge during his lifetime can make people obey and follow him and he is praised and venerated after his death. Remember that knowledge is a ruler and wealth is its subject."[15]

The more liberal among us will surely argue that this concept is not meant to be taken so literally; that it begs us to educate and share knowledge so that all of us may enjoy the societal and personal benefits achieved by shaking off the chains of ignorance. Others will argue more philosophically, saying that the only true power known to humankind is knowledge, and everything of enduring value is derived only from it. Yet, when it comes to establishing competitive advantage, Imam Ali neatly packages the easy justification for why holding back knowledge to the select few may deliver some direct and very powerful advantage, especially in games of confidence and influence.

Before the age of data-driven markets, the concept of competitive advantage was naturally much broader and included any number of barriers, such as geographic location, scale for lower costs and higher profits, differentiated products and services, and myriad tangible and intangible resource-based benefits. But, as we fell headlong into the information revolution, these value-creators became more and more diminished as the importance of the knowledge-based organization prevailed. Then followed a full-blown quest to secure information property rights in markets where it became important to capitalize on new economic asymmetries that would create a positive imbalance of power, which could be bought about simply by virtue of one party's knowing more—that "something special" that would impact a transaction, speed a product to market, increase price, or provide an advantageous contract or negotiating position.

This hoarding of information is a force seen all around us in modern society: certain media outlets will disseminate particular information that helps them further the agenda of their ownership structure; mass surveillance programs hold back information from the public to assert some political or societal goal; exclusive schools may charge higher tuition that affords the affluent certain societal advantages; and, of course, financial market participants have been known to practice illegal insider trading based on privately known data about a company's future performance. Perhaps we got here honestly. After all, the information economy emerged from industrial marketplaces that are enabled by private property rights and the cost-management opportunities that arise from those rights.

As we discussed earlier, a sense of scarcity may cause the hoarding of information and data, but it is a sense of rivalry, which occurs when we prevent

[15] Nakshawani, Sayad Ammar (2014). *The Ten Granted Paradise.* Universal Muslim Association of America. ISBN: 0990374009, p. 186.

someone or something from using our resources, that is the very thing that property rights create. Rivalry, as applied to knowledge—especially digital information—is that moment when holders of information believe that if only their security is good enough, they can hold "it" in the same way as a physical object and extract profit similarly. Yet despite the failures exhibited by increasing levels of "file-sharing" violations and haranguing over DRM-driven contract disputes, these failures certainly haven't slowed down profit-driven organizations and government regulators the world over from working diligently to restrict the uses of information by intellectual property laws that provide the opportunity for the author of an invention or other creative work (or the organization that has the rights to the author's thoughts by contract) to protect the application of their novel idea. Old habits die hard for some, as certain younger companies emerge that, seeming to be unaware of this view of information and how it is produced, are gaining substantial capital investments by "going social" with their content.

1.4 Patents: The Protection Scheme We Most Adore

Protection schemes for information, seen especially in the economy surrounding patent documentation—filing the patent itself, arguing with the examiner, and of course, adjudicating patents after they are granted—are conceivably a multi-billion-dollar business. Patents have created big business across nearly every sector of the knowledge economy. Eric Goldman, a *Forbes* contributor who writes about intellectual property law, describes the problems that especially plague venture-funded startups that are exploited by so-called "patent trolls" with offers that can't be refused: ". . . pay me now or pay your lawyer many times that amount to prove you don't have to pay me. And large companies, especially in the smartphone industry, are paying literally billions of dollars to acquire patent portfolios to keep those portfolios from falling into the wrong hands . . ."[16]

The problem, it seems, is that we are overpaying for innovation because the overall system seems to be built on the idea that wherever we give up the right to prevent others from using our creation, we give up the right to recoup our investment in the development of that idea. This is the assumption that we are challenging here. Perhaps, in reality, the opposite of this assumption is emerging in today's knowledge marketplace—that, smartly managed, unlocking

---

[16] Goldman, Eric (2012). "The Problems with Software Patents." Retrieved May 10, 2016, from http://www.forbes.com/sites/ericgoldman/2012/11/28/the-problems-with-software-patents/.

information and collaboration could accelerate the pace of innovation to reach new heights through organizational structures that leverage altruism, reciprocity, and even free-ridership without trading in corporate value and profits.

Arguably, the walls built with the bricks of intellectual property stricture, especially the patent system, are a real drag on today's pace of innovation. The process as originally designed—generally considered to have begun with the Venetian Statute of 1474[17]—was meant to protect the true novelty of ideas and relies on a condition of nonobvious subject matter as a key condition for patentability. The US code—from which many of today's troubles spring—relates in part to nonobvious subject matter, stating (with my emphasis) that a patent may not be obtained if the ". . . subject matter as a whole would have been ***obvious at the time the invention was made to a person having ordinary skill in the art*** to which said subject matter pertains."[18] A patent must also have some sense of usefulness (utility) and should prevent the fantastic and hypothetical (for instance, a time machine); but this seems not necessarily to apply today, much to the relief of the obviously awesome Motorized Ice Cream Cone (known as US 5971829 A, granted in 1999), which sports a motorized cup spinner for eating ice cream or other similar malleable foods.

Patent examiners have had more of a challenge in their woeful wrestling with software programs, such as in granting the Amazon 1-click shopping checkout button, which transmits previously-entered payment and shipping information to process a credit card and ship an item (US 5960411, also granted in 1999)—an innovation likely worth billions in Amazon's sales and licensing fees (Apple licensed 1-click in 2000 and built it into iTunes, iPhoto, and the App Store). Even patents that arguably should never have existed are just part of the barrage of abstract overclaiming, especially in the area of software, where it has resulted in valuable protections for things like "moving data across a hybrid fiber-coaxial data network" or other situations where the claim is so non-obvious, expansive, or opaque that no one is entirely sure what it actually means.

Many of these patents are so imprecise that it is nearly impossible to avoid transgression, making it hopeless for a software developer trying to steer clear of a violation of use to negotiate the bounds of a patent to even know if they are offending. Patent lawsuits have gotten so extreme that even Jeff Bezos, CEO of Amazon and the winner of 1-click, said in 2012—when his company decided to make a foray into the mobile space—that even he was worried about innovation

---

[17] Venetian Statute of 1471. Retrieved August 13, 2016, from https://en.wikipedia.org/wiki/History_of_patent_law.

[18] USPTO (n.d.). 2141 "Examination Guidelines for Determining Obviousness Under 35 U.S.C. 103 [R-07.2015]." Retrieved May 10, 2016, from http://www.uspto.gov/web/offices/pac/mpep/s2141.html#sect2141.

being stifled by the system, stating that "Governments may need to look at the patent system and see if those laws need to be modified because I don't think some of these battles are healthy for society."[19]

The fact that software programs are a collection of instructions designed to implement an idea to carry out the objectives of the programmer (e.g., an algorithm or set of algorithms, a method perhaps, or even the demonstration of a principle) is considered by many experts (and even a growing number of courts) to be insufficient reason for patentability under existing rules, which seem to require that the implementation of those instructions be nonobvious. This is a difficult charge. Software, by its very nature a method for expressing instructions, is subject to rapid iteration and change (unlike mechanical innovation); and while there is clearly a long tradition designed to protect particular goods and services for some period of time, it seems abundantly clear that patent protection as a way to defend ideas ensconced in software is difficult.

In fact, mind-bending acrobatics are required even to try to assess the likelihood of a successful software patenting endeavor. The US Supreme court has left us with a bit of an eligibility test in its 2010 ruling in *Bilski v. Kappos* (561 US 593) in which Bilski applied for a patent on a method of hedging losses in one segment of the energy industry by making investments in other segments of that industry. Called the *machine-or-transformation test*, it asks that, to be patentable, a process either be tied to a particular machine or apparatus or transform an article into a different state or thing (turn a lump of rubber into a swath of leather, for instance).[20] In the case of software claims, to satisfy the first criterion requires more than the use of a generic computer, but require an acceptable connection to a specific computer. There is still no answer to whether software can be patented in the long term, but the path to protecting computer-implemented inventions is becoming increasingly narrow. Also, more and more, the question emerges whether it even makes sense to do so.

1.5 But, Copyrights—Where the Real Trouble Begins

In the world of future technologies, nearly every innovation will come at a rapid pace that already defies property and protection lines. There is profound and

---

[19] Reisinger, Don (2012). "Amazon's Bezos: Patent Suits 'Might Start to Stifle Innovation.'" Retrieved May 10, 2016, from http://www.cnet.com/uk/news/amazons-bezos-patent-suits-might-start-to-stifle-innovation/.

[20] Watson, James C. (2016). "What Ties to Particular Machines Render Patent Claims Eligible Subject Matter?" Trask Britt. Retrieved May 10, 2016, from http://www.traskbritt.com/what-ties-to-particular-machines-render-patent-claims-eligible-subject-matter/.

significant evidence that hoarding information no longer works when it comes to the kind of exponential growth in benefits we need from our research and development efforts—efforts that will unleash the kinds of discoveries and insights that are beginning to sprout up around us in the world of sensors, robotics, artificial intelligence, nanomedicine, life extension, renewable energy, and other heretofore unimagined enterprises. We have raised concerns about the weakening future of a patent strategy for protecting information-based assets, but copyright is about who owns the information, data, and source code—and maybe even your projects—that employ shared, licensed assets in the first place.

In essence, if you think that moving into an open and common approach to innovation is through the framework of open source, you might be right at least theoretically; but if you or your company does not create or adhere to licensing agreements made by participating in open-source projects, this action puts project collaborators and company assets at risk, even opening up the potential for liability claims.

Whenever software is created, it is automatically copyrighted under the terms of the Berne Convention,[21] which doesn't make it open or "free," but makes it protected under the provisions of the convention and its tenets. The work, such as software, even if it is not registered, enforces the copyright of authors from the signatory countries (the Berne Union) once the work is "fixed." This is part of the reason that open-source advocates claim that for software to be available for use by others it must be licensed. Even that is a tricky business, as there are many ideas and philosophies about freedom and openness, and some licenses even require an assignment of copyright to the project. License violators can be sued, participating companies may be asked to give up all their rights to their development of the openly available code under certain terms, and your bleary-eyed developers may even enter you into an agreement that puts the entire project or company at risk without anyone even knowing it.

It has become such a philosophical quagmire that today nearly any perspective can be protected with an open-source license, such as the GNU AGPL, GNU GPL, GNU LGPL, Mozilla Public, Apache, MIT, or Unilicense. If you are concerned about data or media, there are the CC0, CC-BY, or CC-BY-SA, or perhaps a new font that can be licensed via the Open Font License. If you're not sure, you can even mix them up. Because, as open-source adherents contend, knowledge should be free, entirely free, nearly free, open, libre, commons-based, in the public domain, copylefted, noncopylefted free. Choose one of the above.

Yes, it's confusing at first, but the open-source framework and a study of its evolution is instructive as we move toward defining practical models for

---

[21] Berne Convention (1886). Accessed August 13, 2016, at https://en.wikipedia.org/wiki/Berne_Convention.

open knowledge and collaboration. That is, it's all about defining a strategy for engagement that includes an honest assessment of your corporate strategy, what is core, and understanding that adopting open source is not about "getting stuff for free." If you want to build a quality and valuable differentiated product, then using open source allows you to invest more on innovation and differentiation when the basics of your software are already provided by a community invested in a development model in which rewards are available for all participants.

"Which license?" is the wrong question to start with. Why on earth would you want to deal with the thorny nest of legal obligations to a faceless swarm of developers? And I promise you, "Why not?" is not an answer. When you deploy some variant of open source in your commercial entity, you become part of a community, and you have the obligation to be a good citizen. When you choose open source (trust me, you already have; your developers use it to keep up with your deadlines and to produce higher-quality code), you change the way you perform many functions in your business and how you interact with the greater creative world. It changes how you spend your development money. It changes your product requirements. It changes your hiring strategy, your marketing approach, your public reputation, and maybe even your business model.

Some licenses are onerous, and for most commercially oriented companies, this is because their terms and conditions require derivative works to be licensed under the same license. However, the use of the most restrictive "copyleft" licenses has been declining since their peak in 2006, which may signal a very positive change indeed—indicating that startups and established vendors are driving the shift toward permissive licenses that make cohabitation between openness and commercial entities peaceful. Open-source licensing is out of the scope of this book but receives extensive treatment nearly everywhere that the nature of proprietary software is discussed. What is important is the philosophy of community development, how the open-source community made it work in many important cases, and what it means as we move toward an ever greater ecosystem of open data, information, knowledge, and collaboration.

1.6 Using This Book

The rich and vital field of open-source software has taught us that there is a massive global incubator for both ideas and their realization. With no barriers to entry except the development of programming skills sufficient to the task, nearly anyone can join in and make potentially huge contributions to the community. Open-source systems handle over half of all Internet traffic and are thought to generate tens of billions of dollars in revenue for the myriad companies who use them. What was born from altruistic and idealistic notions (or what Torvalds himself called a "hobby") turns out to be the modern-day capitalist's dream: tax-free labor, virtually free reproduction and distribution, and high added value.

Yet, if this sense of openness is indeed the key to mass innovation for future technologies, its prospects face difficult challenges driven by private industry business models around the ideals of intellectual property and creative culture that must be overcome if the required pace of advanced technology innovation is to continue.

In the world of future tech, we are facing an insatiable demand for information, knowledge, and application as we also face warning signs that our understanding and management of innovation are starting to falter because of a chronic underinvestment in innovation and the people who innovate. To try to make up for this difference, industry has begun to offer "prizes" to innovators, or to cynically leverage "crowdsourcing" as a way to develop new intellectual property. The negative potential of this strategy is not well understood, except that it is an approach that is surely self-limiting in its impact, when the first blush of getting the crowd to do your work begins to attract only mercenary talent.

We must ask whether the best and brightest among us, who thrive in inspired and creative collaborative (and intellectually challenging and politically anarchic) environments, are only attracted to this model? Or is it the very environment defined by the knowledge commons, fairly governed and actively supported, that will bring about the best from the brightest? Like the technologies of aviation, firearms, and the Internet before it, as a society we are beginning to witness that the way we "protect" intellectual property as a business model serves only to inhibit the rapid and required innovation in a world where technology silos and corporate interests are collapsing together.

There needs to be a new model, and with it new strategies for identifying problems, breaking them down into the right questions, directing resources in research and development, interpreting results, disseminating information, manufacturing and distributing products, and, yes, commercializing enterprises that can make it all work to their advantage. This book will define, explore, and provide practical approaches to applying open thinking and systems to our businesses. Together we will work to understand the profound and significant benefits brought to us by the philosophy of the knowledge-commons approach, in which information, data, and content are an accessible resource available to all—to the world of market-driven technology. As common as it is to create scarcity and rivalry for knowledge resources, one day it will be usual and predictable to work together collaboratively in a world where not just our things, but also our brightest minds, are connected.

Liberating information holds the promise to create new traditions in the world of innovation, one in which our common and everyday approach to how we work together in the age of rapidly accelerating technology will positively change the way we think, learn, do business, and live.

Chapter Two

What Open and Free Means to Innovation

Success is the ability to go from one failure to another with no loss of enthusiasm.

— Winston Churchill[2]

---

[1] By British Government. Photograph HU 55521 from the collections of the Imperial War Museums. Public Domain. Retrieved August 21, 2016, from https://commons.wikimedia.org/w/index.php?curid=3884379.

[2] Winston Churchill (n.d.). Quotation. Retrieved from http://quotes.lifehack.org/winston-churchill/success-is-the-ability-to-go-from/.

2.1 Chapter Theme

"Open" and "free" software are considered to be the progenitor of today's open ecosystem of data, information, and content. Yet these movements are still in the domain of human beings, which brings richness, confusion, and consternation to their philosophy and practices. As discussed in Chapter 1, many will freely admit that what we do know about open source and what it can teach us about working together in this type of a collaborative environment is largely anecdotal, because there are actually few studies that specifically examine the nature of collaboration in these environments and, further, how the development of these communities are born, die, handle conflict, and relate themselves to collaboration and capitalism. This chapter explores some of the circumstances that have brought forth the open and free software movements in the hopes of learning what and how we may carry their tenets forward.

2.2 Let's Talk Freely/Openly

For this book to be successful, it is important that the reader understand the differences between the concepts and traditions of "free software" and "open source," not only in practice, but in the historical and cultural impact both approaches have had on the many application domains that have benefitted from them. Free software and open source are not the same thing. This distinction has had a significant effect on software development, and it is vital to make clear what each is and is not.

- *Free software* may be run, shared, studied, and modified by anyone. The term also describes an organized social movement of individuals who advocate for the growing importance of sharing and cooperation in a progressively technology-driven society.
- *Open source* is made publicly available for modification or enhancement by anyone, but the term has also come to describe a development methodology that promotes collaborative participation and community development among contributors.

Both free software and open source express their principles through their recommended licenses; however, true free software activists focus on the ideals of how software should be shared, while open source advocates are more concerned with creating better programmers and better code. Free software adherents rigorously defend the liberties of software users by demanding unflinching adherence to their principles and practices by authors, to the extent of rejecting software that does not sufficiently respect their concept of freedom. Quite differently, open source is concerned with engagement of community, transparency, and communication as it relates to building great software by creating conscious communities of contributors.

One of the most powerful examples demonstrating the distinction between free software and open source approaches is raised by Richard M. Stallman (popularly referred to as RMS), self-described freedom activist, in his article, "Why Open Source Misses the Point of Free Software."[3] He discusses what he calls a malicious feature of software used by movie and record companies that is designed to restrict use of the content, called Digital Rights Management (DRM), which he euphemistically names Digital Restrictions Management. Not surprisingly, he asserts that DRM is antithetical to the "spirit of freedom" that free software affirms. Of course, DRM software would necessarily make it impossible or even illegal to modify the code through which the scheme is implemented.

However, there are open-source DRM projects with the goal of providing basic DRM functionalities that not only strive to answer the call of open content, but also seek to allow copyright holders to receive remuneration for their efforts. In the spirit of open source, they strive to create more powerful and reliable software that enables DRM—although it must be said that DRM projects are considered somewhat ridiculous even in open-source circles, but for technical and not philosophical reasons. Stallman, attacking the issue with perfect logical consistency states, "This [DRM] software might be open source and use the open source development model, but it won't be free software since it won't respect the freedom of the users that actually run it. If the open source development model succeeds in making this software more powerful and reliable for restricting you, that will make it even worse." Such an effort must be eschewed by free-software advocates, but it would not be under open source auspices, simply because someone has an interest in creating and distributing the technology under an open license and there may be a community of interested individuals who will build it. That is all that is required; there is simply no implicit or explicit ethical conflict.

When Mahatma Gandhi said, "The essence of all religions is one. Only their approaches are different," he certainly could have been speaking of the two prongs of free software ideology. Yet, despite their common enemy of proprietary software and a mutual endorsement and advocacy for software licensing that provides for software that is available to study, change, and distribute,

---

[3] Stallman, Richard M. (n.d.). "Why Open Source Misses the Point of Free Software." Retrieved May 31, 2016, from http://www.gnu.org/philosophy/open-source-misses-the-point.en.html. Licensed under Creative Commons CC BY-ND 4.0 2007–2016.

they still cannot unify as a consistent force because of their stark foundational schism. And these battles are often fought in the public view, where certain very vocal members of the two communities expend great effort denigrating each other's efforts. Is it any surprise that the open source and free software movements—and any movement that claims to adopt their philosophies—appear confusing, hostile, and arrogant?

The well-worn groove from business-minded technologists who want Free Software Foundation (FSF) advocates to lighten up serves to drive a further wedge between the two groups as they fight to maintain their independent perspectives; if the broader societal argument between accessible and proprietary software is heated, the debate about how to accomplish the goals of accessible software are even more impassioned (and too often disturbingly arcane) among the free and open tribes. Among the general constituency of software developers, though, whether one adopts the tenets of open-source production or the full-blown ethical system of governing moral principles for free software is likely decided much more by technical interest, curiosity, and practicalities than by a true understanding of how these ideas are symbolically reflected in the license guidelines pursued by the respective sides.

Many would hope that a unified theory of free and open software would emerge that would lend credibility to the idea of open software in widespread development projects, driving further open innovation and collaborative projects. However, the problem with a unification or hybrid approach seems to be impossible especially for FSF advocates, as it would necessarily include a dilution of the very principles of liberty that the FSF espouses and a potentially overly restrictive perspective for open source licensing that violates their own definition.

A deeper investigation of their various viewpoints will take us down a rabbit hole that so many have gone down before and not emerged in very good shape, but we hope to at least find ourselves with a useful, if not entirely novel, understanding of how these two movements need not be mutually exclusive. Open source advocates may argue that an emphasis on "freedom" discourages widespread acceptance, but it is not altogether clear that it has been handicapped by the FSF insistence on principles; the risk, however, is that a race to openness leaves behind a fully explored relationship between technology and users that may be more important now than ever.

2.2.1 Free/Open in Their Own Words

Open-source software (OSS) is defined as computer software with its source code made available *via a license* in which the copyright holder provides the rights to study, change, and distribute the software to anyone and for any purpose.[4] Alternatively, *free software* primarily emphasizes the liberty of the user, which demands rights regarding access to and use of software. Thus, it is sometimes called *freedom-respecting software, software libre,* or *libre software,* and is described by the FSF this way (their emphasis):

> *"Free software" according to the Free Software Foundation (FSF) means software that respects users' freedom and community. Roughly, it means that* **the users have the freedom to run, copy, distribute, study, change and improve the software.** *Thus, "free software" is a matter of liberty, not price . . . you should think of "free" as in "free speech," not as in "free beer."*[5]

To the naïve reader (which seems to be an extensive collection of people), the difference between these two definitions is not immediately apparent, but I hope it will become more clear. As mentioned, free software advocates are represented by the FSF, which curates and serves to help enforce their ideological approach: that free software is integral to personal liberty in a digital world and that the informed should actively prevent those who construct software from wielding it as an unjust instrument of power. Furthermore, freedom is restrictive and clearly defined in its principles and licenses—described as GNU-compatible Free Software Licenses (GNU is a recursive acronym for "GNU's Not Unix!")—to make obvious its differentiation from non-free software. These kinds of restrictive licenses are also called *Copyleft* and mean that any derivative works of the licensed software must also use the same license as the original work.

The Open Source Initiative (OSI)—members of which have named themselves the stewards of the Open Source Definition (OSD), which is largely technical in nature—stresses that open source is "a development method for software that harnesses the power of distributed peer review and transparency of process. The promise of open source is higher quality, better reliability, greater

---

4 St. Laurent, Andrew M. (2008). *Understanding Open Source and Free Software Licensing.* O'Reilly Media, p. 4. ISBN 9780596553951. Retrieved May 30, 2016, from https://books.google.com/books?id=04jG7TTLujoC&pg=PA4#v=onepage&q &f=false.

5 Free Software Foundation (2007–2016). "The Free Software Definition." Retrieved May 30, 2016, from https://www.gnu.org/philosophy/free-sw.html. Licensed under Creative Commons CC BY-ND 4.0.

flexibility, lower cost, and an end to predatory vendor lock-in."[6] The definition itself includes statements about what makes software open source, and tenets include free redistribution, availability of source code, status of derived works, management of derived works to maintain the integrity of the author's source code, technology neutrality, and non-discrimination for peoples or fields of endeavor. But perhaps most notable, in comparison to the FSF, is the ethical criterion that an open source license *may never restrict other software that may run alongside the open source code,* in that it may not require that all other distributed software also be open-source licensed. Number (9) of the OSD reads as follows:

9. License Must Not Restrict Other Software

The license must not place restrictions on other software that is distributed along with the licensed software. For example, the license must not insist that all other programs distributed on the same medium must be open-source software.[7]

Given that statement, it is clear that this very permissiveness is one of the primary reasons that the open source movement is part of a growing market share in the commercial sector, despite being advocates of freely available software for all. And it is this very permissiveness that—along with encouraging engagement as the best way to ensure that we are developing technically good, high-quality software—makes open source, without all the heavy gravy of FSF, to be quite attractive. Having access to study and improve on others' creative work is inherent in this mission but is not the *raison d'etre* of the movement. Software cannot be proprietary if we desire to work across traditional boundaries; therefore, proprietary software is anathema to that mission. But, because free software advocates are moved by liberty and the rights for anyone who uses software—either as an individual or as a collective—to examine it, manipulate it as they will, and be in complete control of what it does for them, they aver that software must be free in any society that claims to value individual independence.

Free software mandates what they call the "four freedoms" as a way of defining what is *essential* to free software, which is legitimized, oddly enough, through the use of international copyright law. The four essential freedoms

---

[6] Open Source Initiative (2007). "About the Open Source Initiative." Opensource. org. Retrieved May 30, 2016, from https://opensource.org/about. Licensed under Creative Commons CC BY 4.0.

[7] Open Source Initiative (2007). "The Open Source Definition." Retrieved May 30, 2016, from https://opensource.org/osd. Licensed under Creative Commons CC BY 4.0.

defined by the FSF and shared here under the Creative Commons attribution (BY-ND 4.0) include:

- The freedom to run the program as you wish, for any purpose (freedom 0).
- The freedom to study how the program works, and change it so it does your computing as you wish (freedom 1). Access to the source code is a precondition for this.
- The freedom to redistribute copies so you can help your neighbor (freedom 2).
- The freedom to distribute copies of your modified versions to others (freedom 3). By doing this you can give the whole community a chance to benefit from your changes. Access to the source code is a precondition for this.[8]

Despite a shared history, OSI and FSF are stylistically, attitudinally, culturally, and ideologically different, but their very public skirmishes overshadow the important possibilities of concordance. One really does begin to wonder if the schism between FSF and OSI is just another example of trying to resolve a false dichotomy, where we believe we must make a choice between either free software or open source because they tell us we must. Maybe not. Consider an example: the children in your neighborhood play games in the summer streets way too far into the night for your taste; they're loud and they impinge on your TV time. So you approach the homeowner's association and make your case that the group should prevent families with children from buying houses in the neighborhood in future. You insist that there is no other way to stop noise caused by children playing but to stop the inflow of children. Obviously, there are other simple options such as talking to the parents, establishing curfews, creating playspaces or even structural elements that could help manage noise; but in a huff to solve the problem, only black-and-white logic is deployed. This is a missed opportunity.

It is possible to adopt a perspective in which OSI and FSF become important partners with each other, as FSF is about ensuring the principle of software freedom, and OSI is about building a case for the widespread adoption of free software. In fact, the two organizations have found occasion to join forces and file statements of support on enforcement cases and lawsuits related to software patent law. Still, it is important to realize that the methodologies that make open source so powerful and attractive not only owe a debt to the principles of

---

[8] Stallman, Richard (2007–2016). "The Free Software Definition." Retrieved July 26, 2016, from https://www.gnu.org/philosophy/free-sw.html. Licensed under Creative Commons CC BY-ND 4.0.

the free software movement, but may strip itself of meaning without them. An open source movement shorn of the principles of the FSF dilutes the important effort of working to ensure the rights of citizens in the face of a technocratic society. At the same time, too heavy a hand from the likes of FSF program licenses has brought adoption struggles and, by some standards, a measurable rejection of restrictive licenses in favor of more permissive licenses.

As we instinctively know, there is plenty of software that meets the criteria for both free and open, and, in an attempt to harness the dualist tension between free software and open source, many have come to define collectively Free and Open-Source Software (FOSS), indicating that the software allows for the use, study, copying, and modification of the source code, but that it also resides in an "open source" form that brings a collaborative methodology to bear on the project. It should surprise no one that the FSF prefers the nomenclature of Free/Libre Open-Source Software (FLOSS), as they hope to stress the philosophical importance lost in the less precise acronym of FOSS. However, except where it is important and instructive to be specific to the principles of either FSF or OSI, we prefer the term FOSS, as its usage in government, academic, legal, and business spheres across the globe is already understood.

2.3 How FOSS Created a Cultural Storm

Our examination of the principles of both the free software and open source movements are key to understanding what we hope to achieve in a greatly expanded movement that brings data, information, and content to a common and accessible space in the world. However, we must also be mindful of falling into the trap of over-analysis and dependence on a single model. Yes, FOSS is an extremely powerful, tested, and observed set of practices, but as our sole source of instruction for how we might practically construct an adoptable and practical framework for our businesses, it does not tell the complete story. And as we'll find, it may tell us even less than we had hoped about how to implement open practices in our own companies. To make substantive organizational change, we must first be willing to understand competing theories and truths that have contributed to open practices, ask probative and clarifying questions that draw out not just history but also our probable outcomes for success, and be impeccable in our interpretations of what we learn without emotionalism and bias whenever possible. If we are truly committed to drawing out the value of openness, we must be honest about the challenges, and that includes the messiness of humanity. And it is true—dogma has been one of the most troubling aspects of the story of FOSS, although certainly not its most important. Indeed, many great stories have a complicated legacy, and this is one of the great ones.

Anyone truly interested in open methods of creative production has likely spent many hours reading the research studies, articles, and books that have attempted to capture some of the common characteristics for the successful open project. And despite the prolific adoption of the word "open" to describe collaborative production—as we have learned in exploring the ideological roots of FOSS—we must not assume that many users of the terminology have a more than rudimentary understanding of what open software is and why and how it generates both excitement and fear.

FOSS projects have changed the face of nearly every industry that relies on information technology. Its positive impact is undeniable, but unfortunately, this success belies the fact that many of these initiatives fail to thrive. When we celebrate only the big wins of the open-source movement, we fail to fully appreciate the formidable challenges of creating a flourishing community of loosely connected contributors that make up a project. Furthermore, do we really know what motivates these groups to flourish or even to sustain themselves? Why do a significant number of such projects die off? Were they bad ideas? Were there personal or political problems in how the project founders tried to negotiate community development? Or is there something more fundamentally troubling about the open-source model itself? It's not as if these questions aren't asked, it's just that the conversation is often arcane and nuanced, stumbling over the seemingly endless worries about values and principles.

2.3.1 A Walk Backward in Time

In the halls of technology companies, the first thing that usually comes up in a conversation about how to rapidly innovate in the world of future technology is how to find and access data, information, and content, and how FOSS can accelerate the progress of any commercial effort. In fact, there seems to be an endless number of "open" initiatives these days, and they are often conflated with this movement, for right or wrong. Figure 2.1 shows how many application domains attempt to leverage open source, but this drawing doesn't even begin to capture the buzzword status of "open." If you call something open today, in nearly any environment, you are taken to mean transparency, fairness, collaboration, and sharing. But, there is no guarantee of any of these characteristics. In fact, the opposite response will occur if you travel a little farther down the hall to the corner office, where the in-house counsel and the COO worry that FOSS has made its way into their company code, creating unknown liabilities, legal quagmires, and a fundamental wrecking of the business plan.

But it's not just the cheerleaders on the engineering team who see relief from FOSS not only in how they manage their work, but in how they might also

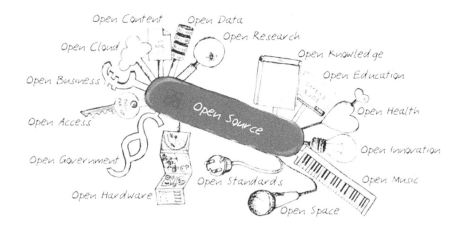

Figure 2.1 Many application domains benefit from the framework of the Open-Source Model.[9]

contribute to the greater good, learn skills from other programmers, and even develop new models of production that feel more like an expression of craft than the arbitrary deadline-driven schedules usual in a corporation. So, yes, while copyright schemes have ruined more than one office freaky Friday party, the FOSS model has done much to teach our organizations about how individuals can successfully bring perspectives and talents to the table, even when contributors may have no interest in the long-term success of the project, or even when it seems that these groups are voluntarily giving up many millions of dollars of profit by working outside proprietary efforts.

2.4 Explore the Past to Shape the Future

As we work to establish a common definition for FOSS, it is safe to say that if we boil it all down, the idea of openness simply describes *access to something,* whether it's a field to play in or a structure for maintaining software, digital media, information, or knowledge. In both cases, the problem seems straightforward: *Can we get what we want when we want it, and what are the terms to retrieve those rights of access?* But we already know that this topic can get messy very quickly, even if we're just talking about a common patch of grass. So what about that field? Is there a fence around the field? If they let you in, do they still

[9] Spielhagen, Johannes (2012). OpenSwissKnife.png. Retrieved May 30, 2016, from https://commons.wikimedia.org/wiki/File:121212_2_OpenSwissKnife.png. Licensed under Creative Commons CC BY-SA 3.0.

own it? Who is they? Who pays the taxes? Who gets the keys? Can anyone go in? And what are the rules once we're in there? Can we take things with us when we leave? Do we have to put things back? Do we have to take a turn cleaning and tending to the grass? What if we see someone not following the rules? Do we take their key away, or tell the person that first gave us the key? So, while reasonable people can agree that openness is about access, as with so many practices that bind together people with a common goal, certain observances are in order, there's lots of tradition, maybe a smattering of ritual, but there is always a place of mutual interest.

That's not necessarily a negative thing, but when it comes to the topic of software, it can become very difficult to understand. Anyone who has ever claimed to have written an "innovative" portion of code or program (or has been close to such an individual, we'll call them *geeks* or, loosely, *hackers*) will recognize the über-geek, that competitive individual who loves to solve problems and learn fiercely. They also enjoy bragging rights when they do something slick, and they will often share it. Some of these individuals will go so far as to find themselves on the FBI's most wanted list, like hacker-extraordinaire Kevin Mitnick, but most are satisfied with just running their stuff on a huge video display for their teammates. Still, most have given up discussing their "special" project at the neighborhood barbecue and instead seek an affinity group, people who speak their language and appreciate the joy of their sweet moment. It is in part this basic human need that underscores the importance and enjoyment of peer learning, the concepts of learning by doing and sharing, and even a sense of freedom.

2.4.1 It Can Happen Anywhere

While much of this connection may happen in cyberspace, with the proliferation of technology creation in the everyday world, physical space has become increasingly important. An article in the *International Journal of Cultural Studies,* which explored the production and governance of commons-based peer production in physical space, described the hacker ethic as one that "include[s] freedom, in the sense of autonomy as well as of free access and circulation of information; distrust of authority, that is, opposing the traditional, industrial top-down style of organization; embracing the concept of learning by doing and peer-to-peer learning processes as opposed to formal modes of learning; sharing, solidarity and cooperation."[10] And while current academic studies on the topic

---

[10] Kostakis, Vasilis, Niaros, Vasilis, and Giotitsas, Christos (2015). "Production and Governance in Hackerspaces: A Manifestation of Commons-Based Peer Production in the Physical Realm?" *International Journal of Cultural Studies,* vol. 18, issue 5, pp. 555–573. DOI:10.1177/1367877913519310.

may be weak and not yet largely convincing, there is every reason to believe that hackers in collaborative settings—physical or virtual—do adopt models of governance, even organizational structures that serve as the foundation of their very principles of production.

As a reflection of this tendency, we are seeing a renewed burgeoning of physical "hackerspaces" designed to nourish individuals by providing community in which the mechanisms of peer learning and knowledge sharing can be experienced. These spaces emerged as early as 1994 and have grown in popularity across the globe, including surprising places such as sub-Saharan Africa, where resource-sharing is vital; and there are even commercial chains across the globe that support community space. We will explore these spaces as a way to enable the social norms that support collaboration, but for now it is sufficient to say that these efforts demonstrate that collaboration with peers is of crucial importance to the craftspeople of software, even when popular culture dresses up these individuals as energy-drink-slugging, chip-eating introverts, and this may especially be true of the FOSS aficionado. Although geek culture doesn't always do a lot to dispel common stereotypes, what we will come to learn is that what often separates geeks from others who participate in collaborative moments is motivation and world view.

2.5 Preinventing the Wheel

Engineering culture has always had its own patois, a sort of well-read, clever short-hand that sometimes describes a wealth of information and history. This tendency came fairly early in the world of computing, with terms such as *Bellcore* (Bell Communications Research) and *CLEC* (competitive local exchange carrier), but this tendency skyrocketed as the Internet became available and the conversation become multifaceted and fast paced, especially among researchers and academics. This special language is pointedly anti-cultural, with the freewheeling use of terms such as *orphans, cluster funk, kill, grok, hairballs, spam, velveeta, scrambled inodes,* and *angry garden salad:* "What a cluster funk. Zombie reaping problem." This kind of language may even be considered a form of ludling, that childhood game to disguise speech from others, usually adults. There are hundreds of gibberish variants that also have more serious uses, such as gaining an advantage in trade or as rapid-form encryption, and geek-speak easily qualifies at least some of the time.

Engineers are not alone in using precise words that have a special professional meaning—it may actually improve communication to a point—but jargon also can form a sense of unity, shape the culture, create meaningless messages, and drive exclusivity—even alienation—for certain group members. And it's not all that popular with every engineer, even if they speak it. Carlos Bueno, a former Facebook engineer, was less generous about his feelings when he wrote in *Lauren Ipsum: A Story About Computer Science and Other Improbable Things,* "Jargon live in the swamps. They feed on attention. If they can't get that, they'll settle for fear and confusion. . . . A little Jargon doesn't look like much. Some people even keep them as pets. But they form packs, and they are very dangerous."[11] So, perhaps it is not that much of a surprise that the idea of open source emerged from the minds of a curious group of individuals, who in many ways adopted attitudes and behaviors that are different than the prevailing cultural norms. A counterculture is often tied to a movement that not only expresses an ethos, but carries aspirations for themselves that they often hope to extend to mainstream society.

The sharing of code in this culture has always happened, and part of this is simply because engineers are mostly not interested in wasting time and resources *reinventing the wheel,* although that doesn't mean there won't be a lot of discussion about who invented the wheel and at least some tentative exploration into whether it could be done better. And if it can be done better, it's called *redefining the wheel.* Of course, to be in a position to improve, one must understand existing solutions and at all costs avoid *preinventing the wheel* (that's when someone else is already working on that same wheel-redefining project). You may be lost by now, but there is one kernel of truth worth taking from the way sharing happens in a state of FOSS-lessness or an overly restrictive FOSS license: reinventing the wheel is a common occurrence, and it is done to avoid copyright issues. Unfortunately, when engineers can't or don't share their solutions to solving a problem, they are sometimes forced to reinvent a square wheel, which can easily result in suboptimal results and certainly lost time for things more useful, creative, fun, productive, and perhaps even innovative.

Since the early days of complied language, sharing has been important, as has free access to tools and code (in the context of free beer). Especially if you wanted to do something better, faster, more efficiently, or your code just wasn't working, sharing happened and help (sometimes with a healthy dose of scathing sarcasm) was provided. And today, the unrestricted use of free compilers, interpreters, and development systems for many programming languages is widely available, and many of the most in-demand languages have a free option, including SQL, Java, JavaScript, C++, C#, Python, and PHP. As described in Figure 2.2, FOSS is now found throughout the technology ecosystem and serves to help software engineers focus on innovation and differentiation, not

---

[11] Bueno, Carlos (2014). *Lauren Ipsum: A Story About Computer Science and Other Improbable Things* (1st ed.). San Francisco, CA: No Starch Press, p. 6. https://www. nostarch.com/laurenipsum.

Figure 2.2   FOSS is found throughout the technology ecosystem in applications, frameworks, and languages.

drudgery and redundant undertakings. That doesn't mean there aren't non-free ways to build your software with those languages, just that you don't have to.

The official beginnings of collaboration and sharing as methodology in software has often been attributed to Eric Steven Raymond (we'll call him ESR, as everyone does), a software developer who wrote a 1997 essay and follow-up book called *The Cathedral and the Bazaar* (called, of course, *CatB*). If you're interested in a deep exploration of the origins of the open-source community, buy the book or, at the very least, read the essay online. *CatB* was and in many ways still is a seminal and guiding work for the adoption of FOSS in the commercial enterprise, as it brought one of the first companies to its source code (on purpose): Netscape, through Mozilla. But really what ESB did was observe, synthesize, and document a phenomenon that was already occurring in open software communities, in which high degrees of productivity occurred as the supposed result of the special nature of community building and social management mechanisms that were being deployed in the Linux project.

As a method of exploration, ESR wrote *CatB* and defined and contrasted two development models for free software: that it is built either in the "cathedral" under lock and key and a mechanistic cadence, or in the bazaar of public scrutiny. His central thesis, or Linus's Law, is that "given enough eyeballs, all bugs are shallow." This is a deeply important perspective, which has come to form the central thesis of the open-source movement: that source code available for public review, experimentation, study, and use has the best chance to be of the highest quality.

So in the end, there are many good reasons that the mother of all *open* and the key for understanding nearly any other open movement is FOSS. But still, this movement is one of human beings, and that can cast confusion on our understanding of why such projects succeed or fail. As discussed in Chapter 1 of this book, any honest observer is forced to admit that what we do know about open source and what it can teach us about working together in this type of a collaborative environment is largely anecdotal, because there are actually few studies that primarily examine the nature of collaboration in these environments, and further, how the development of these communities are born, die, handle conflict, and relate themselves to collaboration and capitalism. To be sure, there is no shortage of opinion on these topics, but not enough study and research. This begs the question: can we really make the concept of *open* work at all? Meaning, do we have any idea of the circumstances that could create a successful open-source project outside of those circumstances? Do we have any idea how to practically achieve this? Or is it only luck and circumstance?

This is a matter for our later discussion.

Chapter Three

Innovation in an Open World

[1]

*It's not the strongest of the species who survive, nor the most intelligent
that survives. It is the one that is most adaptable to change.*

— Charles Darwin

---

[1] Barraud, Herbert Rose (1881). Charles Darwin. Retrieved from https://commons.
wikimedia.org/wiki/File:Charles_Darwin_photograph_by_Herbert_Rose_Barraud,
_1881.jpg.

3.1 Chapter Theme

There is big money and big hope in innovation. There are hundreds of inspirational quotations, books, consulting companies, and business and cultural philosophies that hold high the concept of innovation. In the world of technology, especially, it's an obsession, it's an imperative, it's terrifying, it's an expression of true creativity and passion, it's grit, it's sparks, it's working with others, it's working by yourself, it's specific, it's big, it's winning—and without it you will most certainly fail. But many of us are also in awe when we see the flash of inspiration move from impulse to impact. How do we work to avoid inertia and adopt innovation-oriented processes not only for ourselves, but for our communities and companies, where so much creativity is translated into existence?

3.2 The Fashionable World of Innovation

The "halo effect" is typically ascribed to a respected person, when others assume that nearly everything they say must necessarily be true. It is a cognitive bias in which a general impression of a person, a brand, or even a word influences a person's thoughts and feelings about the characteristics or properties of that entity.

This effect is not always positive and glowing, and it can drive misconception in many directions. For example, Bob in the accounting department can work the bookkeeping software like nobody's business. He knows every arcane key combination and how to restore lost data, saving the day more than once. Everyone seems to go to Bob at least once for help, and they are always grateful for his cheerful assistance.

At promotion time, Bob's boss notes that he has served the organization well, and, despite his singularly focused background as a certified public accountant, his technical proficiency and willingness to support others has brought the growing company to the moment when they are thrilled to offer him the position of Director of Information Technologies! (*Halo effect:* if he's good at the accounting software, he must be good at all technologies and is probably generally gifted enough to be a manager. Besides, everyone likes him.) Bob is thrilled, takes the promotion, gets a corner office and a big bump in his paycheck. However, all the things Bob likes to do, such as figure out accounting software, are no longer in his purview. Now he manages a chronic barrage of problems—hearing complaints from staff, managing assets, and dealing with stressed-out personnel. And, it turns out that Bob has little talent or interest in running IT, he doesn't really understand how networks operate, and he's terribly ineffective as a manager. Consequently, the IT workforce falls desperately behind in their work, they can't do their jobs effectively, and they are frustrated with Bob and the company. At the end of the day, the entire IT team takes a hit, and the regulars in the company assume they are just incompetent individuals and incapable of doing their jobs (*Negative halo effect:* because Bob can't actually manage IT, the whole team is perceived as unskilled and inept).

Clearly, if we are to explore the relationship of *openness* to *innovation*—two words that exhibit the halo effect so distinctly that the cover of this book may be glowing—we must expunge the poorly evidenced reliance on the glamorous idea of both concepts, so that we can make real, rational progress toward creating a culture in which our ambitions for future tech can be met with accelerating innovative capability.

3.2.1 Under a Cloud of Jargon

When it comes to certain buzzwords and jargon in the business of high technology, we may have reached peak ridiculousness, as Scott Adams's Dilbert has been forewarning since 1989. In 1995, Adams consecrated his incredulity with what he termed the "Dilbert Principle," that ". . . the least competent, least smart people are promoted, simply because they're the ones you don't want doing actual work."[2] For Adams, lampooning techno-management-speak is his greatest weapon, as the point-haired boss says in the January 9, 2010, strip: "Let's schedule a scenario-based roundtable discussion about our enterprise project management. We'll use our infrastructure survey tool to architect a risk-based tiering system."[3] Despite the light humor, what makes Dilbert so hilarious is the biting satire—but unfortunately, the real irony is that despite our widespread recognition of this ridicule-worthy gobbledygook, we seem to have become drunk on special words and have a hard time putting the drink down.

Some of us treat our ability to understand jargon as a badge of honor. Perhaps, we even claim in certain circles, our special language brings enhanced precision and understanding to the conversation, and often it really does; the whole truth, though, may largely include the opposite—not only may the use of jargon cloud meaning, it is also a way to lose trust with others who can't follow along, suggesting a lack of candor or, worse, a lack of understanding of the issues with a smokescreen of syllables. At its worst, jargon is used as a tool to mark who is in

---

2 Eveleth, Rose (2012). "Your Boss Gets Paid More Than You Because They Get More Done." Smithsonian.com. Retrieved on July 26, 2016, from http://www.smithsonian mag.com/smart-news/your-boss-gets-paid-more-than-you-because-they-get-more-done-30365265/.

3 Adams, Scott (2010, January 9). Dilbert. Retrieved on July 26, 2016, from http:// dilbert.com/strip/2010-01-09.

and who is out, as Steele Champion, corporate-culture consultant and author of TalkLikeTheBoss.com claims, ". . . the primary reason business buzzwords occur is to convey connection. It's similar to an inside joke, where a few individuals get it while outsiders do not. If you have ever been one of the people in on the joke, think about the immediate connection you felt to those who also understood it."[4] Even our conversations have become proprietary.

To demonstrate the halo effect in the fast-track world of "open," here is an imperfect list that seeks to demonstrate the halo effect of the word *open*. Several things are at play here; the use of the word *open* as a lever to show the commitment of the project/entity/movement to transparent practices; a moral and ethical position implied with regard to freedom of access; and in some cases, an implied set of benefits related to individual potential and societal benefit:

> *open data, open source, open data, open innovation, open collaboration, open research, open leadership, open government, open standards, open education resources, open content, open library, open world, open proxy, open publishing, open thesaurus, open learning, open core, open society, open collector, open access initiative, open science, open firmware, open inventor, open geospatial, open directory, open constitution, open text, open kimono, open cities, open StreetMap, open adoption, open management, open university, open 'zine, open publication, open-source intelligence, open comments, open education, open mediation, open meditation, open API, open marriage, open door, open office, OpenGL, open access, OpenFS, open economy, open utility, open assessment, (massive) open online courses . . .*

This leads us naturally to the not-surprising emergence of the term *open washing*—calling something open when it really isn't. So why is it so compelling to be "open" these days? There must be benefits, real or perceived.

The most powerful reason to "go open" in a business context is related to the extensive and oft-enumerated significant benefits that promise unparalleled performance, higher quality, and even acclaim by sharing community values. Here are some words that are often positively associated with the massive improvements wrought by being open in approach and practice:

> *innovation, reliability, stability, auditability, efficiency, cost containment, flexibility, freedom, respect, accountability, supportability, transparency, democratic participation, security, self-empowerment, better products,*

---

[4] Vaccaro, Adam (2014, March). These Buzzwords Make You Look Bad (and Hurt Business). *Inc.* Retrieved on July 26, 2016, from http://www.inc.com/adam-vaccaro/buzzword-engagement-interview.html.

> *better services, better government, efficient government, better governance, better analytics, new knowledge, integrity, experienced, good designers, standards focused, quality, motivated*

These are wonderful words—they are ideals, they represent much of what many of us want to use to describe our work lives and the companies we are associated with, especially as leaders of companies, communities, and nations. These words satisfy our imagination of what is desirable and quintessential—the gold standard—particularly with regard to the dreams of personal liberty that so many open advocates hold so dear in their quest to build the foundations of more vibrant, transparent, accountable, and open societies.

3.3 Ideals Are Not Required to Make a Good Business Case

However, other than as broad goals and even claims for the prospect of greatness, these are not really sound reasons to "go open," nor do they lend much to the poor analyst left with the charge to convince their companies that they should take the significant risk of changing their entire business model. Yes, being principled might represent a personal or corporate ethos, but principles are not benefits, nor are they even outcomes. They are a system of belief. When we open up our systems and companies and strive to build a business strategy on hopeful concepts, we had better be very successful, very quickly, because building a business on the oftentimes illogical, hyperbolic, and largely untested benefits of adopting openness in society and industry only serves to obscure the real benefits that open culture can bring to global development, urban development, finance, health care, nutrition, agriculture, and the future of technology that will drive these sectors and the manner in which such an approach can be reasonably adopted.

3.3.1 The Perils of Openwashing

A lack of rigor in understanding the principles of openness may be the leading reason for a disturbing trend in openwashing claims, especially against multinational technology companies such as Apple, Inc., and Microsoft Corporation. Researcher and software engineer Dr. Roy Schestowitz frequently writes about fair competition and directly points the finger at these two significant companies that have made public moves to embrace open source. In his commentary, he draws a parallel between openwashing and the marketing efforts of other multinationals, especially in the environmental sphere, writing,

"Non-technical folks may easily be led into the illusion of 'open' Microsoft and 'open' Apple (openwashing), much like that of 'green' (and yellow) BP or 'green' Shell (greenwashing). . . . They all involve mass deception with a huge budget. It's quite a theatre!"[5]

These are heated words, for sure, but they underscore the expected emotional tension among open software advocates and open claimants. However, this also indicates another interesting trend—this somewhat arcane movement, which confuses even those who develop software, has caught the eye of companies that make billions of dollars through proprietary technologies. Obviously, these moves are not directed at the average iPhone user or Excel spreadsheet junkie, but at the ever-increasing segment of open-influencers, such as the environmentalists who do so much to shape the story of the anthropogenic impacts on our natural ecosystem before the supermajor oil and gas companies even show up for the conversation. In this case, it is the developers who rely on the ease of availability, low barriers of entry to participate, and widespread feature sets offered by open source that are of interest. This is especially true where their work impacts the push and pull of content to consumers, like every app not owned by Apple in the App Store. In any case, like any deceitful reputational defense, openwashed claims of open-source compliance may be overstated in an attempt to credentialize, protect, and enhance a brand's reputation, in part based on the phenomenon of the halo effect.

3.4 Innovation Inertia

> It's funny. All you have to do is say something nobody understands
> and they'll do practically anything you want them to.
>
> — J.D. Salinger, *The Catcher in the Rye*

There is big money and big hope in innovation. There are hundreds of inspirational quotations, books, consulting companies, and business and cultural philosophies that hold high the concept of innovation. In the world of technology, especially, it's an obsession, it's an imperative, it's terrifying, it's an expression of true creativity and passion, it's grit, it's sparks, it's working with others, it's working by yourself, it's specific, it's big, it's winning—and without it you will most certainly fail.

---

[5] Schestowitz, Roy (n.d.). "The Disturbing Rise of Openwashing: Today's Case of Apple and Microsoft." Retrieved June 6, 2016, from http://techrights.org/2015/06/12/openwashing-apple-and-microsoft/.

One thing is clear: while innovation is about ideas, it's much more than the simple flash of creative inspiration, as beautiful as that moment may be. Instead, innovation defines how we choose to do the work to bring our meaningful, impactful impulses to life. But it is how we define that process—how we "get it" ourselves, in our companies, and in our communities—where so many breakdowns begin, bringing inertia instead of the innovation we so desire. In many ways, this is because not only are we poor translators of the methods of innovation, but also we lack an understanding of the rigor and risk-taking required to innovate, not just imitate.

3.4.1 The Challenge of Tortilla Chips and Underwear

In companies, many blame internal bureaucracy for being the major impediment to innovation. But I think it is somewhat more reductionist in nature, as Brené Brown, University of Houston Research, says when talking about jargon: "You can often chart the demise of a good word or phrase to the minute advertisers start using it to sell us everything from underwear to tortilla chips," even when the need for intimately understanding what it is—innovation in this case—remains.[6]

When a leader stands up in front of her team and proclaims, "We must innovate!" it may feel immediately inspiring, but it is not a formula for change. When a CTO says, "We are going open! We want to engage the open source community! We want all ships to rise!" we are roused, our venture capitalist may write us a big check, our shareholders are titillated, but so often these steps are too small to empower those who aspire to transform our world with pivotal ideas, and at worst, they are just an empty turn of phrase.

This lack of inspiration, this emptiness, likely isn't because a business leader is overtly trying to manipulate or deceive, but is simply careless and ignorant about the nature of innovation. Misinterpretation of the idea of innovation is so profound that, too often, even the mere utterance of the word "innovation" can create a room full of eye-rollers. The eye-rollers may be on to something. Alfred North Whitehead identified the "fallacy of misplaced concreteness," also called the "fallacy of reification." This is the error of treating an idea as equivalent to the thing to be represented by that word or idea.[7] And in complex

---

[6] Brown, Brené (2016, June). "My Response to Adam Grant's *New York Times* Op/ED: Unless You're Oprah, 'Be Yourself' Is Terrible Advice." LinkedIn. Retrieved July 26, 2016, from https://www.linkedin.com/pulse/my-response-adam-grants-new-york-times-oped-unless-youre-brené-brown.

[7] Whitehead, Alfred North (1929). *Process and Reality*, New York: Harper.

domains, in which words seem to be used more for marketing caché and buzz than precision, this tendency to abstract appears with greater intensity and consistency, especially in advanced technology domains. As Brown warned, talking about "innovation" and "open" is a lot like selling undergarments and snacks.

This isn't some new phenomenon, although it seems to be a very loud one in the socially connected world; the fallacy of reification is all around us. Read any article in the newspaper, listen to the news, even pick up a popular business book, and you'll identify it very quickly: the War against Drugs, the War on Poverty, Stifling Innovation, or even, on the positive side, How to Grow Innovation. Let's be straightforward: these statements make no sense.

3.4.2 Why You're Not an Innovator

First, why do we do this? And second, why do we even care about such precision? A bit of indulgence is requested:

So, let's imagine a war. It typically involves parties made up of people who are trying to kill each other and prevail in some way at the end of all the killing (even if "killing" is just meant in a competitive way); or it can loosely imply a struggle. Now think about poverty. Poverty is a term that describes the state of people who are without resources, typically chronically. Let's look at the "War on Poverty": the idea is that we want to enact policies that eradicate the condition of indigence. That is a worthy goal; however, poverty cannot be shot or killed, and it certainly cannot sign a treaty putting an end to aggression, declaring it has been beaten and it will now be rich. The problem is that the phrase "War on Poverty" does not represent a model for change, and it results in many billions of dollars being spent on trying to implement something that is largely symbolic and that exists only in our thoughts. It is not real and does not define a path forward, even if it represents an important concept.

This idea of treating a conception as concrete (poverty is a conception, even though the consequences of poverty are very real) is called "reification" or "thing-making." It is a popular tendency among politicians of every ilk as well as those who don't like to muck about in the details, and we can fully expect to find reification occurring when a concept is not well understood or is complex, complicated, and inconsistent. Humans as a rule like to measure things to make them real. For example, temperature is an idea, but we can measure it, which makes it an actual thing that we can confidently express as meaningful. Poverty, on the other hand, is an issue about the conditions of a human life that is lacking something (which is sometimes relative). The Word Bank describes poverty, in part, as, ". . . a situation people want to escape. So poverty is a call to action— for the poor and the wealthy alike—a call to change the world so that many more may have enough to eat, adequate shelter, access to education and health, protection from violence, and a voice in what happens in their communities."[8] When do we win the War on Poverty? Well, it depends.

The important point of avoiding symbolic language to encourage substantive changes in the way we do business at its core is that, even if we optimistically attempt to simply bring consistency, we may actually be saying very little of shared meaning. Promoting "innovation" or "openness" as symbolic principles will in the end not unify a company or a team, but clear and consistent communication will. Depending on reification to inspire is likely to create an ambiguous, confusing mess that uses an abstract belief or construct in place of a concrete, precise—real—strategy. Otherwise, it bewilders us.

So, now the news.

You are not "innovative" and you never will be—nature has been making humans just fine for thousands of years; *your company is not "innovative" no matter how much you say it is*—it's an entity defined on paper. You might have an innovative idea, method, product, or way of solving a problem. Or you may be an inspiration of innovation in the work of other people or those in your company. Or your company may be organizationally structured to promote innovative thinking. But if we want to authentically pursue innovation and open thinking in our work cultures, we need to recognize that concepts don't get the work done, whether it is finding a cure for cancer, colonizing Mars, cloning a pig, or finding a silver bullet to end anthropogenic climate warming. In our guts, we can understand the ideals implied, but they are ideals with a lot of skills, development, humility, and truth-telling required. And those behaviors are not natural for those struggling to do new and creative things in our hierarchical ranks—we are calling for a messy, inefficient, and risky process; a tolerance for failure; and an emotional rollercoaster.

By the way, *you're also not "open."* The same problems inherent with "being innovative" emerge for those who declare that they are "open"; it is a bold idea that indicates an important willingness to modify the corporate and legal boundaries of assets, be it with its data, source code, designs, or other inventions. It is a perspective that in itself is not inherently meaningful (because "open" is not real, and it means very different things to different people), even if as a society or organization we believe that it may lend itself to fulfilling some higher order. For example, the US government has designed a secure way for you to download your household energy data electronically as part of their open data efforts. At last count, many millions of households could access their data,

---

8 Economic and Social Inclusion Corporation (2008). "What is Poverty?" New Brunswick, Canada. Retrieved July 26, 2016, from http://www2.gnb.ca/content/gnb/en/departments/esic/overview/content/what_is_poverty.html.

but to be clear, this ability does not confer a condition of liberty. Green Button Data comprises literally a spreadsheet of consumption values, and so is just a tool in our quest for that condition.

Both innovation and open thinking may certainly require an attitude shift and a new framework for achieving success in business, but at the end of the day, they are empty constructs that require new behaviors and thinking. The business of innovation and open thinking requires a precise intent, not pabulum.

3.5 Let's Get Real

If making a concept seem "real" and "thingy" when it may be ineffective in practice can also have damaging impacts when we push them too far into made-up exactitudes. In the book *The Mismeasure of Man,* Stephen Jay Gould describes these risks in explaining the dangers of using a manufactured intelligence quotient to score human intellect. We don't want to give up on the idea of an intelligence score because it implies that intelligence can easily be measured, like reading a thermometer. The impact has been devastating for many: consider children with learning disabilities, such as visual perception problems, who score poorly on an IQ test and hence are treated as not being smart, resulting in educators glossing over their low educational achievement with a convenient label. Gould warns us about "the use of these numbers to rank people in a single series of worthiness, invariably to find that oppressed and disadvantaged groups—races, classes, or sexes—are innately inferior and deserve their status."[9] This great book goes on to describe how quantifying a claim makes things feel scientific and correct, and this can contribute to a fundamental and dangerous social impact that, in Gould's belief, alters our social organization and the perceived worth of individuals, both to themselves and to others.

This commentary is given both to suggest an approach for how we deploy the heady concepts of innovation and openness in our companies, and to underscore that how we frame what we know in practice is never without sociopolitical and cultural implications. Without getting further lost in this ontological nightmare, reductionism of the complexities of moving a novel idea into a process is surely to be controversial—as it should be. Strangely, the tomes and articles and models that have been raised up thus far to help us pursue innovation and openness have perhaps been too easily accepted, instead of raising the kind of argument and debate we need to move forward consciously and deliberately.

---

[9] Gould, Stephen Jay (1996). *The Mismeasure of Man* (Revised and Expanded). New York City: W.W. Norton & Company, p. 57.

3.5.1 Toward Developing a Model

Given the extensive body of both academic and popular work done over the decades on the process of innovation, it is tempting to provide a survey of the literature. However, that would be redundant and also so disparate, given the interdisciplinary perspectives on the topic, that there would be little value. Furthermore, the perspective of innovation and openness for future tech applications is somewhat unique in that we are not compelled to force a fit with the traditional boundaries of manufacturing or even non-virtual companies, although the outcome of such innovative practices may serve such entities. Also, we sense in future tech a changing perspective on the sources of innovation that have been well defined in most linear and end-user models of innovation, in which we innovate either to sell our idea or because there is a perceived need.

It also seems that future tech violates the most fundamental tenets of innovation. Joseph F. Engelberger, a robotics engineer, physicist, and entrepreneur, stated precisely that an innovation (and by extension, the process of innovation) only requires three things: a recognized need, the right people with relevant technology to solve the problem, and money.[10] The "Father of Robotics" was correct *in his context;* however, in a time that can only be described as a technological revolution, we need to consider expanding Engelberger's requirements. Our sources of innovation are much fuzzier and much faster. The half-century-old Moore's Law (the number of transistors per square inch on integrated circuits will double every year for the foreseeable future) has been declared dead and buried, rendered moot by the ability to scale processing power by exotic techniques with different quantum effects.

When it comes to innovation, even engineers have changed their theories of development: they use *lean*, they are *agile*, and these practitioners have learned how to use these ideas to accelerate their work. They use analytics and machine learning to drive new discoveries, and they confirm such discoveries using massive datasets pumped out by the Internet of things, cell phones, and anything else that can produce and transmit a bit. They rely on their robots to scale manufacturing and on advanced models to identify markets, assess human behavior, and manage learning and adaptation—and they even train machines with ethical models to help solve some of the most intractable human problems. The rules have changed, and the rules of innovation have changed along with them. Except for money—that part stays the same.

We have moved way beyond the major change agent of failure as driving—or sustaining—innovation in the field of advanced technologies when we simply

---

[10] Engelberger, Joseph F. (1982). "Robotics in Practice: Future Capabilities." *Electronic Servicing & Technology Magazine.* [Out of print, not electronically available.]

seek continuous improvement. Innovation cycles are moving so rapidly that they must necessarily be revealed outside of traditional intellectual property boundaries to allow further development, especially when they have massive social meaning and impact. Open methods of ideation, exploration, and transformation are required in future tech. No one company can ever hope to maintain the intellectual capability and resources required to operate in the world of advanced technology. It's a dead model, just like Moore's Law. Innovating with an open approach will become the common way to innovate in future tech.

Table 3.1 shows at a high level how this new way positions the idea of openness and collaboration—at any level, including machine or human—as the central feature of this approach. Innovation is about relationships in future tech, not always real-time and not even always human. When we let the walls fall around our organizations, our data, our source code, and the way we collaborate and innovate, we evolve not just our way of building better things, but our economic philosophies and business structures as well. The traditional

Table 3.1 The Principles of Open Approaches to Innovation Are Focused on Relationships

Closed Approach to Innovation	Open Approach to Innovation
Collaboration is a characteristic of the strategy of adopting open principles for internal projects.	Collaboration between internal and external project contributors is central to innovation.
Clear demarcation exists between external and internal project assets.	Relationships are the key asset managed between internal and external project stakeholders.
IP management is explicit and based on protection.	Intellectual property is used to grow intellectual capital through shared ownership, investment, and capitalization.
Social participation is an input.	Social participation is integral.
New ideas are funneled through a process and shaped by risk and expense analyses.	Ideas are seen as products themselves and are refined based on their fit to the business model.
New ideas are designed to fit the current market or create an entirely new one.	The idea is permitted to test, change, or even break the business model.
Cultural boundaries are distinct, even when they are flexible.	Cultural boundaries are fuzzy and may even be vague.
Value networks as represented by the nodes (such as people) between interactions are connected by both intangible and tangible deliverables, and the nodes are managed contractually.	Value networks as represented by the nodes between interactions are connected by deliverables and creative actions, including problem solving and idea generation. Nodes are managed by reciprocity.

framework of innovation may change more slowly in some markets, and there are many guides to instruct, advise, and teach how to cope with those practices. But where we believe that future technology is not just an engine of global growth but is also the catalyst for positive changes in organizational productivity, quality, and competitiveness, we must refocus our everyday relationships to each other and our creative processes.

3.6 Innovation for More than Innovation's Sake

At its simplest, innovation spins on two dimensions: its *novelty,* which describes the newness of the innovation, and its *type,* as a product or a service. In addition, the nature of an innovation may be either *disruptive* or *sustaining.* Harvard Business School Professor Clayton M. Christenson is easily the world's foremost authority on disruptive innovations, identifying them as those that create new markets with new systems of values and that ultimately decimate existing markets, much as the Ford Model T crushed the market for the horse-drawn buggy or Wikipedia pushed the *Encyclopedia Britannica* out of print production after over 244 years.[11] A sustaining innovation improves a product in largely expected ways, such as a faster computer. (This is not a truism, as Apple has come to push surprises into its iPhone, despite its being a sustaining innovation.)

The conventional wisdom is that the most likely sustainers are the incumbents, because sustainers are bound to their model of the market and that is what they play to. Disrupters, on the other hand, don't tend to have customers or well-defined value networks that describe the relationships within and between businesses. So, disruptors can perceive different and novel things and take the risk of attacking the disruptive technology, even with the prospect of more certain failure. Christenson's words have seeped into our everyday language about innovation, but there are other perspectives, including Michael Porter's "continuous" and "discontinuous" change,[12] Michael L. Tushman and Philip Anderson's ideas about "incremental" and "breakthrough" innovations,[13]

---

[11] Christenson, Clayton M. (n.d.). "Disruptive Innovation." Accessed from http://www.claytonchristensen.com/key-concepts/.

[12] Porter, Michael E. (1985). "Technology and Competitive Advantage," *Journal of Business Strategy,* vol. 5, issue 3, pp. 60–78. DOI: http://dx.doi.org/10.1108/eb039075.

[13] Anderson, Philip and Tushman, Michael L. (1990). "Technological Discontinuities and Dominant Designs: A Cyclical Model of Technological Change." *Administrative Science Quarterly,* vol. 35, issue 4, pp. 604–633. Available at http://www.jstor.org/stable/2393511. DOI: 10.2307/2392832.

or William J. Abernathy and Kim B. Clark's framework for analyzing the implications of "conservative" and "radical" innovations.[14]

All of these theories are available for the serious student of innovation or the academic theorist to pore over, and all deliver a deep examination of the nature of innovation, its history, and its influence on economic market behaviors and structures. With regard to the software industry alone, Edison at al. took note of these myriad approaches and performed an extensive literature review on the term *innovation,* finding over 40 distinct definitions that underscored the difficulty in managing and measuring innovation efforts in the software industry. They identified what they determined was a complete definition, which hangs on the two axes of novelty and type.[15] In the end of what seems to have been quite a Herculean effort, they chose to accept possibly the most comprehensive definition they could find, proposed by Crossan and Apaydin:

> *Innovation is: production or adoption, assimilation, and exploitation of a value-added novelty in economic and social spheres; renewal and enlargement of products, services, and markets; development of new methods of production; and establishment of new management systems. It is both a process and an outcome.*[16]

This definition has become quite acceptable to those who prefer high observability, because it seems to give us established rules for what innovation is, although it is quite broad and confusing even in itself—especially in its rather poetic conclusion that innovation is *both* a process *and* an outcome, as it is clear that "innovation" by their definition can be one, the other, or both. Confounding the discussion was the idea of "being innovative," which is to describe an attitude that is almost sure to be part of the process of innovation (and maybe even an outcome of capturing innovation), but we must not confuse it with a practice itself, because it is not overly useful for defining a methodology to enable innovation.

---

[14] Abernathy, William J. and Clark, Kim B. (1985). *Innovation: Mapping the Winds of Creative Destruction.* North-Holland: Elsevier Science Publishers B.V. Available at http://www.sciencedirect.com/science/article/pii/0048733385900216.

[15] Edison, Henry, Bin Ali, Nauman, and Torkar, Richard (2013). Author's personal copy, "Towards Innovation Measurement in the Software Industry." *The Journal of Systems and Software,* vol. 86, issue 5, pp. 1390–1407. Retrieved from http://www.torkar.se/resources/jss-edisonNT13.pdf.

[16] Crossan, Mary M. and Apaydin, Marina (2010). "A Multi-Dimensional Framework of Organizational Innovation: A Systematic Review of the Literature." *Journal of Management Studies,* vol. 47, issue 6, pp. 1154–1191. DOI: 10.1111/j.1467-6486.2009 .00880.x.

In the unique model we are defining in this book, we will quibble with the usefulness of the comprehensive definition for innovation by arguing that *innovation is always a process,* never just an outcome. It starts when we begin to think differently about solving a problem in an open forum, explore that idea in depth through collaboration, and attempt to develop it. In the chapters that follow, we will discuss how a common process of open innovation flows from the flash of insight to the iterative cycles of prototyping, testing, and checking for fitness against our product and market fit—allowing us to optimize our idea (this is loosely called a *pivot,* which is the opportunity to explore the hypothesis of our idea in relation to our business model, where something may be subject to change)—and finally transforming our representation design into a thing or a way of doing new things.

We will not limit ourselves to preconceived ideas about the market, as future tech is not well served by such limitations, nor are we necessarily bound to an idea's marketability, perception of customer need, or other extrinsic value, although we may choose to build that model into gauging which ideas have found their moment and which have not. These factors may even be the defining characteristics for how and what we choose to invest in as part of an overall business strategy, even if the idea stresses the business strategy to the point that it must be redesigned.

Perhaps unique to future tech, it is not only feasible but likely that technology itself will drive the innovation process, potentially improving velocity and efficiency, although that is hardly a guarantee in the short term. In the next chapter, we will not only explore this model in the context of openness but also begin to discuss how such practices benefit from the extended value networks of community across the globe. We hope to demonstrate how the flash of insight, the real "aha" moment, the true "new" is not when we see the world with new eyes and think "what if we did it this way," but when we build the organization that enables bold thinkers to develop an idea collaboratively, and set out to do it, for better or for worse.

Chapter Four

Innovation Is Natural

Leonardo da Vinci (1452–1519) studied birds, observing their anatomy and flight to understand how one might construct a "flying machine."[1]

---

[1] Image retrieved from the public domain at https://commons.wikimedia.org/wiki/File:LEONARDO.JPG.

4.1 Chapter Theme

In seeking inspiration for driving innovation into our work, natural ecosystems may represent our greatest opportunity to understand the patience, invention, and collaborative thinking required. Learning from the designs of nature is already serving as a key accelerant in the field of future tech and may hold the keys both to a sustainable future and to how we learn to better innovate in our businesses. Design thinking, Agile, and peer production approaches are singular approaches that all happen to be focused on people-first in bringing new ideas to market, but they have much more in common than just their philosophy. The following discussion helps to frame the OpenXFORM model within the context of these approaches in a natural setting.

4.2 Imitation Is the Sincerest Form of Inspiration

Despite the proverbial expression that imitation is the sincerest form of flattery, in the practice of innovation, stealing someone else's work is unacceptable. And in academic settings, simply drawing on an idea, even if it is unintentional or just sloppy, may even be considered plagiarism. Stealing an idea by taking credit for someone else's research or results is seen as an offense against the soul of creative enterprise, especially in research circles. It makes innovation in the realm of future tech particularly challenging. Yet many of the same scientists and researchers whose work contributes to the most cutting-edge advancements in society today are looking to nature for their inspiration. It serves as the very source material for their designs. In many ways, nature has become our greatest mentor for future technology progression and innovation. Nature itself may represent the greatest genius in the field, a mentor of sorts that embodies both the spirit and the ethos of patience, invention, and open thinking. Truly, learning from the designs of nature is a key accelerant to future tech and holds the key not only to a sustainable future—by definition, the most efficient way to design—but also to how we innovate in our businesses.

Biomimicry is about connecting with just this ethos and spirt. And while the term "biomimicry" is easy to define, it is important also to discover why it is useful and how the process of connection with nature changes the way we collaborate and design. Biomimicry, also called *biomimetics,* literally means to "imitate life" (from the Greek, *bios* = life and *mimesis* = imitation). But the pursuit of biomimicry is also related to inspiration from the forms and materials found in nature, rather than just clever reproduction. Janine Benyus, an American author and natural sciences writer, describes in her work how nature provides us with broad models for processes. She writes, "Biomimicry is basically taking a design challenge and then finding an ecosystem that's already solved that challenge, and literally trying to emulate what you learn."[2] In this context, the practice of emulation is not just a technique but an aspiration and an ambition for learning from nature, wherein we explore the principles of all natural systems, including the social, to inform our study of the process of innovation.

4.2.1 Inspiration

Many of us have been enthralled by the stories of Leonardo da Vinci, who studied bird anatomy and systems of flight, among his other keen observations and remarkable visual studies. The Wright brothers' studies of these materials led them to understand how the shape of the wing was so crucial to creating lift. Many have called human flight the greatest innovation of mankind, but perhaps the most remarkable feat of these inventors was their ability to find novel ways to apply the principles they captured from studying bird flight to actually effect human flight. There are innumerable examples of how nature has informed some of our greatest and most useful human innovations, such as resilient buildings that mimic the shape of human bones or the hexagonal structure of the cavities that form beeswax honeycombs. Here are some of the most commonly referenced examples of biomimicry:

- **Fasteners**. In 1941, Swiss engineer George de Mestral was removing burrs from his dog. Like so many engineers before him, he became curious, and looked a little closer to see how these burrs worked. What he found were small hooks at the end of the burr needles that inspired him to create what we now call Velcro.
- **Self-Regulating Ventilation**. Mick Pearce was one of the architects of Eastgate Shopping Centre in Harare, Zimbabwe, which opened in 1996. One of Pearce's goals was to minimize damage to the environment and to improve the sustainability of the building. The average high temperature in Harare throughout the year hovers at around 27 degrees Celsius, or just over 80 degrees Fahrenheit. To control the temperature in the building to maximize energy savings, he mimicked the construction of termite mounds.

    A termite mound can withstand dramatic outside temperature variations throughout the day and stay comfortable (according to the termites surveyed for this study) inside by a system of chimneys and

---

[2] Benyus, Janine. Quoted in: Martin, Rebecca (2014). "Naturally Inspired Design." Catapult. Retrieved August 1, 2016, from http://www.abc.net.au/catapult/indepth/s1683782.htm.

tunnels. Pearce studied these and applied his findings to the construction of the over 300,000 square foot Centre, which has been reported to consume *90 percent less energy* to heat and cool than similar buildings. His design incorporated chimneys that draw in cool air at night to lower the temperature of floor slabs. During the day, the slabs retain the coolness and reduce the need for air conditioning.

- **Aerodynamics**. In 2004, scientists at Duke University, West Chester University, and the US Naval Academy discovered that the bumps at the leading edge of a whale fin greatly increase efficiency in the water by reducing drag and increasing lift. It violated all the popular thinking about fluid dynamics. Today, several designs leverage this concept to improve the efficiency of cooling fans, airplane wings, propellers, and wind turbines, in which the design is purported to boost the amount of energy created per turbine.

It seems that humans are very inspired by the structural forms and biomechanical designs found in nature. This is especially true when researchers and new product designers want to develop techniques to put materials together, to discover new materials, or to modify existing materials to be lighter, more efficient, or even just more beautiful. But there is so much more to discover. As we garner more and more insight into how animals, plants, and their ecosystems operate holistically, we are learning how systems are balanced in the natural environment; also, future tech researchers are finding ways to emulate entire physiological systems by developing a deeper understanding of the complex mechanisms that keep plants and animals alive and adapting in every stage of their lives, from biochemical functions to the cellular level.

This approach for studying natural systems is called *systems thinking,* the study of how communities thrive, survive, or perish. As a management discipline it helps us understand the interactions of the entities and resources in our sphere of concern (usually our companies), a sphere which is challenged by open resources and processes, pressure to innovate more quickly, and the need to adopt new principles for working. In stressing the interactions and dependencies among designers, builders, peer groups, and open resources and methods, we can start to conceive of better models that represent that changing landscape and learn how to create, deploy, and adapt better and more effectively. Through nature, we have learned to think about whole systems; it is this study and appreciation that have indeed connected the world through the web we call the Internet.

With a few definitions and concepts, we can begin to examine the entities involved in a system of innovation and work toward synthesizing a new model that comprehends the new boundaries of our whole system.

4.2.2 Translating Natural Models

It's not just in yoga class or at the gym that we often see ever more curious exercises that incorporate animal-like moves—such as crouching, hopping, slithering, crawling, standing like a mountain, or extending like a tree—into routines designed to strengthen human muscles and align our musculoskeletal systems. While we have not always been literal in our use of natural models, we have certainly been metaphorical (have you ever done the "downward dog" in yoga class?). To some, this is a spiritual pursuit driven by existential challenges to bring together the power of nature-inspiration and the very health of our planet, as researchers pursue more sustainable designs. Others are perhaps less poetic, but no less interested. When we study nature, we are well advised to begin with biological principles, and perhaps there is no better (or no better funded) domain than sports from which to explore some of the most advanced techniques to mimic the functions of animals.

Many, many dollars (state economies worth of dollars) have been dumped into performance enhancement, from pharmaceuticals to physical fitness. A quick overview of human fitness techniques reveals many nature-inspired designs to provide the perfect circumstances for maximum conditioning, peak performance, and healing. High-performance athletes are highly motivated to win, but at the top of mind for coaches, investors, and athletes themselves is avoiding injury that would take down a prized competitor. When injury does occur, it can ruin seasons, cause missed events, and even destroy careers. For those times when injury does occur, injury management is crucial. And if we think that nature is only inspiring shark-skin swim gear or ever-tighter biking shorts, we find that it's in the trainer's office where some of the most remarkable bio-empathetic magic happens.

Apart from every nature-inspired strategy designed to avoid injury—such as metabolically-oriented base training or special shoes—there are key fitness technologies that focus on rapid healing in a body that, under normal conditions, requires rest, ice, compression, and elevation (RICE) to bring pain and swelling under control. However, advanced technologies allow us to do much more than hang around waiting for a sprain to heal. It is possible to simulate certain natural processes in the body to create enhanced conditions for self-repair. One approach is to simulate intense physical exercise using a device that electrically stimulates the athlete's muscles, as if he or she were in active training. This "activity" causes the body to respond with the production of lactic acid, which in turn causes the brain to respond with a message to the metabolic system to release certain hormones whose job it is to quickly act to repair damaged tissues. Thus, the body is signaled to renovate itself by being tricked into thinking it is "bonked" and in need of assistance to recover.

Other machines that have employed biological inspiration use cooling systems of cold compresses placed strategically on the body to lower the athlete's body temperature. A lower body temperature allows oxygen to remain in the bloodstream for a longer period of time. For any athlete looking to maximize training, this is a massive benefit—with access to more oxygen, physical exertion becomes much more efficient, creating enhanced benefit without further stress that might bring injury or exhaustion.

4.3 The Strategies of Life

Biomimicry is a profound inspiration to engineers such as George Devol, inventor and science fiction aficionado, who created the first digital and programmable robot in 1953, named Unimate. Unimate consisted of a large control box with an arm that transported die castings in an assembly line, which it welded to auto bodies (a tremendously dangerous job for humans, and quite poisonous from the fumes emitted during the process). But now, more than ever, biologically inspired engineering is not only the stuff of great comic books and movies, it's a scientific discipline unto itself that is driving future tech solutions in medicine, industry, environmental sciences, and other fields.

The principles of biology, organismal and chemical engineering, and the physical sciences are not only informing how new products can work, but also translating nature at every level into new products that carry the form and function of living systems. These designs seek to maintain complex natural network structures, to provide the ability to self-repair and heal, and, of course, to evolve. Yet, despite the fascination with and interest in biologically inspired design, especially in sustainable development and future tech innovation, the focus is nearly always on developing solutions to engineering problems. Strangely and sadly overlooked are the interactions among communities themselves within a given ecosystem's organization. This is certainly not a truism, but, apart from the domain of social network analysis (SNA), it is certainly a largely untapped reservoir of inspiration for new models of digitally mediated social organization.

4.3.1 Natural Networks

To be clear, the study of the principles of social and self-organization is widespread, finding support from natural systems, especially with ideas for understanding human behaviors by studying swarming, crystallization, and natural neural networks. In the area of self-organization, especially, the more it is studied the more complicated it appears to become. And the profound impacts of progress in the domain of self-organizing entities can be great, because it builds the foundation for potentially dramatic and meaningful shifts in physics, economics, education, psychology, urban design, cybernetics, and spatiotemporal phenomena—including even the improbable, such as collecting water from thin air by mimicking the behavior of desert beetles.[3]

Unfortunately, using nature as a reference point for human communities is surprisingly difficult to master in the modern era, because the common application of design principles still seems to rely heavily on the theological belief in human sovereignty and dominion over nature itself. This perspective is still quite influential in many countries and organizations, and it demonstrates a subtext of moving away from natural systems, not toward them. Many people prefer to think of disruptive innovation as solving problems in a wonderful new way, not assuming that a similar problem may have already been solved by a bug living on a cactus in a desert. And while it seems that the biomimicry movement brings highly relevant solutions to human problems with tested patterns and strategies, humans are slower to adapt when compared to nearly every other living creature.

Given this framework of thought about innovation, perhaps it is not entirely surprising that the biomimicry movement tends to focus on the physical design and production aspects of innovation, in which new material resources, structures, and systems are modeled on those found in nature. In many cases, their designs focus solely on physiology or perhaps some other aspect of biological behavior, but less often on learning and applying aspects of community interaction.

4.3.2 The Balance of Life

Any ecosystem, whether it be forest, grassland, desert, tundra, or marine, represents a rich tapestry of interactions among the living organisms and nonliving features within it. Science classifies these two major components of an ecosystem as *biotic* and *abiotic*. Biotic features are the plants and animals within the community of the ecosystem, and abiotic features include the non-living parts of the environment that affect the functioning of the biotic components in the ecosystem, especially in terms of growth, maintenance, and reproduction. Abiotic resources include water, sunlight, temperature, soil, humidity, the

---

[3] Medlock, Katie (2016, February). "Harvard Taps Biomimicry to Harvest Water from Thin Air." Inhabitat. Retrieved August 1, 2016, from http://inhabitat.com/harvard-taps-biomimicry-to-harvest-water-from-thin-air/.

quality of the atmospheric chemistry, and even pressure and sound waves in a marine ecosystem.

All ecosystems have *carrying capacity* and *limiting factors*; the carrying capacity of an ecosystem is the greatest number of community members that can be healthfully sustained, and limiting factors are anything that control growth in the systems, such as the availability of water, sunlight, or food. Thus, every ecosystem has contention and competition for resources, which in an uninterrupted state are managed through a system of *ecological regulation* that includes the diversity of interaction among members of the community, ecological succession, and various forms of cycling, such as food chains, trophic levels, and energy flow.

A prejudicial summary of biological ecosystems for our focus in this work is that the abiotic resources are those that create the conditions for growth of biotic organisms, and it is the amount and availability of these resources that accelerate or inhibit growth. This is important to understand as we move forward.

4.3.3 Is There an Innovation Ecosystem?

If we believe that innovation is a process, then there is no such thing as an "innovation ecosystem." An ecosystem is a biological community of abiotic and biotic factors and interactions, and, as we previously described, for this study we see innovation as a process. With that perspective, innovation is better compared to how photosynthesis converts sunlight into energy, where the process of innovation takes an idea and provides a framework within which to transform it into a different idea, a new device, or a fresh method for solving a human complication. However, there is definitely an ecosystem within which the innovative process will be able to flow efficiently, with maximum efficiency, within its carrying capacity, and with an implicit acceptance for its limiting factors. There is no question that the interactions within a natural ecosystem provide a rich and abundant representation of ideas that support what we hope to achieve in encouraging rapid innovation with the resources of open data, information, and content.

There is a notable movement that seeks to define and drive an *innovation economy* through an *innovation ecosystem*. This form of economics has been broadly championed by many, including Michael Porter, and calls for economic policies that spur productivity through innovation. This community of stakeholders argues that innovation fuels the creation of ancillary products and services that may include resource centers comprising research, technology, and business development players who serve these markets that drive regional economic growth.

We mention this economic framework simply to distinguish it from our goal of defining a model that is divorced from (even if it is useful to) any particular economic theory or development initiative.

What is most extraordinary about natural ecosystems is their natural efficiency, where nothing is wasted—a tree dies and it decomposes, decays, and in that state creates the conditions for new life to emerge through the quiet persistence of beetles, woodlice, fungi, and earthworms. It may not always smell perfect but, over time, that fallen tree unlocks new life. This is precisely what we strive for in bringing new ideas to markets, and why we seek accelerants, such as new processes, research, money, and methodologies, that we hope will throw fuel onto the barbeque. We argue these processes academically, in our business news feeds, and in the open bar after any Agile development conference. In the halls of business schools and engineering classrooms, with the well wishes of psychologists, sociologists, and anthropologists, we keep looking for the Holy Grail.

Yet when it comes to innovation in future tech, the imperative for transparent systems of information, data, and content that hold transformative capital within them, and the market potential of companies that rest their business models on open resources, suggest that we must do much more than just unlock data sets with equality of access. We must also examine the interactions between our abiotic resources and their biotic consumers to understand how we may best collaborate and compete in a manner that doesn't predicate the annihilation of either our own ecosystem or another's.

There are both anecdotal and strong patterns of reference in this field of inquiry we call biomimicry (or biomimetics) that have convinced a generation of engineers that the practice of deeply studying nature, learning how to imitate a natural model or system, can go a long way toward enabling us to create new, and often sustainable, solutions to our human problems. Just since 2015, graduate programs in such centers of learning as the Massachusetts Institute of Technology (MIT) and Harvard University are emerging that offer biomimicry studies through engineering, sustainability, and design programs.

Even so, while the practices of biomimicry may change how we approach the development of new technologies, as a community of future thinkers, we have largely overlooked some of the most important lessons that the ecosystem from which our inspiration springs also has to teach us about how we do the work of innovation. What we learn from studying how certain biologic entities achieve things so resourcefully in their biome can also bring critical learning about adaptation efficiency to our own process of invention, in very much the same way that the abiotic features of a natural ecosystem contribute to the life of its natural community—with highly efficient systems for self-healing, the ability to withstand stress, the capacity for self-organization, and the ability to harness and efficiently consume resources without waste.

4.4 We Must Adapt, Again

The idea of a common innovation is bound to our bio-empathetic model we call the Open Idea Transformation model, or OpenXFORM. This model is founded in the practices of the commons-based peer production communities and inspired heavily by the practices of Agile methodologies and design thinking, all three of which attempt to methodize human-centered practices with a people-first mentality, organized to balance efficiency and high-quality outcomes in a constrained, limited, and dynamic world of the customer or user.

To facilitate and later explore the fully-fledged model in future chapters, a short discussion of these three methodologies is helpful:

- **Peer Production.** The commons-based peer production system, sometimes called *social production* or *mass collaboration,* is also a model documented by Harvard Law School professor Yochai Benkler. We explored some of the key influences and components of Benkler's ideas earlier when we discussed the cultural structure and other issues, such as personal liberty and methodologies, found in the world of FOSS. The community and composition of what we generally call FOSS has indeed done much to forward the feasibility for a real-world system of production that does not rely on proprietary knowledge while it simultaneously encourages a decentralized and participant-driven method of working in collaboration. We participate in peer production every time we contribute to a crowdsourced effort, whether it is an open-source project or a church cookbook.

  Benkler explores both the features of and issues with social production approaches in his 2002 book, *The Wealth of Networks,* and in it identifies principles that attempt to comprehend the wide variations in human creative impulses that emerge under the auspices of peer governance or that otherwise depend on free cooperation. He describes cooperative enterprises as those in which "the inputs and outputs of the process are shared, freely or conditionally, in an institutional form that leaves them equally available for all to use as they choose at their individual discretion."[4] He has published frequently on this topic and fully examines the correlations between production scale and the openness of the outputs generated by the peer community. One of his most interesting conclusions is that peer production has challenges outside of the production of primarily functional works (something that has a specific purpose or goal) as opposed

---

[4] Benkler, Yochai (2006). *The Wealth of Networks.* Yale University Press. ISBN 978-0-300-11056-2. Retrieved on August 1, 2016, from cyber.law.harvard.edu/wealth_of_networks/Sentence-sliced_Text_Chapter_3. p. 62. Available under CC BY-NC-SA 2.5.

to an open-ended effort, which raises questions of peer governance. Questions of peer governance are also raised in the context of Agile—specifically, whether a team should be free to acknowledge limitations, discuss progress on discrete tasks, and employ collective problem-solving as key functions of a fully transparent effort. However, like peer production, Agile always depends on some level of self-selection and individual action for an effective result.

- **Agile Methodology.** Agile was first described within the Agile Manifesto (www.agilemanifesto.org), which emerged in early 2001 after a gathering of independent thinkers and software development professionals agreed that they wanted to work in communities of practice that emphasized basic human values, transparency, and adaptive behaviors as foundational to creating great software products that were in the interest of the customers' needs. Their hope and optimism was great—as with all declarations that claim to put the interest of people first—that through Agile, the Dilbert-esque organization would die quickly and quietly, thereby creating workable approaches to production that would help teams respond to unpredictability with incremental and iterative work rhythms.

  Agile has been one of the most oft-discussed approaches in the modern software-driven development world. It has been applied widely to other disciplines without regard; in some ways it is still seen as a bit of a novelty. However, an honest Agile expert who has watched projects rise and fall will tell you that it is not a one-size-fits-all approach. In fact, some say that if the team knows what they're doing, they've worked together, and they're familiar with the project domain, Agile is just not useful.

  Mike Cohn, an experienced Agile trainer and founder of Mountain Goat Software, says, ". . . agile is most appropriate on any urgent project with significant complexity and novelty—and that includes software development and weddings. It does raise the question though of whether a couple's first kiss at the end of the ceremony is a product backlog item or part of the done criteria for the overall product."[5] His humor underscores how the efficient system of Agile production can get caught up on arcane details and disruptions as well. To summarize, Agile can been a positive choice for teams, especially when there is confusion and when focus could easily be lost.

- **Design Thinking.** Design thinking describes an approach to solutions-oriented problem solving, which at its core focuses on meeting people's

---

[5] Cohn, Mike (2011). "Deciding What Kind of Projects Are Most Suited for Agile." Retrieved August 1, 2016, from https://www.mountaingoatsoftware.com/blog/deciding-what-kind-of-projects-are-most-suited-for-agile.

needs; it is a method of thinking about designing new products or processes. The methodology of design thinking—like Agile's iterative approach and peer production's focus on discrete tasks—codifies a cyclic process that moves between prototyping, testing, analyzing, and refining to achieve its goals. Also like Agile, there are as many variations on design thinking as there are designers who use the process. This is not really surprising, because design thinking mostly represents the mere desire to transform our perspective from technology-centric to human-centric. This means creating meaningful products that strive to balance a world of constraints and competing requirements of both people and systems in a way that is positive, useful, and viable within that world.

Tim Brown, president and CEO of IDEO ("*eye*-dee-oh"), who is in many ways the world's pre-eminent go-to guy when a company wants to build or fix their creative culture, describes design thinking as, "a human-centered approach to innovation that draws from the designer's toolkit to integrate the needs of people, the possibilities of technology, and the requirements for business success."[6] As broad as that statement might sound, it is significant in explicitly making space for creators to help them identify the tools they need to express their best ideas in a forum that provides the means to bring inspired thinking to life.

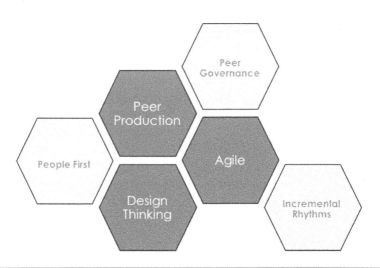

Figure 4.1   Like the honeybee's honeycomb, peer production, Agile, and design thinking approaches share key principles for efficient and collaborative production.

---

[6] Brown, Tim (n.d.). Quoted in: "About IDEO." Retrieved August 1, 2016, from https://www.ideo.com/about/#EBHlW2wBQIRkmDMZ.99.

Figure 4.1 describes how peer production, Agile, and design thinking approaches share key principles of people first, transparent governance, and incremental rhythms, among others—principles reminiscent of the honeybee's perfectly shaped hexagonal honeycombs, which appear to maximize every available efficiency in managing collective labor and the availability of raw materials. Where these approaches diverge is in their intended application: peer production helps us understand and design the relationships that make up the ecology of information and knowledge in the service of human freedom and development; design thinking attempts to formalize the best of the creative process to solve for solutions (instead of problems) to difficult human problems; and Agile brings much to those who work every day to build things of value for customers in responsive, collaborative, and self-organizing teams and can scale effectively with the needs of the organization.

4.4.1 The High Costs of the Next Best Thing

All these approaches are about "doing the right thing"—encouraging joy and inspiration for the designers and developers who bring meaningful innovation quickly and efficiently to the customer—which will naturally benefit the company sponsoring the effort, perhaps even massively. Both Agile and design thinking specifically include principles that attempt to capture the creative process of design and the craft of building those designs and that may often be ambiguous and depend on iterative improvement to reach the right outcome, but the two approaches are different in their gaze. The design thinker embraces a thorny problem, because he or she has a way to solve for it, while the Agile purist takes joy in the revelation of a working product that emerges from the efforts of well-oiled, collaborative, self-organizing teams, which can rapidly and flexibly respond to change, all supported by the resource-rich world of the knowledge commons and a world of like-minded peers. Agile and design thinking *seem* similar because they *are*—philosophically—in that they are oriented toward empowering the people involved in the creative process and flexible enough to find the right solution for the challenge at hand. However, the two are different, even if one were to use Agile principles in their design thinking efforts or vice versa. The important distinction is that the creative process of design thinking offers an excellent way of getting to the best solutions, and Agile will take them to scale.

4.4.2 An Anti-Case Study

So, what could possibly go wrong? Well, much has, and the trouble stems from two things—evangelism and its evil twin, *co-optation*.

First: an anti-case study based on the author's experience (with some facts obscured to shield the most dreadful parties) in the Agile trenches:

The team sitting around the table looked terrible. The two senior-most engineers on the team sat across from each other, the elder hunched forward, tapping a blue EZ-erase marker, while the other fell back in his seat, running his hands through his thinning hair, shakily managing his third energy drink of the morning. Andy and Phil always seemed exhausted. The two had developed a system in which the first one would code from the afternoon through the night, hanging it up at about 5 A.M., when the next engineer would pick up the problem and press on. Despite being terribly honest engineers, brilliant, who played for the game of it and the big startup win, hardly anyone knew of their round-the-clock arrangement.

The feisty startup, which was working on one of the first real-time search engines for mass public use, was certainly the prettiest girl at the party those days—one of the first to draw down serious venture funding after the first bubble burst at the turn of the century.

And the company was frothy; they claimed to be an "Agile shop," to self-organize around the tenets of the Agile Manifesto and people before tools, to hold its members in esteem, to maintain working code, and above all, always to deliver working software. Only they were none of those things. Andy and Phil ran the show, handing out meaningless tasks to the other engineers as a smokescreen to cover up their private scheme, and leaving the hand-waving to an irascible, heavy-drinking front-end man who smoothed over the engineering lead's concerns time and time again with a cloudy form of transparent hedging. It was an industrial, steampunk office, which passed out the free beer and mounted whiteboards on every wall, which were covered with colorful little sticky notes marking tasks that were never completed—a team haunted by a growing mountain of technical debt. There was very little sanity, and certainly nothing even remotely close to a product.

This was a very tired team, and binge drinking was its greatest stress reliever. They bought the idea of solving a very difficult and nearly intractable problem that would bring a new world of internet browsing with a design for a social-internet-thingy that was founded in the head of a guy calling himself "the creative." Unfortunately, Mr. Creative was so "creative" that he couldn't keep a single idea in his head, showed zilch respect for anyone else's workstreams and deadlines, and consequently was left to inspire a team of people who weren't sold on his vision at all, because they couldn't afford to be.

Still this team was tough, with changing requirements and complicated features that would shift and twist, sometimes in days (called business *pivots*), and consequently, almost ensured an utter failure to execute on both the product vision and the marketing story. Most of the team was sure they had ruined their future careers by aligning with a well-known-crazy company, but hardly anyone left, because they liked the idea of being in a well-funded startup in a hip town.

But the last day, when the worm finally turned, the team were sitting in their Agile sprint planning meeting, hangovers nursed, markers tapping, and energy drinks flowing. They were just about done with grooming the backlog, when in walked the CEO. He was excited, and looked remarkably like a hip, wind-up kewpie doll. Kewpie nearly hopped into the room, dark Prada glasses perched easily in the dips of his jelly-coiffed hair, in unabashedly tight low-hipped stitched jeans, d-toe leather shoes, and (black) T-shirt that clung unconvincingly to his slight, pale arms.

"Guys, Guys! I have a great idea!"

It was the sort of moment that ends great movements, as each worn-out body and mind raced with endless memories of 100 work-weeks of trying to make it work for Kewpie—hours of pure frustration, missed school plays, no sleep, and unhealthy amounts of caffeine, alcohol, and salted almonds. No one got up and walked out, they couldn't afford to. The high salaries had resulted in another form of servitude, called debt. Kewpie CEO was met with blank stares, not one verbal stroke for his mind-blowing new idea, not a single marker tapped. A few feet shifted under the long tables. Feet that were going to walk away from this Agile company the first moment a new job could be landed that had decent psychiatric benefits.

Anyway, Kewpie flushed what was left of his start-up goodwill story and other-people's money (OPM), the layoffs finally—and blessedly—began as no product shipped, engineers started to walk away, and deadline after deadline soaked into the mist. The hardcore startup boys stayed behind, and the edgy entrepreneurs sold off their wares, unbelievably, to the IT department of a discount store. All the preferred shareholders got a payday, of sorts, and a few people went along for the ride, but the dream had died many months before. It was Kewpie's final words to the blank faces of the team, as he skulked out of the fake garage door that day, that put the nail in the coffin of inspiration and innovation, "What is wrong with these people, I thought they were Agile!"

Because after all, shouldn't an "Agilist" be able to keep up with the random spinning of "the creative"? Doesn't the Agile Manifesto specifically say that their process helps teams in "responding to change over following a plan" to keep up that constant pace of production, indefinitely?[7] It does, but it left out

---

[7] Beck, Kent, et al. (2001). "Manifesto for Agile Software Development." Retrieved August 1, 2016, from http://www.agilemanifesto.org/.

the part about how if a team must fight the powers that be to maintain the discipline of Agile or they are condemned to use Agile as a smokescreen for their own private process. This is the moment when Agile becomes the same old way of forcing an outcome that will surely underperform any innovative idea that was ever envisioned.

4.4.3 Highly Principled Disruption

The evangelistic touting of Open, Agile, and Design Thinking have many times over led to the gimmicky and artificial manipulation of the creative process in the service of mediocrity and, sometimes, utter calamity. This is not because it is wrong to be excited about seeking and sharing about a better way to do work, and it certainly isn't wrong to try to bring in new ways of solving difficult problems. But excessive enthusiasm has resulted in a watering down of the process by attempts to standardize and normalize what is dangerously cast as "freedom." As new adherents—such as a Fortune 1000 financial company or others that are compelled to measure every minute of time for contractual reasons, or that are oriented to manage their production very closely in the name of efficiency—attempt to push the process into very different contexts, things don't always go smoothly. Agile just isn't an easy fit for companies with public reporting requirements; C-suites that demand daily productivity updates; or, most especially, marketing departments that want to schedule their press releases, product launches, and social media strategies way out front.

It is often the most enthusiastic who push the hardest to force a new process into a one-size-fits-all model with the idea that adopting *something* is better than adopting *nothing*, because Agile (good) is measurably "better" than the waterfall methodology (bad). David Thach and Rick Rene discuss their experience with large companies that have attempted to wrap discipline around Agile adoption. Their observations are easily recognizable to many anticipative Agilists. They describe how companies that attempt to adopt Agile with the singular goal of enhanced efficiency not only will have a tough time, they may also find themselves in a worse condition—sometimes utter disaster. The consequence is that internal adopters who don't really understand the history or principles of Agile may find themselves with a costly endeavor and a resulting team that cannot seem to meet management's goals, which often exist under uniquely *un*-Agile conditions that demand traditional reporting requirements, rewards, oversight, and strict project management.

Thach and Rene write that companies that have much "technical specialization, complicated reporting structures and governance committees, long-term roadmap planning and budgeting, conglomerate and subsidiaries in geographically dispersed locations, multiple shared product owners, mature legacy third-party installed applications, inherited roles absent in purist Agile teams, a variety of IT vendors and partners with near-shore and off-shore blended workforces, and entrenched waterfall frameworks . . ." are going to be in for a very rough ride.[8] They further state that this doesn't mean that a simpler adoption of Agile isn't possible and potentially helpful, but what they are underscoring is that going full bore to standardize "Agile" behavior and practices with documentary canons and strict adherence to the artifacts of the process will find the achievement of their goals of a streamlined and adaptable production process to be illusory at best.

Design thinking also suffers from unprincipled short-cutters looking for massive, innovative breakthrough. Yet design thinking depends (without apology) on messy conflict, loopy looping, ugly prototypes, and even tears of frustration. But, of course, brazen design consultancies will claim they can straighten all this out, and their evangelists start touting the next process trick to finally, once and for all, capture the creative process for a few bags of cash. Obviously, there is no way that all that messiness can be accepted in any so-called serious company.

Tim Brown, both a champion and a critic of design thinking, had this to say as early as 2011, when asked about the perceived low rate of success with the design thinking process, where he dumped an awful lot of the blame on the way that it has been framed by many design consultancies who widely deployed the methodology. He says that they were ". . . hoping that a process trick would produce significant cultural and organizational change. From the beginning, the process of design thinking was a scaffolding for the real deliverable: creativity. But in order to appeal to the business culture of process, it was denuded of the mess, the conflict, failure, emotions, and looping circularity that is part and parcel of the creative process."[9] Understanding the reality—that processes do not change companies—the company must first begin to change itself.

And finally, the legions of "open" advocates get their day, as many companies that want to get ahead of the innovation curve are aggressively and quickly adopting myriad open approaches. They plan on succeeding in today's digitally disrupted world. And thus, it is no longer taking a radical position to say that open innovation/collaboration/data/information/knowledge/etc. is

[8] Thach, David and Rene, Rick (2013). "Implementing Agile in Fortune 1000 Companies." Retrieved August 1, 2016, from https://www.agileconnection.com/article/implementing-agile-fortune-1000-companies.

[9] Brown, Tim. Quoted in: Nussbaum, Bruce (2011). "Design Thinking Is a Failed Experiment. So What's Next?" Retrieved August 1, 2016, from http://www.fastcodesign.com/1663558/design-thinking-is-a-failed-experiment-so-whats-next.

the only way to authentically accelerate to innovative success. As things such as open innovation or consultancies that desire to assist such companies begin to flower, it is worth a moment of short reflection. Consider the following commentary from a chief corporate marketing strategist, when discussing the role of open source in today's companies. Tom Wentworth, CMO of Acquia, a cloud platform company, emphasizes the importance of open source, saying that such a strategy ". . . allows enterprise business to place its bet on the freedom to innovate. The global developer communities bring unforeseen development speed, and the lack of high license fees mean that resources can be invested in a great digital experience . . . open source provides the freedom to innovate, plan out your own product road map, and respond quickly to market demands. That equals survival."[10]

To be fair, Wentworth was offering a broad view of the impact of open source in his enterprise for a blog author; he was hardly offering a firm position. But his optimism makes a point about the danger of unbridled exuberance. While optimism has a role, woe to those who read Wentworth's words and, hearing only the exuberant assessment of open trends, decide to power it into their companies without acknowledging the critical importance of fit and context. Understanding fit and how it could serve a company strategically requires understanding the principles that help shape the forces for an open perspective to begin with. Like Agile and design thinking before it, peer production and going open are not "tricks" for reducing operating and development costs, improving productivity, and forming fresh, new relationships with partners and customers. They are simply models for collaborative design and development that have worked for many and that may enhance efficiency and output for others and might even bring remarkable returns.

4.4.4 Patterns of Co-Optation

Michael O. Church is well known in Silicon Valley circles for his relentless drubbing of high-tech culture. In one of his criticisms, he exposes a very important concern about the blind adoption of Agile. He writes, ". . . creative people lose their creativity if asked to explain themselves while they are working. It's the same with software. Programmers often have to work in an environment of one-sided transparency. These Agile systems, so often misapplied, demand that they provide humiliating visibility into their time and work, despite a lack of

---

[10] Wentworth, Tom (2013). "Acquia Says Open Source Helps Enterprises Thrive in Today's Digital Disruption." Retrieved August 1, 2016, from http://sandhill.com/article/acquia-says-open-source-helps-enterprises-thrive-in-todays-digital-disruption/.

reciprocity."[11] In the end, the result is that organic, highly adaptable, bottom-up approaches to creative design, production, and knowledge sharing that are enthusiastically and zealously encouraged as the new "keys to the kingdom" end up being thrown out as failures, and the proverbial baby goes out with the bath water. If, when such a process is implemented, a company knew that they would be asked to violate their well understood, measurable frameworks and customary, comfortable approach to management, such adoption would be more measured in and of itself.

Whereas autonomy and freedom are at the heart of many initiatives that enter the organization from the bottom up, shoehorning such approaches into traditional top-down hierarchies will often cause a flexible process to grow rigid and ultimately to break down. The problem is not so much that a community of practice has gone off the rails, it's more that trying to force a community into the wrong ecosystem will never work. A fish can't survive on the beach. It needs water. And a beagle can't live under water. When companies require precise measurability and where they simply cannot change quickly as an organization, can they ever take advantage of the benefits offered by approaches such as design thinking, Agile, and peer production?

The answer may be found in nature itself, as expressed in the principles of ecological regulation, in which living communities, simply as a byproduct of their natural and normal behaviors, ultimately support the health of the overall ecosystem.

4.5 That's Not What We Meant

My goal is fairly modest: to tell a few stories of how unintended consequences occur, to speculate about their significance, and to inspire more research and discussion about this often mentioned but infrequently explored theme.
    —Steven M. Gillon, historian and author of *That's Not What We Meant to Do*[12]

When IDEO wanted to help companies unlock their creative potential by introducing design thinking, they surely weren't envisioning a workplace in

---

[11] Church, Michael O. (2015). "Why 'Agile' and Especially Scrum Are Terrible." Retrieved August 1, 2016, from https://michaelochurch.wordpress.com/2015/06/06/why-agile-and-especially-scrum-are-terrible/.

[12] Murray, Philip (2001). "That's Not What We Meant to Do: Reform and Its Unintended Consequences in Twentieth-Century America by Steven M. Gillon." Retrieved August 1, 2016, from https://fee.org/articles/thats-not-what-we-meant-to-do-reform-and-its-unintended-consequences-in-twentieth-century-america-by-steven-m-gillon/.

which the master "creative" would swoop down and tell the "Agile people" how to make his or her idea a success. Or when the authors of the Agile Manifesto believed that focusing on relationships was important to building a great software product and an ultimate victory for lower-cost software production, but they shied away from the disturbing vision of dashboard management that turned Agile tasks into de-facto punch cards. And when the enthusiasts of open collaboration insist that open and accessible resource sharing is critical to rapid evolution in business, they are certainly hoping for more than a dominant management strategy that means "we'll just take what we need here." Tim Brown himself actually made the poignant observation and disappointing revelation about how leadership who want to drive innovation into their companies have failed to lead by example (Brown's emphasis):

> *Creative leadership isn't about leaders simply becoming more creative. It's about individuals **leading for creativity**. That means you, as a leader, must unlock the creative potential of your organization, no matter the industry. It's your job to set the conditions for your organization to generate, embrace, and execute on new ideas.*[13]

Still, with a good ecological risk assessment and a realistic plan, all need not be in vain. We still can find opportunity to persistently (even if not always delicately) venture forward into unchartered territory, where it is possible to speak openly about what is happening for good or ill in our projects, work to inspire each other, and reflect on how to improve our collaboration in an engaged way. Inspired and pragmatic leadership is still the best way to clear the pathways for the innovative process to take place and to make a space where risk-taking and the prospect of small and frequent failures are accepted as important tools for the greater good of the company.

4.5.1 It's Still About the People

In the beginning, all of these approaches were about helping people to reflect openly on their work efforts and adapt with resilience to changes in their momentary conditions without losing momentum or a sense of mission. Most bottom-up methodologies are in fact about finding a way to solve complex problems in a cost-effective way that meets customer needs, and by the way enjoy the experience of creating with others, even when that means adjusting to all kinds of dysfunction. It's still mostly about that; after all, ever since we got

---

[13] Brown, Tim (2016). "Unlock Your Organization's Creative Potential." Retrieved on August 1, 2016, from http://designthinking.ideo.com/?p=1474.

tools in our hands that allow us to massively accelerate what we can achieve with our ideas, they will be picked up even if the directions are never taken out of the box. The question is if companies want to make space for authentic innovation, whether it resides inside or outside of their walls; and if peer production does emerge as imagined, companies will be scrambling to hire a whole new batch of relationship managers.

It's time to stop blaming a methodology as "wrong" or "not being done right" or "just a bad idea," especially when flexibility and resiliency define those very processes, even if it cannot be adequately adapted as useful during an age of digital disruption. In many ways, design thinking, Agile, and peer production are nothing more than attempts to write down what seemed to be working among certain individuals and share it with others. But when top-down organizations construct rigid frameworks that focus solely on encouraging measurement (even arbitrary measurement), this tears away the prospects of achieving a long-term mission and getting atoms of work done. In many ways, these ideas will fail when they are perceived as a gilded gift for in-crisis organizations that use them as a controlled-chaos smokescreen to cover up their dysfunctional organizations while blaming their most curious and productive contributors for failing to lay golden eggs. After a while, the shiny buzzwords become secret code for "trash bin of ideas," "waste of time," or "working from home."

4.6 A New Model? You Can't Be Serious

Robby Krieger is an American guitarist and singer-songwriter best known for his affiliation with The Doors. The author of *Light My Fire* and *Love Her Madly* has been inducted into the Rock & Roll Hall of Fame, is named by *Rolling Stone* magazine as one of the greatest guitarists of all time, and is one of the creators of the music for Jim Morrison's poetry on the stunning 1978 album *An American Prayer*. Krieger knows a little something about how to successfully shepherd collaboration from the caverns of creative inspiration through technical craft.[14] He once said, when asked about the nature of creative inspiration in the band, that, "In The Doors we have both musicians and poets, and both know of each other's art, so we can effect a synthesis . . . All of us have the freedom to explore and improvise within a framework."[15]

---

[14] Krieger, Robby (2016, July 30). "Wikipedia: The Free Encyclopedia." Wikimedia Foundation, Inc. Retrieved on August 1, 2016, from https://en.wikipedia.org/wiki/Robby_Krieger.

[15] Gaar, Gillian G. (2015). *The Doors: The Illustrated History*. ISBN: 9780760346907. Minneapolis, MN: Voyageur Press. p. 33.

Krieger was alluding to the general idea that when two or more ideas come together, they can—with a certain form of regulation—bring forth something altogether new and innovative. In chemistry, *synthesis* stands for many different types of complex processes, as in physics, electronics, sound, the creative arts, linguistics, and of course philosophy, in which the triad of thesis, antithesis, and synthesis are the formula for thought called the *dialectical method*. This method of collaborative problem solving is one that, when honestly and openly applied, can bring its contributors to a point of resolution or synthesis, where a common truth forms a new beginning in which the dialectic begins again with a response to a new truth. It is the very thing that keeps us moving forward in the world of ideas—that we can always make progress, incrementally and steadily, in a way that is satisfying both emotionally and logically. It's unbelievably simple, but it's not always easy.

As described in Figure 4.2, our "regulated ecosystems" are also an expression of the dialectic method. We often call them companies, and as research experience is beginning to show, they can benefit greatly by connecting to the opposing unregulated resources found in open information, data, and content. Not only can companies benefit from open thinking, collaboration, and innovation, any company may come to find that it is establishing a firmer stand in delivering on their strategic goals, whether they are founded in new products or services, by focusing on their core strengths rather than pre-creating or re-creating the wheel. When it comes to innovation, the further we are able to balance our corporate ecosystems by establishing a synthesis with open approaches and by pushing the edges into the areas of transition that form *ecotones*—the regions

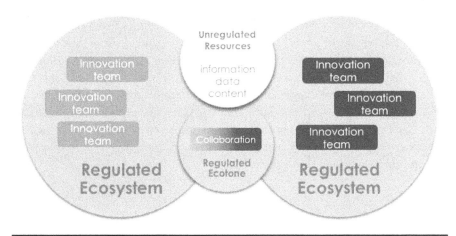

Figure 4.2 A synergistic approach to innovation helps balance regulated and unregulated ecosystems.

of transition between other biological communities—with our partners and collaborators, the greater our potential returns.

That is the dialectic demonstrated by the model presented fully in the next chapter, called *Open Transformation* (OpenXFORM), which seeks to propose a natural approach to the process of innovation. We will delve into the nature of these systems—how they adapt and decompose information—and discover ways to find the points of synergy among the tested methodologies that put human relationships first—design thinking, Agile, and peer production.

The dialectical method is as old as every story ever told among human beings; it describes the tension of natural systems and has been a key feature in many philosophical tomes, from Hegel to Marx. It is this: that survival relies on the forces of opposition; and that it is actually the phenomenon of resistive force that holds everything together physically, biologically, chemically, emotionally, and logically. The whole requires its parts, an atom needs its electrons, living creatures need the sun and the rain, designers need inspiration, and craftspeople need their tools.

Chapter Five

Building an Ecosystem

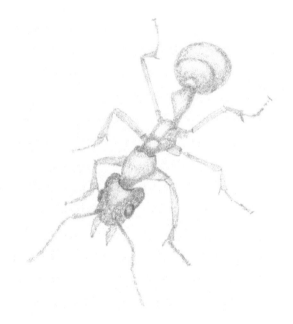

A pencil drawing of a meat ant (*Iridomyrex*), considered to be the most ecologically important group of ants to farmers in Australia, who use them to manage animal carcasses.[1]

---

[1] Coleman, Peri (2009). Retrieved, July 3, 2016. Released into the public domain by https://commons.wikimedia.org/wiki/File:Meat_ant.jpg.

5.1 Chapter Theme

Those who want to encourage creativity and innovation recognize that open thinking and sources of data, content, and information help achieve and realize strategic goals that have previously been out of reach. Bio-empathetic designs, especially from the organizational perspective, seem like the perfect way for any motivated business entity to achieve those sought-after qualities. Yet even if it makes good sense to mimic natural forms for innovative new functional designs—such as copying the shape of a whale fin for ergonomic advantage—taking natural systems too literally is counterproductive, especially when we want to transform the way we work to drive peak performance. The OpenXFORM methodology helps facilitate the uncertain and difficult relationship between open resources and the private world of the innovating company entity.

5.2 Agents of Innovation

When it comes to biomimicry, bio-empathetic designs, or simply nature-inspired solutions, the topic of ants will surely emerge. Social insects, such as ants, have all sorts of fascinating behaviors, including the sharing of food, highly efficient food-tracking behavior, recruitment strategies, and even group-level personalities. A good naturalist who studies ants (a myrmecologist) can share a mythology of ants to enthrall any listener, including the fate of virgin queens, old male ants being sent to the front lines where their loss of life would not be devastating to the colony, and yes, even ants eating their own offspring. The world of ants across the globe seems almost otherworldly and impossibly diverse, but there's no question that while we fight with them over food left on the countertop, they are amazing. The authors of the dedicated myrmecology website, atark.net, states, "Ants have efficient and organised societies which are much more human like than we think. Ant colonies with millions of individuals seamlessly perform: public health, movement of goods, infrastructure, climate control, defense systems, child care, livestock farming, food cultivation and traffic flow control. Their presence on planet Earth is essential, their techniques for survival are unrivalled, these creatures are definitely worthy of study."[2]

It should therefore surprise no one with more than a passing interest in teamwork and leadership that there is a widespread fascination with the self-organizing principles of ants. Some of the most advanced and lauded management

---

[2] About antARK (2016). Retrieved August 1, 2016, from http://antark.net/about-and-acknowledgements/.

publications describe what ants can teach us about teamwork and leadership, how to better understand our roles on a team, and even in-depth discussions of the ant colony work ethic. Ants get work done, they don't complain, and they certainly don't strike or ask for wage hikes or better working conditions.

Ted Lewis, one of the authors of the Ubiquity blog of the Association for Computing Machinery (ACM), an international computing society, asks, "Why Can't Programmers Be More Like Ants?" He explores how, under a decentralized model of software development, it is the code itself—not the organization—that has become central to the structure of a project. He references this as *stigmergy*, an entomological term that defines a mechanism in which work done stimulates the work to be done. He writes, ". . . the emergence of stigmergy among programming teams has gone largely unnoticed. But once we get it, software development teams can improve quality and lower costs even more by duplicating ants, bees, and other insects that have perfected stigmergy over the past million years."[3] So, for example, when an ant is on the hunt for food and identifies another one of her colony on the same path, the series of near-collisions stimulates a natural, mutual adjustment in foraging patterns.

Humans have already adopted these strategies algorithmically in different applications and variations as *Ant Colony Optimization* (ACO), first proposed by Marco Dorigo in 1992 in his PhD thesis and published in 2007 in Scholarpedia.[4] ACO has been adopted for solving problems that involve finding the best way through a graph (represented mathematically as a series of nodes interconnected by vertices), including vehicle routing, scheduling problems, and image processing. If ACO can help robots find explosive mines in a desert, then surely a team of human workers can learn something of value from them. There are other interesting ant behaviors that also have meaning to observers, such as the chemical trail of pheromones that some ants excrete to "recruit" other ants to help move a big haul of food back to the nest. When the resource is tapped out, the trail is abandoned and soon dissipates. Humans, too, leave markers in their digital world, such as comments, chat logs, documentation, and meeting notes.

Others have gone even further to name the collaborative behaviors among ants as an expression of trust. Ndubuisi Ekekwe, founder of the non-profit African Institution of Technology and chairman of Fasmicro Group, wrote in

[3] Lewis, Ted (2015). "Why Can't Programmers Be More Like Ants? Or a Lesson in Stigmergy." Retrieved August 1, 2016, from http://ubiquity.acm.org/blog/why-cant-programmers-be-more-like-ants-or-a-lesson-in-stigmergy/.

[4] Dorigo, Marco (2007). "Ant Colony Optimization." *Scholarpedia*, vol. 2, issue 3, p. 1461. Retrieved September 13, 2016, at http://www.scholarpedia.org/article/Ant_colony_optimization.

the *Harvard Business Review* about the unity he observed among ants. In his personal piece called "The Leadership Lessons of Ants," he describes how, during a troubled project, he found himself dejectedly watching ants at work while he sat at a rest stop on his way to a meeting. "As I watched them, the theses project flashed to my mind. Wouldn't it be good to trust others to help you?"[5] To adopt ant behaviors, he re-grouped the project, instituted focused deadlines, made more focused assignments, and improved his own communication skills, which led him to develop a willingness to collaborate in a trusting way. The entire project progressed well from there.

The wisdom of ants! They work hard, they are disciplined, they collaborate, they teach us important lessons not only about planning, strategy, leadership, and management, but also about how to develop a greater faith in and practice of human trust. But it is also true that ants are very simple organisms that rely on non-reflective communication principles. They seem to exist only to serve as members of the greater colony. Is this really the right model upon which to construct a framework for human collaboration?

5.2.1 Stigmergy for the Masses!

As already implied, stigmergy is an organizing principle. It allows the members of an ant colony to communicate indirectly, perhaps even unintentionally, and exchange key information simply by modifying their local environment. The result is that a very complex structure can be arranged without planning, control, or even intentional communication between agents in the system. Consider ants leaving a pheromone trail for others to find the pathway to a food source. At its simplest and perhaps most efficient, these agents may not have any facility for memory or any awareness of other agents in the system, even if their individual behaviors collectively create a complex and advanced network and a shared memory. And it's not just ants who use environmental prompts; many other cooperative creatures follow decentralized rule sets to keep their world going.

It was only a matter of time before human social movements were analyzed and new ones proposed in which stigmergy was considered not only a defining characteristic, but also a positive framework or set of practices through which to perform complicated, cooperative tasks. Perhaps not surprisingly, the open-source movement has been considered in this light in a variety of academic journals and studies sponsored by both government and technology laboratories that explored the idea that it is the code base itself, rather than a centralized

[5] Ekekwe, Ndubuisi (2010). "The Leadership Lessons of Ants." Retrieved August 1, 2016, from https://hbr.org/2010/10/business-lessons-from-the-ants.

leader, that stimulates the next right action of any agent in the project. A 2009 work sponsored by US Oak Ridge National Laboratory has been particularly influential in examining the phenomenon as a collaboration model.[6]

The principles of stigmergy have been proposed as the foundation of peer production and what has come to be called the "gift economy," in which we give without any promise of a future reward, considered by many to be a defining feature of FOSS culture. In part because of the success of FOSS, others have proposed a purposeful implementation of new social systems in which collaboration is enabled not by representative democracy or consensus, but by stigmergic societies that require no committees, corporations, or commissions to operate. Heather March, a human-rights and internet activist and the author of "Binding Chaos,"[7] writes about life in a stigmergic world: "Workers are free to create regardless of acceptance or rejection; . . . some work may be accepted by the largest group, some alternatives for a different user group, some only by a small group, and sometimes the worker will be alone with their vision. In all cases the worker is still free to create as they wish."[8]

5.2.2 The Extent of Empathy

Some might complain that even when it makes sense to mimic natural forms for innovative new functional designs—such as copying the shape of a whale fin for ergonomic advantage—taking natural systems too literally is counterproductive, especially when we want to transform the way we work to drive peak performance. It seems that we have found ourselves engaging in what might seem a strange twist to the literary device of anthropomorphism, where we ascribe human traits and emotions to non-human animals (and sometimes even natural phenomena or inanimate objects). In literature, one of the functions of anthropomorphism is to make the core message of a story more accessible to many readers by delivering the dialogue through animal characters. It is an important tool in satire of both a political and social ilk. One of the most compelling examples of the use of

---

[6] Cui, Xiaohui, Pullum, Laura L., Treadmill, Jim, and Potok, Thomas E. (2009). "A Stigmergy Collaboration Approach in the Open Source Software Developer Community." Oak Ridge National Laboratory. Retrieved from http://cda.ornl.gov/publications/Publication 15641_Cui_062009.pdf.

[7] Marsh, Heather (2013). "Binding Chaos: Mass Collaboration on a Global Scale." Create Space (an Amazon Company). Available at https://www.createspace.com/4292129.

[8] March, Heather (2012). "Stigmergy." Retrieved August 1, 2016, from https://georgiebc.wordpress.com/2012/12/24/stigmergy-2/.

this device is found in George Orwell's *Animal Farm,* the dystopian novel written about the events leading up to the Russian Revolution (1917), in which the barnyard animal leaders must inspire the others to defeat the human enemy. Old Major, the pig, says "Man is the only creature that consumes without producing. He does not give milk, he does not lay eggs, he is too weak to pull the plough, he cannot run fast enough to catch rabbits. Yet he is lord of all the animals. He sets them to work, he gives back to them the bare minimum that will prevent them from starving, and the rest he keeps for himself."[9] Anthropomorphism can give even pigs superpowers, but what can the pigs do for us?

We so desire the seemingly perfect outcomes produced by the hyper-efficient behaviors of the ant colony that we express our desires to be equally efficient by adopting ant-like behaviors and ascribing ant-like traits to human beings. Thus, not only are we inspired by these social insects, we want to behave as if we're ants ourselves. Perhaps we may even feel a little humiliated by the ants, as Matt Schlosberg, the managing director of Hanna Concern, avers: "Humans are obsessed with leadership. Ants don't have any leaders. Humans build huge inefficient organizations. Ants are very efficient, but their organizations are thousands of times larger than those of humans. Humans learn management, performance, quality, and productivity. Ants don't worry about it but perform better than humans."[10] Ants not only do the jobs they have been born to do without complaining, they keep their communication to the pertinent, they are productive, and they do it all without leadership. In fact, that may be the source of greatest fascination with ant colony behavior: they seem to focus on each other as a prerequisite to the common mission of survival, rather than following the whims of some leader or earning a paycheck.

The study of stigmergy has been an area of inquiry for decades, and it has been applied in many cases to improve coordination mechanisms among simple agents, such as vehicles, robots, and "resources." But clearly, there is an impulse among researchers to apply ACO to human behavior by using virtual pheromones or markers to coordinate mechanisms between so-called intelligent agents (we can call these people, too) in a distributed environment, especially to drive optimal practices in the ecosystems of peer production, open collaboration, and open innovation. After all, the benefits derived from mimicking nature to improve the shape of a wing, or an all-weather jacket, better fasteners, more efficient buildings, and even improved medications and disease treatments, have

---

[9] Orwell, George (1945). *Animal Farm.* Retrieved August 1, 2016, from https://en.wikiquote.org/wiki/Animal_Farm. CC BY-SA 3.0.

[10] Shlosberg, Matt (2010). "Hack: What Ants Can Teach Us About Leadership." Retrieved August 1, 2016, from http://www.managementexchange.com/hack/what-ants-can-teach-us-about-leadership.

driven an entire wave of positive innovation. What stops us from designing and implementing collaborative systems that deploy human beings in the same way as successful ants in a colony—naturally avoiding negative impacts, automatically choosing the next right action, and working not for the benefit of the self-realized ant, but for the team?

We don't, because human beings collaborate and communicate intentionally, with expression, gesture, and purpose, to persuade others of our perspective, to make decisions, and to get things done with awareness of ourselves and others.

It is far out of the scope of this work to posit a philosophy of consciousness or an argument for free will and determinism, as tempting as that is. And it is doubtful that any philosophical framework would capture without excessive discussion why so many innovation frameworks "feel funny" or flame out. Let's let the author Neil Gaiman try: In his novel, *Anansi Boys,* a work of speculative fiction complete with family dysfunction and killer birds, he includes the following truism, "Human beings do not like being pushed about by gods. They may seem to, on the surface, but somewhere on the inside, underneath it all, they sense it, and they resent it."[11] That is, as human beings, we sure seem to show a preference to think for ourselves, even if we don't always exercise it or even seek to understand the nature of free thought.

5.3 From Ants to Innovation

Philosopher George Santayana is known for describing fanaticism as consisting of "redoubling your effort when you have forgotten your aim."[12] As discussed previously, we have seen exuberance from the bottom up to bring more people-centric processes into the corporate institution that are then standardized or misapplied from the top down, resulting in either failure or the loss of some of the most fundamental parts of the process. The same can occur when we want to imitate a natural model or system to solve our own complex human problems. We are tempted with a sort of fanaticism that ultimately limits our ability to debate and synthesize what we can learn from nature by treating it as a perfect system outside of any context. We simply trade the value of advancement for the cost of dogma. We become unproductive in our quest to become

---

[11] Gaiman, Neil (2005). Quotable Quote. Retrieved August 1, 2016, from http://www.goodreads.com/quotes/57780-human-beings-do-not-like-being-pushed-about-by-gods.

[12] Santayana, George (1905). *Life of Reason: Reason in Common Sense.* New York: Charles Scribner's Sons. p. 13.

productive because we are focusing on technique at the expense of motivation and inspiration.

This sort of thinking is logically problematic, because it promotes a fallacy called *affirming the consequent*. The fallacy goes like this:

> *If my cousin owns a castle with a turret, then he is obviously super-rich. It turns out my cousin is super-rich, so he must also own a castle with a turret.*

Anyone can see how silly this is. And you'd be smart to question my logic, because he got rich by inventing the super-thin skins for the supersonic jet, not by owning a castle with a turret. Clearly, there are lots of ways to get rich.

Yet we persist in this type of flawed thinking in other, subtler situations, especially when it comes to introducing methodologies and techniques into our companies to promote reliable innovation. If Company Zed "innovates," then it will be terribly successful. Company Zed is a member of the Fortune 50, so obviously the company "innovates." That is also flawed thinking. Innovation will not make any company necessarily successful, even should one claim that innovation is the only way to ensure the bounties of survival in the digital arena. Context is always important, including questioning if innovation is always beneficial and good.

5.3.1 The Value of Context

If we agree that the purpose of innovation is to help us take an idea and transform it into something of value, then we must embrace the conditions within which breakthrough thinking happens as well as the ways in which our companies create customer value. The process of innovation itself must be flexible and resilient enough to meet idiosyncratic circumstances. Rigid process and management approaches that attempt to inculcate normalization tend to completely wring out adaptability. Most often, this is done to establish a system of measurement to mark if things are on track and within expected operating parameters, but it is a poorly informed instinct if it is fixated upon as an end in and of itself.

Whereas the process of innovation begins with a spark of human imagination—no matter its inspiration—the process of drawing out that idea to the moment at which it becomes something of significance to someone depends wholly on a deep understanding of the conditions under which we innovate—who our customers are, what we want to do for them, how we will deliver it to them, and the economies of delivering that value. It is this very ability to operate in an adaptive milieu that allows a company with an open ecosystem of data, information, and content to more rapidly and powerfully execute on strategic plans, and, more importantly, to create rich opportunities for the sorts of collaboration and partnership that are the foundation of accelerated innovation.

We still have much to learn and appreciate from the approximately 12,000 species of ants, each of which, to survive, uses a different variant of a similar algorithm to solve its specific core problems within its particular ecosystem. Human beings all have different brains, different ways of learning, feeling motivated, performing, and communicating. Yet there is much evidence that as individuals we are more alike than different, a fact which can serve to give us inspiration for creating the desired conditions for creativity and innovation while still acknowledging the power of context as we interact within the huge diversity of environments in which we think, work, and produce.

In our prior, more deterministic work environments, rigid rules had their place in creating scale. Today, in a decentralized world, it is the relationships among our ideas, knowledge, and values that will have a more profound influence on our behavior within open ecosystems and ecotones. Reframing innovation as a context-sensitive process that is inherently adaptive will help us find new ways to address more complex problems by eschewing didacticism in favor of more holistic thinking, within which we accept that our systems can—and will—change over time.

5.4 The Open Effect

Forming a corporate ecosystem in a company that must balance the forces of infrastructure, products and services, customers, and finances that encourage innovation comes down to aligning goals with trade-offs. There are endless models describing how to create that equilibrium, derive the best conceptualizations, and develop strategies for implementation and growth. Over the last two decades, these models have become largely data driven. But to manage risk and unlock value in both innovation and performance, the major driver has been the availability of data—open data. Open data companies have emerged and now comprise their own market of open data analytics providers, consultants, lead and advertising generators, and specialized curators and aggregators.

These companies emerged because the data-driven company is considered to be an imperative for survival; even the electric company has been hauling in data from their customers, despite very low levels of innovation, in working to make their businesses thrive (or even survive). Nearly every sector benefits from open data, and it is becoming clear that there is a multiplier effect when datasets are made accessible in a common manner: any company that makes a business from enriching, supplying, or enabling open data access establishes this multiplicative impact. There are key datasets already available that facilitate international trade, provide educational resources, drive opportunities for clean energy and sustainability, improve the production of food and agriculture, sell real estate, and improve consumer advocacy. Astounding shifts in research, particularly healthcare, have been made possible by virtue of wide-ranging types of accessible scientific data, especially as relates to the human genome. It is there that we see the most exciting area of growth, as even more mundane uses of data have been able to effect powerful change.

In the article "Driving Innovation with Open Data," Joel Guerin notes that, "Healthcare has become a proving ground that shows how the four different kinds of data—Big Data, Open Data, personal data, and scientific data—can be used together to great effect. By analyzing *Big Data* (the voluminous information on public health, treatment outcomes, and individual patient records), healthcare analysts are now able to find patterns in public health, healthcare costs, regional differences in care, and more."[13] In the United States, government insurance agencies work with other entities such as the Food and Drug Administration (FDA) to merge personal data with open data to improve the opportunity for individuals to manage their own health, such as with inexpensive devices networked with their smart phone. The accessibility of myriad data and the ability to analyze such data in unique ways has broken open new markets and helped existing markets deliver entirely new products and services that have been innovative from the ground up.

Open data is part of the big business of big data. In fact, the revenue portion from big data in some companies is significant to the bottom line. Revenue opportunities include consulting as provided by PWC and Accenture; software and services through companies such as Palantir, Oracle, Teradata, and SAP; hardware providers such as Dell and HP; and mega-players such as IBM, in which the amount of money sifting through our public markets, as relates to the massive volumes of data now available, is of tremendous value and importance. Open data matters, its benefits and successes are instructive to the proponents of FOSS and any "open" initiatives related to content and other forms of information.

The truth is, we don't fully know how business will evolve to leverage new ways of innovation based on open data, information, and content. We are just starting to see the new forms of business innovation and creative endeavor that can be imagined by breaking the shackles of knee-jerk private ownership of intellectual property. It is without question, though, that we will see accelerating advancements related to nearly every human endeavor as we learn to coexist

[13] Guerin, Joel (2014). "Driving Innovation with Open Data." In: "The Future of Data-Driven Innovation." Chapter 5. Retrieved August 1, 2016, from https://www.uschamberfoundation.org/driving-innovation-open-data.

as private entities with non-public data, public data, government data, and other data sources, including citizen engagement, social media, scientific research, and business reporting.

The future tech landscape is sure to be one of shock and awe, but business models and strategies take a while to form and implement. The goal of any person charged with implementing new processes to meet their goals in a swiftly moving world will seek to bring facilitative mechanisms to bear that can inspire self-organization with simplicity like an ant colony, while thriving within an intelligent ecosystem that is uniquely human.

5.4.1 The OpenXFORM Ecosystem

In the previous chapter, we presented the concept of "regulated ecosystems" as way to discuss how private companies with trade secrets and proprietary methods and data could find balance with the unregulated forces found in open data, information, and content, and to explore operating at the edge of their corporate ecosystems in a blended ecotone. In this chapter, we have further explored how companies benefit from more adaptive forms of thinking, collaboration, and innovation to deliver on their strategic goals.

Most important, when it comes to innovation, the further we are able to balance our corporate ecosystems by establishing a synthesis with the open, unregulated (or self-regulated but without an authoritarian presence) world by identifying the areas of transition that form ecotones with our partners and collaborators, the greater our potential returns. There have been three major sticking points for this, though, for many private companies:

- The idea that it is dangerous to share intellectual property, because there is inherent value in that property.
- The belief that it is impossible to partner with a self-regulated economy of heterogeneous and distributed bodies of information, data, content, and communities that trade on the currency of ideas and competition among those ideas.
- That we cannot create value in a mixed economic system in which one system defends the private ownership of property, capital, and even wage labor as fundamental to innovation, versus the other system that collectivizes property, where work is based on collaboration and where there is no express expectation of a personal return.

In response, Open Transformation (OpenXFORM) seeks to define a bio-empathetic approach to the process of innovation—one that is not so literal as to propose that we must manage ourselves just like the ants do, but that is inspired by the way in which social beings in nature coordinate to evoke problem-solving methods that are graced by the uniquely human gift of highly flexible and context-sensitive intentional communication.

It is true that when ants face each other in a territorial dispute over food or nesting rights, a colony might seek to destroy its intruders. But even ants know enough not to participate in a scenario of mutually assured destruction; intruding ants will often employ ritual displays of aggression to prevent real risk to the lives of their workers. In fact, if one colony would be destroyed in a heated battle, ant puffery can lead to the ceding of territory to the assumed stronger party, simply to prevent actual physical destruction. Truly, defining new social and economic relationships is not for the faint of heart, but business stakeholders and strategists are well advised to revisit their business school assumptions that would lead them to think that in a digitally mediated world, data, and by extension, information and content, is in any way scarce. Such beliefs are profoundly self-limiting, especially if open resources can be freed from excessive regulation and governance and provided in a way that is sufficient to fulfill every want and need related to digital property. Until now, scarcity has framed value. If there is no paucity or scarcity of resources, because digital resources are limitless in every useful measure of the term, then that construction holds no merit.

These ideas are not novel, but because so many of our companies operate within traditional business structures, the very human problems of collective behavior and irrational human behavior make the development of repeatable models difficult if those models require the creation of new rules, motivations, and incentive structures. This is because we are trapped in a system of perverse incentivization, one which Thomas Jefferson recognized two centuries ago. He once wrote to Isaac McPherson on the topic of invention and the idea of exclusive right to inventions, which he noted were never provided by nature, but only by the law of the state, saying, "He who receives an idea from me, receives instruction himself without lessening mine; as he who lights his taper at mine, receives light without darkening me. That ideas should freely spread from one to another over the globe, for the moral and mutual instruction of man, and improvement of his condition, seems to have been peculiarly and benevolently designed by nature, when she made them, like fire, expansible over all space, without lessening their density in any point, and like the air in which we breathe, move, and have our physical being, incapable of confinement or exclusive appropriation."[14]

The idea of innovation built on scarcity is no longer useful, it's destructive. Tammer Kamel, co-founder and CEO of the Quandl data platform, notes that any company that attempts to manifest a winning strategy by defending

---

[14] Jefferson, Thomas (1813). *The Founders' Constitution* (Volume 3, Article 1, Section 8, Clause 8, Document 12). Retrieved August 1, 2016, from http://press-pubs.uchicago.edu/founders/documents/a1_8_8s12.html.

(or creating) scarcity will face increasing difficulty as they "fast [become] yet another case study on the consequences of trying to execute a business model whose efficacy is being diminished every day by the Internet itself. When your core innovation is built on the scarcity of a resource and that resource suddenly becomes ubiquitous, you've got a problem."[15]

Data is not scarce anymore, nor is information or content. It is cheap to acquire, store, analyze, and share. Its status as a scarce and valuable resource will not be reinstated. In fact, any organization that tries to do so may soon be spending the morning downloading their own proprietary information from a website from a former eastern bloc country, or discovering that it has been re-created more cheaply and sustainably by an open source project. Even ideas are cheap these days.

5.5 The OpenXFORM Ecosystem

Figure 5.1 describes how the OpenXFORM ecosystem works to flexibly accommodate the uncertain and difficult relationship between abiotic resources and the biotic world of the innovating company entity. The points of connection between the two are symbiotic and generally described as the functions of *adaptation* and *information decomposition*.

Figure 5.1 Balancing the self-governed commons by adapting materials and returning benefit.

Adaptation

In natural systems, adaptation is a change to an organism that helps it survive in its environment. Often, mutations that create the change are a sudden variation in the genetic makeup of the organism that is somehow helpful in the mission

---

[15] Kamel, Tammer (2013). "The Travails of the Closed Data Industry in an Open Data World." Retrieved August 1, 2016, from https://www.quandl.com/blog/the-travails-of-the-closed-data-industry-in-an-open-data-world.

of survival and, because of the increased survivability of those with the muta-tion, gets passed down to the next generation until it becomes a standard part of the species: thus, an adaptation. As the *National Geographic* authors note, "An adaptation can be structural, meaning it is a physical part of the organism. An adaptation can also be behavioral, affecting the way an organism acts."[16] When open data is released, there is no requirement for it to be in a specific format or standard (although a well-documented interface is appreciated by its users). Thus, any consumer of open data, information, and content will be required to adapt not only to its structure but to transform that raw information into useful knowledge that best fits the unique way in which your company hopes to use it, especially in the process of innovation.

As we will discuss with regard to the OpenXFORM Model of Innovation itself in the next chapter, a company can dramatically accelerate and improve quality by access to the commons in all phases of innovation, including ideation, new product exploration, and transformation at scale to a fully-fledged product or service offering. The most important thing to understand at this point is that adaptations typically occur to assist an organism to respond to change in its habitat or ecosystem. For example, as we discussed previously, ants in general will excrete pheromones to recruit other ants to help them forage, but carpenter ants, specifically, have adapted to nighttime activity to reduce predation. Thus carpenter ants have refined their pheromone skills to help all colony members, not just foragers, by creating what are called "trunk trails" that provide access to long-term sources of food, such as nectar or aphid colonies.[17]

The data, information, and content that live in the commons only become valuable when placed in the context of a unique idea—one that will distinctively draw out useful insights to meet the strategic goals of a business, including pumping value into proprietary algorithms, improving customer relationships, or building an application to perform heart surgery into a smart phone with a 3D holographic screen. The data, information, and content in the commons only become valuable when adapted to a goal and given meaning for customers who are seeking value from a company offering.

But, what about giving value back?

Information Decomposition

Decomposition gets a bad rap; it's true that it's about rotting and decay, often quite smelly, and explicitly suggestive of death. But decomposition plays a vital

---

[16] National Geographic Society (2011). Adaptation. Retrieved August 1, 2016, from http://nationalgeographic.org/encyclopedia/adaptation/.

[17] Harris, Rob (2016). "Carpenter Ant Adaptations." Retrieved August 1, 2016, from http://animals.mom.me/carpenter-ant-adaptations-6502.html.

role in the cycle of any ecosystem, because death and decay unleash nutrients into the system that are crucial for new growth. Like chemical decomposition, information decomposition breaks down the components of the corpus and its previous structural integrity.

Thus decomposing information reduces the system from its context level to progressively smaller, but well-defined, objects. In and of themselves, they do not describe a domain or a system; but in their independent parts, they become available to other functions, processes, organizations, or even entirely alternative subject areas. To take the physical example to its logical conclusion, when a carcass has nearly completed its cycle of decay, the soil around it measures a marked increase in carbon and crucial nutrients, at which point it is quite common to see a resurgence of plant growth around the decomposition area until the nutrient pool at that site normalizes. And thus it can be with information, data, and content in the commons—understandable, useful, maintainable, but not necessarily in the context from which they came.

5.6 From Adaptation to Innovation (and Back Again)

We want to encourage creativity and innovation in our companies—they are the key factors that help us achieve and realize options that previously have been out of strategic reach. And it's not that hard if companies can lay down the mythology of the creative genius and instead embrace the idea that innovation can become a common occurrence if we don't waste our resources locking down what is inherently a social process. If we were to plot innovation as a journey of sharing, connection, and learning that must be enriched in many ways, then we could create a map that can be referenced over and over again. A. G. Lafley and Rom Charan, the authors of *The Game Changer: How Every Leader Can Drive Everyday Innovation,* remind us that there really is nothing mystical about it, writing, "Collaboration is essential; failure is a regular visitor. Innovation leaders are comfortable with uncertainty and have an open mind; they are receptive to ideas from very different disciplines. They have organized innovation into a disciplined process that is replicable. And, they have the tools and skills to pinpoint and manage the risks inherent in innovation."[18] Of course, these people are not gurus either, but they must be cultivated within the company—this cultivation can change everything, including entire business models.

---

[18] Lafley, A. G. and Charan, Rom (2008). *The Game Changer: How Every Leader Can Drive Everyday Innovation.* London, UK: Profile Books. eBook available at https://profilebooks.com/the-game-changer-ebook.html.

Chapter Six

An Evolutionary Model for Innovation

[1]

We must not forget that when radium was discovered no one knew that it would prove useful in hospitals. The work was one of pure science. And this is a proof that scientific work must not be considered from the point of view of the direct usefulness of it. It must be done for itself, for the beauty of science, and then there is always the chance that a scientific discovery may become like the radium a benefit for humanity.

— Marie Curie from a Lecture at Vassar College
Poughkeepsie, New York, May 14, 1921.[2]

[1] Photo of Marie Curie by unknown. Retrieved on July 11, 2016, from user Tekniska Muskeet at https://www.flickr.com/photos/tekniskamuseet/12835367815. Available under CC-BY-2.0.

[2] Marie Curie. Wikiquote.org. Retrieved on July 11, 2016, from https://en.wikiquote.org/wiki/Marie_Curie. Available under CC-BY-3.0.

6.1 Chapter Theme

The study of morphology lends a bio-empathetic perspective to our research by encouraging investigation not just of structure, but also of how an organism works to exist sustainably within its ecosystem. With greater tools of examination at our disposal, we can learn to understand how an organism works within a system, in this case how a breakthrough idea can move through a process that persuasively supports our best innovative thinkers to test their assumptions, validate their hypotheses, and tune and tweak their ideas not only to drive solutions for users but also to meet the strategic goals of their companies. The anatomy of OpenXFORM (Open Transformation) contains the process for moving from a flight of fancy to a readiness to produce.

6.2 The Form of Things

In biology, *morphology* is a term rooted in the Greek word morphé, for "shape" and refers to the study of the form and structure of living organisms. In working to reveal a bio-empathetic process that adequately captures the potential for innovation in the overwhelmingly data-driven world of technology development, we are well served to deeply question the morphology of our typical new product development (NPD) process. After all, not only are today's companies increasingly dependent on the virtual world, which extends far beyond the proprietary, they are participating in mixed economic, cultural, and societal systems that are often fundamentally different in terms of capital markets, personal motivation, and ownership. All of these factors are forcing companies into an adaptive phase that pushes them beyond cost-cutting and containment and toward disruptive innovation as a practice, not a talking point.

Morphology once comprised two separate branches of study—*anatomy* and *eidonomy*. Early biologists who studied eidonomy, which is concerned with classification and taxonomy, focused mainly on the external appearance of an organism; but over time it became clear that little new information could be revealed simply by looking at an organism only from the outside in. Frustration with the superficiality of eidonomy was in part due to the phenomenon of *convergent evolution*, which describes analogous structures with similar functions or traits. This parallel evolution occurs when there are similar environmental factors in which similar solutions are arrived upon to solve the problem at hand. One can easily see these analogous structures in many mammals and insects—for example, the wings of a moth, the wings of a butterfly, and the wings of a bat—which are all meant for flying but have different evolutionary origins. Or consider the fins of a goldfish and a mammalian whale, both of which require stability and propulsion in the water but are not closely related animals. The important point when thinking about analogous structures is that, whereas they are superficially similar, their internal structure—their anatomy—is quite dissimilar. And thus, to many morphologists, outward appearance became quite uninteresting for seeking deeper understanding of an organism.

With technological advancements, what has become much more fascinating and useful to modern biologists is anatomy—the study of how an organism's pieces connect and work together to tell a rich story about the life of that creature. Anatomy helps scientists understand structure and functions in a specific context, including the parts of an organism and the materials, locations, and relationships with other parts within. As techniques for study and measurement have progressed, such as the use of x-ray, magnetic resonance imaging, and positron emission tomography as found in nuclear medicine, our understanding of organismic structures has dramatically increased.

6.2.1 And What of the Anatomy of Our Organizations?

For our purposes, we consider the anatomy of future tech corporations and their structural relationships to data, information, content, and the individuals and teams seeking to innovate rapidly, efficiently, and powerfully. So, while the study of external appearances has become more the place for evolutionary historians, the field of morphology is now much more defined by the quest for the deeper learning provided by understanding how things work within a system, whether it is chemical, muscular, connective, or nervous tissues. And as it should be in our companies today, we must put aside a singular (and somewhat obsessive) focus on how to fit innovative processes into our organizational structures. Collaboration and innovation are not corporate departments, and such rigid stances help us little in our efforts to revolutionize future technologies not only for material success, but also for the advancement of society in medicine, energy, artificial intelligence, robotics, nanotechnology, space exploration, and every aspect of our built and natural environments that might make the world that much more civilized and verdant. Innovative models of design that are implemented for their external benefits, optics, measurability, or ease of communicating up the chain are insufficient.

Ron Adner has written extensively about collaboration strategies, and in his 2013 book *The Wide Lens,* he writes about the benefits of working with others to accomplish greater things with improved efficiency, but he also locks into the mortal fear in organizations related to working outside of a comfortable sphere of influence when he writes, ". . . your success now depends not just on your own efforts but on your collaborators' efforts as well. Greatness on your part is not enough. You are no longer an autonomous innovator. You are now an actor within a broader innovation ecosystem. Success in a connected world requires that you manage your dependence."[3] Adner challenges the idea that we can ever succeed as innovative companies if we continue to adopt organizational attitudes and structures that do not fully comprehend the wide-ranging external dependencies embedded in the federated value chain that makes up our markets today.

6.2.2 Failure Is Not a Strategy

Pick up nearly any of the leading business magazines over the past fifteen years, and you'll find article after article on the topic of the "failure to innovate," which expose the most shattering and iconic failed efforts from Betamax, Newton, QR codes, DIVX, and laser discs. At the same time, there seem to be just as many articles about how failure is key to the process of innovation. This is distraction. Popular blame is placed at the feet of the dysfunctional organizational structure, but the work to improve such systemic problems is too often shallow and makes only small dents in identifying the underlying problems. While there always seems time for hyperbole—such as the "top ten things that an innovative company did that you should do too!"—most articles leave issues beyond the structural and organizational unexamined. Yet the structure of the organization is only a part of the picture, as eidonomists learned; it's the way things work inside—the company anatomy—that tells us much more about how we might make positive change that embraces learning, not failure, as always a certain outcome.

Perhaps our fins are not propelling or stabilizing us the way we would like, but instead of finding new fins, companies must first consider how their internal relationships and collaborative processes are helping them navigate today's broader challenges. Every future tech entity must honestly assess the risks of integration with the external sources of data, information, and content, as well as of the impact of avoiding such assessment on the entire value chain, which is often required to harness a new idea and drive a rapid and successful outcome.

Even when we optimistically push new ideas for collaboration or production up from the bottom of an organization and have every intention of focusing on helping people find original solutions to our many problems, wiring in dials like streaming KPIs (key performance indicators) that allow managers to

---

[3] Adner, Ron (2013). *The Wide Lens.* (Introduction). Retrieved July 11, 2016, from http://thewidelensbook.com/excerpt.html.

calibrate and correct is self-limiting. Sure, it seems tautological that we must measure to manage, but that assumes that everything is accessible for measurement. In an interconnected world, in an open world, the only things that can be managed directly are our access to broad and diverse relationships and their quality. Perhaps we must remind ourselves that the highly specified process for launching a rocket is a very different process than thinking about how we might get there. Don't confuse the process of learning and adapting ideas to meet customer needs with designing sealing joints on a rocket booster; learn to appreciate the difference between conceiving new ideas and products and implementing complex systems.

It should not need restating, but this in no way means that a company bent on innovating should quickly fire all the project managers and send them packing, tossing the keys to the company to its "creatives." Eidonomists didn't quit the field of morphology because new techniques allowed them to see beyond the external manifestation of an organism; instead, when handed new tools, they found new ways to learn. In fact, their world of study may have even become more interesting and challenging, and much more powerful and profound in providing the ability to learn more about how natural systems work and how living organisms work within them. Companies that want to drive innovation in an open world are well served to deeply consider that traditional systems of innovation and production that rely on fixed measures are old, broken tools. We can do better. And that requires investigating the messy world of human relationships, systems of motivation, and new patterns of communication and collaboration to capture and amplify the new perspectives that successful innovation in the open world demand.

6.3 The Morphology of Innovation

In the previous chapter, we discussed how OpenXFORM works to flexibly accommodate the uncertain and difficult relationship between the company and the commons. The points of connection between the two are symbiotic and are generally described as the functions of *adaptation* from the commons to the business enterprise and *information decomposition* from the business to the commons.

In the case of adaptation, we argued that company survivability depends on the ability to adapt to changes, be they cultural, economic, or other modifications, such as performance development or decentralized work models. Some adaptations are structural and some are behavioral, but when it comes to interacting with open data, information, and content or experimenting with other principles of open culture, many companies are finding that transformations of both form and function are necessary.

If a company is looking for new ways to dramatically accelerate the process and improve quality through access to the commons in all phases of innovation—including ideation, new product exploration, and transformation to a readiness to produce—then not only must we make credible suggestions for change, we must deeply investigate the generative impact that might occur when an organism begins to respond to changes in its habitat or ecosystem. Meaning, considering the self-contained systems we think of when we consider a private entity, when we begin to co-create, generate, and advance in technology, a unique organization is sure to emerge. Generative changes are often unanticipated in one way or another, as new interactions and patterns of structure and behavior emerge. This idea of generativity is important to our future discussions of the OpenXFORM innovation model.

In our attempt to extract a meaningful bio-empathetic approach from natural systems of adaptation to the process of innovation, it is worth remembering that the data, information, and content that lives in the commons only becomes something of value when placed in the context of a unique idea. Otherwise, we are only staring at puddles of regurgitated data that signify nothing. Data and evidence should not be confused with truth; there is nothing inherently valuable in a stream of numbers, nor does even a clever analysis make one complete in their knowledge. Studies tell us that too much salt will kill us; studies tell us that too little salt will kill us even faster. This is why truly innovative companies still seek to hire the best and the brightest and will invest in their people even as they invest in artificial intelligence. They know that to draw out the insight that is available to meet the strategic goals of a business requires human imagination and inspiration, even if it is informed, encouraged, and accelerated by the availability of profound volumes and varieties of data, information, and content. Like the 20,000 species of ants who adapt to their distinctive environments, the real value of any data, information, and content—open or not—becomes apparent only when it is given meaning within the boundaries of specific design goals.

6.3.1 The Anatomy of Innovation

Insect morphology includes three major body regions: the head, the thorax, and the abdomen. As described in Figure 6.1, the *head* is designed for sensory input and food ingestion, the *thorax* anchors the legs (and wings, if they exist) and manages other systems that are specially designed to propel the insect, and the

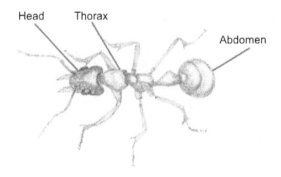

Head   Thorax

Abdomen

Figure 6.1   Insect morphology defines insects as having three regions: head, thorax, and abdomen.[4]

abdomen digests, reproduces, excretes, and sometimes even defends (most of us have been stung by an angry bee at least once in our lives). There are no hard lines between the regions of the insect, and these structures are quite variable among the different species of insects, which allows them to adapt to nearly every ecological niche except the most uninhabitable, such as the deepest oceans or the cold, dry, and windy regions of Antarctica. It is these variations in the basic and recognizable physical form of the insect that permit them to run, fly, swim, jump, see or be sightless, depending on the requirements and challenges to their survival and perpetuation.

Insects are the very definition of resilience in the face of change, and even a cursory study of their forms and functions provides fertile ground for the inspiration of adapting our processes of innovation in a world that benefits from the commons. In the world of insects, as with all creatures, when their form and function is well suited to their niche, business as usual is sufficient; but when environmental pressures mount and begin to challenge the survivability of a species, change happens. And for ants, the pace of change is an incredibly rapid one of emerging mutation and supercolony development. Humans are not nearly so quick to adapt, although change certainly happens in our species too. And so it is in a world in which the pressure for innovative products and services driven by advanced technology shows no sign of abating in the data-driven and ubiquitously connected world. The question is, what does your company need to do to survive?

---

[4] Released into the public domain by Peri Coleman (2009). Retrieved July 3, 2016, from https://commons.wikimedia.org/wiki/File:Meat_ant.jpg. Labels added by Carol L. Stimmel, July 12, 2016.

6.3.2 Comparing Form and Function

Table 6.1 compares the form and functions found within the insect world and the innovation methodology defined in the OpenXFORM model. The structural regions and their functional purposes are made up in the insect as the head, thorax, and abdomen and in OpenXFORM as ideation, exploration, and transformation. The characteristics of their respective morphologies are presented from a bio-empathetic perspective that may serve to inspire the innovation practitioner looking to nature for adaptive and resilient organizing principles.

Table 6.1 Comparison of the Form and Functions Found Within Insect and Innovation Morphologies

FUNCTION	STRUCTURAL REGIONS		CHARACTERISTICS	
	Insect	*Innovation*	*Insect*	*Innovation*
Input	Head	Ideate	Brain Center Seeing Sensing Ingestion	Seeing Feeling Qualifying Expressing
Propulsion	Thorax	Explore	Locomotion Nervous System Circulation Respiration	Showing Testing Assessing Refining
Output	Abdomen	Transform	Digestion Excretion Reproduction Defense	Scaling Validating Designing Specifying

Figure 6.2 helps us see the interaction and flow between the regions of effort, as the head of the insect is where they recognize and make sense of the world, and ideation is how we intuit and give shape to our qualified ideas for what we sense and believe. The thorax is the engine room of the insect, and in OpenXFORM it is the region that represents a spiraling process that takes a prototype that has emerged from the ideation phase and tests, assesses, and refines it based on the goals and limits established for the project. The abdomen, or transformation, region defines the work that must be performed to move a vetted idea to scale and specification wherein proper execution establishes an innovative result. Furthermore, the connective tissue between the regions are the structures used as design and verification gateways between the structural and functional specialties of the organism; in the case of OpenXFORM, we

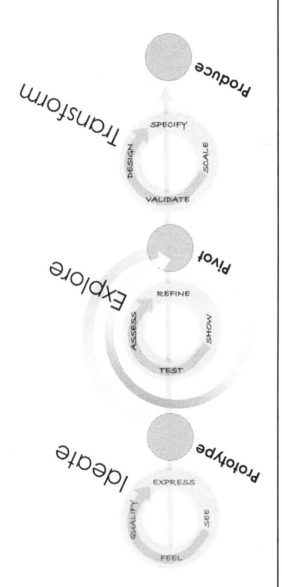

Figure 6.2 The bio-empathetic anatomy of OpenXFORM is inspired by insect morphology.

connect with *prototypes* and *pivots,* which are described in great detail in the next section and throughout the implementation recommendations and case studies further in the book.

6.4 OpenXFORM Terminology

To prepare for our further discussions in applying OpenXFORM, Table 6.2 provides a list of terms used in the model, deconstructing and explaining them at a high level. This list can be referenced at any point that clarification is needed in the course of working with the methods and applications for deployment of the model within the organization. For the sake of brevity, the word *product* may represent a physical thing, a digital application, a service, or even an experience.

At this point, the model is fully realized, having set a foundation for discussing practices, deployments, and organizational impacts in the next portion of the book.

Table 6.2 OpenXFORM Terminology by Region

REGION #1: IDEATE	
See	The entry point to the ideation process, refers to the notion of "seeing" a solution to a problem in the mind's eye, as an inspiration, a spark of a new idea, or the viewing of a problem with new eyes.
Feel	This is a technique that brings imagination to the act of discovery and refers to the conscious manipulation of the mental lens. Methods can be applied that aid in thinking about the contours of the idea and imagining it at work within a context, without details or opposition, from the user's perspective.
Qualify	This is the time to start a conversation about the idea and elicit enough feedback to begin to arrive at how it may be concretely expressed to others. The qualification stage allows the formulation of a research question or hypothesis based on working assumptions that are oriented toward establishing the value of an idea to its users.
Express	This is the moment of arrival at the proverbial "drawing board." At this time, it should be possible to express a lightweight representation of the idea. It doesn't have to be a computer design, or even a physical object. It could be a dramatic endeavor or a poster. The most important aspect to the prototype is that it is clear enough to garner specific feedback. If the idea cannot be expressed, then the idea is not testable and has no means to progress.

PROTOTYPE
The research question is posed, the prototype shows a design that might answer that question, and it is clearly identified through the prototype that we want to test.

REGION #2: EXPLORE	
Show	This is a team effort now, and that team includes those who will be served by the idea. Showing the prototype to users is communicating the idea through a conveyance that is specific and concrete enough to be understandable.
Test	Testing the viability of the idea represented by the prototype means being open to feedback. Test every prototype extensively enough to inform the next prototype or to agree that it is complete. Testing at the exploratory stage should be focused mainly on the user's experience and reaction to the design, and not on being "right."

(Continued on following page)

Table 6.2 OpenXFORM Terminology by Region (*Cont'd*)

REGION #2: EXPLORE (*Cont'd*)	
Assess	When assessing the feedback from the prototype, the open-minded team will look not only for ways to refine their prototype, but also for an understanding of whether the problem was framed correctly. A complete testing effort will likely expose unexpected insights in the form of additional unmet needs among users.
Refine	At this stage, the team is ready not only to reconstruct the prototype, but to tune the research question to better reflect context. Since this is an iterative and not a top-down process, such a refinement doesn't mean that the effort has failed, only that there is an additional opportunity to invalidate poor solutions and improve the overall likelihood of adjusting the product to more appropriately meet the user's needs. If the assumptions were wrong, reject them and try again.

PIVOT
We have validated our idea with a design to the extent that we know the form or structure that the idea should take. The pivot is the opportunity to tweak the outcome of the exploratory phase to allow it to simultaneously meet company strategic goals and satisfy the needs of the actual market of consumers represented in user-feedback testing.

REGION #3: TRANSFORM	
Scale	What's it going to take for the company to deliver this product to the customer? What are the channels, types of infrastructure, or marketing capability required? Much of this information may have been loosely acquired in the exploratory phase, especially if other teams have been included during the exploratory phase. Scaling efforts also focus on developing customer personas as artifacts that will serve the progressive product development effort.
Validate	Are the designers, developers, and product managers all on the same page? What are the priorities for the company in supporting this idea? This is the time to flesh out the assumptions built into the refined design; document technical, business, and user requirements; and validate business goals, objectives, and capabilities.
Design	Design steps may be unique to every team, but every design should reflect enough detail to build a complete story for the customer that builds on the raw information from the exploration phase. This should include designing toward specific success metrics.

(Continued on following page)

Table 6.2 OpenXFORM Terminology by Region (*Cont'd*)

REGION #3: TRANSFORM (*Cont'd*)	
Specify	The proper specification depends on the idea itself and the fact that every successful team has developed their own way to develop requirements. However, any specification must represent the authentic experiences and plans drawn out during discovery, or something entirely different will be built that drives the value of the very process asunder.

PRODUCE

Stay connected to the user experience of the product, system, or experience. It is important to continuously test, incrementally improve, verify, and seek to understand the resulting context of an idea as it is built and released, especially as a way to harvest new solutions to emerging problems.

Section One

Review of Themes and Concepts

Chapter One: Reconsidering Information Freedom

The Challenges of Freedom and Abundance

Emerging innovations in the realm of future tech are not only changing the world, they are creating jobs for inventors and designers; and as they become accessible and affordable, we need people to build, distribute, sell, and service these products. They expand opportunities for many, including investors and companies that seek more adaptable forms of economic value and growth than offered by the tired tradition of invention that defines profitability by the height of a stack of inert dollar bills. Open data, content, and information may indeed be the key to mass innovation for future technologies, although they bring difficult challenges to private industry business models that depend on the established ideas of intellectual property.

Key Concepts

- Our digitally enabled society is faced with the colliding traditions of property ownership and the use of incentives for efficiency to increase profits. The role of this book is to explore these issues and suggest a new way of thinking about how to mitigate the stresses brought about by our current system of production and distribution, which have been rocked by the exploding availability of information and knowledge in the connected world.

- The threat of open data, information, and content is real for any orthodox corporate entity, especially when viewed at the most fundamental level of the predominant economic systems based in capitalism. In part, capitalism thrives on the notion of scarcity, but with digital assets, scarcity is not natural—it must be forced on the system.

- There is a traditional and persistent belief among information-property-rights advocates that if they share their knowledge, data, or content, it will be depleted in some way that will destroy their business, if not collapse the entire capitalist system. This is consistent with thinking that if we achieve power and advantage through our information resources, our ability to rapidly innovate will diminish. This does not make sense in a world of information abundance, in which even where it is not free, it is cheap, and certainly not limited.

- In the interconnected world of knowledge and information, the potential for rapid growth is becoming inextricably linked to the fulfillment of human potential through technology, where the creative process is the economic engine that drives a growing and increasingly powerful social agenda to create jobs in a sustainable way. Innovation can transform the comic-book dreams of future technology, complicated and expensive, into products from which many—the commoners—can benefit. Furthermore, the process of innovation is becoming easier and easier, as we learn to collaborate and create over a global network and share open technologies, data learnings, wisdom, and understanding.

- New models for innovation must include strategies for identifying problems, breaking them down into the right questions, directing resources in research and development, interpreting results, disseminating information, manufacturing and distributing products, and commercializing enterprises in an open environment.

- We must define, explore, and provide practical approaches to applying open thinking and systems to our businesses and come to understand the profound and significant benefits brought to us by the philosophy of the so-called "knowledge commons" approach, in which information, data, and content are accessible resources available to all.

Chapter Two: What Open and Free Means to Innovation

Being Open and Free

Open source and the free software movement are considered to be the progenitors of today's open ecosystem of data, information, and content. Yet, these movements are still the domain of human beings, which brings richness, confusion, and consternation in the form of philosophy and practices. As discussed in the first chapter of this book, many will freely admit that what we do know about open source and what it can teach us about working together in this type of a collaborative environment is largely anecdotal, because there are actually a very small number of studies that explore the nature of collaboration in these environments as the key research question. Further, we know much less than we'd like about how the development of these communities are born, die, handle conflict, and relate themselves to collaboration and capitalism. This chapter explores some of the circumstances that have brought forth the open and free software movements, in the hopes of learning what and how we may carry their tenets forward.

Key Concepts

- To understand the roots of open thinking, it is important to understand the differences between the concepts and traditions of "free software" and "open source," not only in practice, but in how historically and culturally both approaches have impacted many application domains.
- Both free software and open source express their principles through their recommended licenses; however, free-software activists focus on the ideals for how software should be shared, while open-source advocates are more concerned with creating better programmers and better code. Free software adherents rigorously defend the liberties of users of software by demanding unflinching adherence to their principles and practices by authors, to the extent of rejecting software that does not sufficiently respect their concept of freedom. Quite differently, open source is concerned with engagement of community, transparency, and communication as it relates to building great software by creating conscious communities of contributors.
- Despite a shared history, the Open Source Initiative (OSI) and the Free Software Foundation (FSF) are stylistically, attitudinally, culturally, and ideologically different, but their very public skirmishes overshadow the important possibilities of concordance. One really does begin to wonder

if the schism between FSF and OSI is just another example of trying to resolve a false dichotomy, where we believe we must make a choice between free software or open source because they tell us we must. This is left as an exercise to the reader.

- Not surprisingly, it is difficult to harness the dualist tension between free and open software, but except where it is important and instructive to be specific as to the principles of either FSF or OSI, we prefer the term Free and Open-Source Software (FOSS), as its usage in government, academic, legal, and business spheres across the globe is already understood.

- As we work to establish a common definition for FOSS, it is safe to say that if we boil it all down, the idea of openness simply describes *access to something*, whether it's a field to play in or a structure for maintaining software, digital media, information, or knowledge. In both cases, the questions are straightforward: *Can we get what we want when we want it, and what are the terms to retrieve those rights of access?*

- As described in the following figure (referenced in Chapter 2 as Figure 2.2 and repeated here as Figure 1), FOSS is now found throughout the technology ecosystem and serves to help software engineers focus on innovation and differentiation, not drudgery and redundant undertakings. That doesn't mean there aren't non-free ways to build your software with those languages, just that you don't have to.

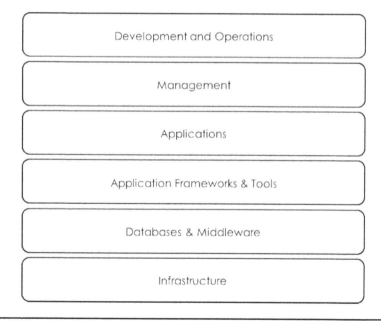

Figure 1. FOSS is found throughout the technology ecosystem, in applications, frameworks, and languages.

Chapter Three: Innovation in an Open World

Translating Openness into Innovation

There is big money and big hope in innovation. There are hundreds of inspirational quotations, books, consulting companies, business and cultural philosophies that hold high the concept of innovation. In the world of technology, especially, it's an obsession, it's an imperative, it's terrifying—an expression of true creativity and passion; it's grit, it's sparks, it's working with others, it's working by yourself, it's specific, it's big, it's winning, and without it you will most certainly fail. Many of us experience awe when we see the flash of inspiration move from impactful impulse to reality. But, how do we work to avoid inertia and adopt innovation-oriented processes not only for ourselves, but for our communities and companies, where so much creativity is translated into existence? By building relationships.

Key Concepts

- If we are to explore the relationship of *openness* to *innovation*, we must expunge the poorly evidenced reliance on the glamorous idea of both concepts, so that we can make real, rational progress toward creating a culture in which our ambitions for future tech can be met with accelerating innovative capability.
- When it comes to certain buzzwords and jargon in the business of high technology, such as *innovation* and *open*, we may have reached peak ridiculousness. Some of us treat our ability to understand jargon as a badge of honor. Perhaps, in certain circles, we even claim that our special language brings enhanced precision and understanding to the conversation, and often it really does; the whole truth, though, may largely include the opposite—not only does the use of jargon cloud meaning, it is also a way to lose trust with others who can't follow along, suggesting a lack of candor or, worse, a lack of understanding of the issues hidden behind a smokescreen of syllables.
- A lack of rigor for and understanding of the principles of openness may be the leading reasons for a disturbing trend in openwashing claims—which includes the notion of being "innovative" to credentialize and enhance a brand's reputation.
- It is important to avoid symbolic language in discussing open thinking and innovation, even if we are optimistically attempting to bring consistency to the conversation. Promoting "innovation" or "openness" as symbolic principles will, in the end, not unify a company or a team—that is

done only with clear and consistent communication. Otherwise, expect an ambiguous, confusing mess that not only defines a poor strategy, but may be downright bewildering.

- If we want to authentically pursue innovation and open thinking in our work cultures, we need to recognize that concepts don't get the work done—whether finding a cure for cancer, colonizing Mars, cloning a pig, or finding a silver bullet to end anthropogenic climate warming. In our guts, we can understand the ideals implied, but they are ideals that require skills development, humility, and truth-telling. And those behaviors are not natural for those who are struggling to do new and creative things in our hierarchical ranks—we are calling for a messy, inefficient, and risky process; a tolerance for failure; and an emotional rollercoaster.

Table 1. The Principles of Open Approaches to Innovation Are Focused on Relationships

Closed Approach to Innovation	Open Approach to Innovation
Collaboration is a characteristic of the strategy of adopting open principles for internal projects.	Collaboration between internal and external project contributors is central to innovation.
Clear demarcation exists between external and internal project assets.	Relationships are the key asset managed between internal and external project stakeholders.
IP management is explicit and based on protection.	Intellectual property is used to grow intellectual capital through shared ownership, investment, and capitalization.
Social participation is an input.	Social participation is integral.
New ideas are funneled through a process and shaped by risk and expense analyses.	Ideas are seen as products themselves and are refined based on their fit to the business model.
New ideas are designed to fit the current market or create an entirely new one.	The idea is permitted to test, change, or even break the business model.
Cultural boundaries are distinct, even when they are flexible.	Cultural boundaries are fuzzy and may even be vague.
Value networks as represented by the nodes (such as people) between interactions are connected by both intangible and tangible deliverables, and the nodes are managed contractually.	Value networks as represented by the nodes between interactions are connected by deliverables and creative actions, including problem solving and idea generation. Nodes are managed by reciprocity.

- The previous table, referenced in Chapter 3 as Table 3.1 (repeated here as Table 1), shows broadly how this new way moves the idea of openness and collaboration, at any level—machine or human—right to the center, as the core feature of this approach. Innovation is about relationships in future tech, not always real-time and not even always human. When we let the walls fall around our organizations, our data, our source code, and the way we collaborate and innovate, we evolve not just our way of building better things, but our economic philosophies and business structures.

Chapter Four: Innovation Is Natural

Seeking Inspiration from What Is Before Us

In seeking inspiration for driving innovation into our work, natural ecosystems may represent our greatest opportunity to understand the patience, invention, and collaborative thinking required. Learning from the designs of nature is already serving as a key accelerant in the field of future tech and may hold the keys not only to a sustainable future but also to how we learn to better innovate in our businesses. Design thinking, Agile, and peer production are singular approaches that all happen to be focused on people-first in bringing new ideas to market, but they have much more in common than just their philosophy. The following discussion helps frame the OpenXFORM model within the context of these approaches.

Key Concepts

- Many scientists and researchers whose work is leading to the most cutting-edge advancements in society today are looking to nature for their inspiration through the discipline of *biomimicry*, which serves as the very source material for their designs. In many ways, nature has become our greatest mentor for future technology progression and innovation. Nature itself may represent the greatest genius in the field, embodying both the spirit and the ethos of patience, invention, and open thinking.
- Biomimicry literally means to imitate life, where *bios* comes from the Greek for life and *mimesis* for imitation. But the pursuit of biomimicry is also related to inspiration from the natural forms and materials found in nature, rather than just the field of clever reproduction. There are innumerable examples of how nature has informed some of our greatest and most useful human innovations, from buildings to airplanes to clothes fasteners.

- We are often inspired by the structural forms and biomechanical designs found in nature, especially when we want to develop techniques to put materials together, or even discover new, lighter, more efficient, or even just more beautiful materials. But as we garner more and more ability and insight into how animals, plants, and their ecosystems operate holistically, we are also learning how systems are balanced in the natural environment; and future tech researchers are also finding ways to emulate entire physiological systems by developing a deeper understanding of the complex mechanisms that keep plants and animals alive and adapting in every stage of their lives, from the biochemical to the cellular level. This is a largely untapped reservoir of inspiration for the pursuit of future technologies.

- All ecosystems have *carrying capacity* and *limiting factors*; the carrying capacity of an ecosystem is the greatest number of community members that can be healthfully sustained, and limiting factors are anything that inhibits growth in the systems, such as the availability of water, sunlight, or food. Thus, every ecosystem has contention and competition for resources, which in an uninterrupted state are managed through a system of *ecological regulation* that includes the diversity of interaction between members of the community, ecological succession, and various forms of cycling, such as food chains, trophic levels, and energy flow.

  A prejudicial summary of biologic ecosystems for our focus in this work is this: *The abiotic resources are those that create the conditions for growth of biotic organisms, and it is the amount and availability of these resources that accelerates or inhibits growth.* This is a key concept in thinking about innovation.

- Open Transformation (OpenXFORM) synthesizes an approach to the process of innovation, inspired by natural systems and human-centric design processes. OpenXFORM describes how an open system of innovation can adapt to the unregulated world of information, data, and content; decompose its own information to release to the open world; and discover ways to find the points of synergy among the studied and tested methodologies that put human relationships first—design thinking, Agile, and peer production.

- Chapter 4 includes Figure 4.2 (included here as Figure 2), which describes how "regulated ecosystems" are an expression of the dialectic method. Companies can benefit greatly by connecting to the opposing unregulated resources found in open information, data, and content. Not only can companies benefit from open thinking, collaboration, and innovation, any company may establish a firmer stand in delivering on their strategic goals, whether they are founded in new products or services, by focusing on their core strengths rather than pre-creating or re-creating the wheel. When it comes to innovation, the further we are able to balance our corporate ecosystems with open approaches by pushing into more creative relationships with partners and collaborators, the greater our potential returns.

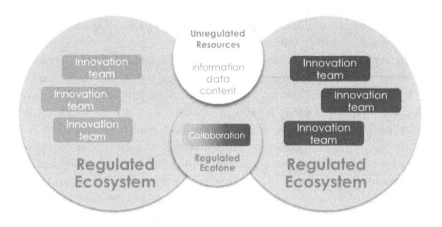

Figure 2. A synergistic approach to innovation helps balance regulated and unregulated ecosystems.

Chapter Five: Building an Ecosystem

The Extent of Bio-Empathy

Those who want to encourage creativity and innovation recognize that open thinking and open sources of data, content, and information help achieve and realize strategic goals that have previously been out of reach. Bio-empathetic designs, especially from the organizational perspective, seem like the perfect way for any motivated business entity to achieve these sought-after qualities. Yet, even if it makes good sense to mimic natural forms for innovative new functional designs, such as copying the shape of a whale fin for ergonomic advantage, taking natural systems too literally is counter-productive, especially when we want to transform the way we work to drive peak performance. OpenXFORM ecosystem works to the uncertain and difficult relationship between open resources and the private world of the innovating company entity.

Key Concepts

- Many who have more than a passing interest in teamwork and leadership are familiar with the widespread fascination with the self-organizing principles of ants. Some of the most advanced and lauded management publications write about what ants can teach us about teamwork and leadership and how to better understand our roles on a team, and even include in-depth discussions of ant colony work ethic. Ants get work done: they don't complain, and they certainly don't strike or ask for wage hikes or better working conditions.

- In exploring decentralized models for project management, terms from the insect world become useful, such as *stigmergy*, an entomological term that defines a mechanism whereby work done stimulates the work to be done, and Ant Colony Optimization (ACO), which captures ant food-seeking behaviors for solving problems that involve finding the best way through a graph (represented mathematically as a series of nodes interconnected by vertices), including vehicle routing, scheduling problems, and even image processing.

- Human social movements have been analyzed and new ones proposed in which stigmergy is considered not only a defining characteristic, but a positive framework or set of practices through which to perform complicated, cooperative tasks. Even the open-source movement has been named as one of those movements that benefits from a stigmergic model of collaboration, with the idea that it is the code base itself, rather than a centralized leader, that stimulates the next right action of any agent in the project.

- For all the benefits of studying ant behavior, there is an impulse to apply their behavior models to human management paradigms by using virtual pheromones or markers to coordinate mechanisms between so-called intelligent agents (we can call these people, too) in a distributed environment, especially to drive optimal practices in the ecosystems of peer production, open collaboration, and open innovation. This is rife with danger, simply because human beings collaborate and communicate intentionally, with expression and gesture, and purposely for effect, to persuade others of our perspective, to make decisions, and to get things done with awareness of ourselves and others, and with purpose.

- Even if the process of innovation begins with a spark of human imagination—no matter its inspiration—the process of drawing out that idea to the moment where it becomes something of significance to someone depends wholly on a deep understanding of the conditions under which we innovate, including who our customers are, what we want to do for them, how we will deliver it to them, and the characteristics related to the economies of delivering that value. This requires the human capacity to empathize with a huge diversity of environments in which we and our customers think, work, and produce.

- In natural systems, adaptation is a change to an organism that helps it survive in its environment. Similarly, decomposition plays a vital role in the cycle of any ecosystem, because, firstly, death and decay prevent resource scarcity; and secondly, it unleashes nutrients into the system that are crucial for new growth. Like chemical decomposition, information decomposition breaks down the components of the corpus and its previous structural integrity. Chapter 5 includes Figure 5.1 (included here as Figure 3), which describes how the OpenXFORM ecosystem works to flexibly accommodate the uncertain and difficult relationships between abiotic resources and the biotic world of the innovating company entity. The points of connection between the two are symbiotic and generally described as the functions of *adaption* and *information decomposition*.

Figure 3. Balancing the self-governed commons by adapting materials and returning benefit.

Chapter Six: An Evolutionary Model for Innovation

The OpenXFORM Anatomy

The study of morphology lends a bio-empathetic perspective for not just structure, but for how an organism works to exist sustainably within its ecosystem. With greater tools of examination at our disposal, we can study an organism within a system and apply our learnings to organizational problems—in this case how a breakthrough idea can move through a process that encourages innovative thinkers to test their assumptions, validate their hypotheses, and tune and tweak their ideas to not only drive solutions for users but also to meet the strategic goals of their companies. The anatomy of innovation through OpenXFORM contains the process for moving from a flight of fancy to a readiness to produce.

Key Concepts

- In biology, morphology is a term rooted in the Greek word *morphé* for "shape," and refers to the study of the form and structure of living organisms. In working to reveal a bio-empathetic process that adequately captures the potential for innovation in the overwhelmingly data-driven world of technology development, we are well served to deeply question the morphology of our typical new product development (NPD) processes to explore new approaches.
- To many morphologists, outward appearance is quite uninteresting when seeking a deeper understanding of an organism. In our study, we put aside a singular focus on how our processes of innovation *fit* into our organizational structures. Collaboration and innovation are not corporate departments, and such rigid stances help us little in our efforts to revolutionize future technologies, not only for material success, but for the advancement of society in medicine, energy, artificial intelligence, robotics, nanotechnology, space exploration, and every aspect of our built and natural environments that might make the world just that much more civilized and verdant. Innovative models of design that are implemented for their external benefits, optics, measurability, or ease of communicating up the chain are insufficient.
- Companies that want to drive innovation in an open world are well served to deeply consider that traditional systems of innovation and production that rely on fixed measures are broken. To improve requires investigating the messy world of human relationships, systems of motivation, and new patterns of communication and collaboration as we attempt to capture and amplify the new perspectives that successful innovation in the open world demands.
- In our attempt to extract a meaningful bio-empathetic approach from natural systems of adaptation to the process of innovation, it is worth remembering that the data, information, and content that live in the commons only becomes something of value when it is placed in the context of a unique idea. Otherwise, we are only staring at puddles of regurgitated data that signify nothing. Data and evidence should not be confused with truth; there is nothing inherently valuable in a stream of numbers, nor does even a clever analysis make one complete in one's knowledge. Information becomes valuable only when it is given meaning within the boundaries of specific design goals.
- Insect morphology defines insects as having three regions: head, thorax, and abdomen. Chapter 6 includes Table 6.1 (shown here as Table 2), which compares the form and functions found within the insect world and the

innovation methodology defined in the OpenXFORM (Open Transformation) model. The structural regions and their functional purposes are made up in the insect as the head, thorax, and abdomen and in OpenXFORM as ideation, exploration, and transformation. The characteristics of their respective morphologies are presented from a bio-empathetic perspective that may serve to inspire the innovation practitioner who is looking to nature for adaptive and resilient organizing principles.

- The chapter text provides a list of terms used in the model, where each term is deconstructed and explained at a high level. This list can be referenced at any point that clarification is needed in the course of working with the methods and applications for deployment of the model within the organization.
- Figure 4 (from Chapter 6, Figure 6.2) describes the bio-empathetic anatomy of the OpenXFORM model.

Table 2. Comparison of the Form and Functions Found Within Insect and Innovation Morphologies

FUNCTION	STRUCTURAL REGIONS		CHARACTERISTICS	
	Insect	*Innovation*	*Insect*	*Innovation*
Input	Head	Ideate	Brain Center Seeing Sensing Ingestion	Seeing Feeling Qualifying Expressing
Propulsion	Thorax	Explore	Locomotion Nervous System Circulation Respiration	Showing Testing Assessing Refining
Output	Abdomen	Transform	Digestion Excretion Reproduction Defense	Scaling Validating Designing Specifying

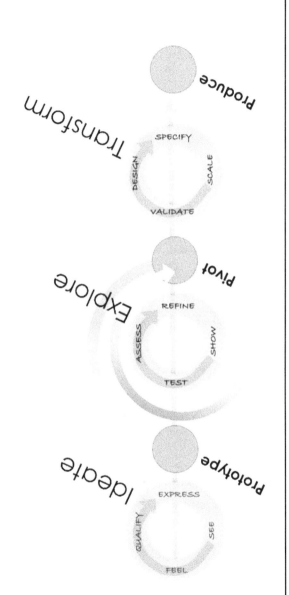

Figure 4. The bio-empathetic anatomy of OpenXFORM is inspired by insect morphology.

Section Two

The Anatomy of
OpenXFORM

Chapter Seven

Setting Organizational Intention

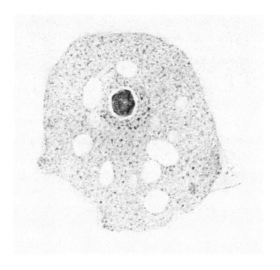

1

The process which led from the amoeba to man appeared to the philosophers to be obviously a progress—though whether the amoeba would agree with this opinion is not known.

— Bertrand Russell

---

1 *Popular Science Monthly* (1907). Vol. 71. Retrieved August 28, 2016, from https://commons.wikimedia.org/wiki/File%3APSM_V71_D368_Amoeba_coli_highly_magnified.png [Public domain] via Wikimedia Commons.

7.1 Chapter Theme

There are documented benefits to incrementalism, including improved efficiency, greater collaboration capabilities, and enhanced quality. However, serious questions are raised about applying the principles of incrementalism as a corporate strategy toward improving the processes of innovation within the firm. Incrementalism plays a role in problem management, preventing overinvestment in the wrong solutions, but many push for its operational use. This chapter argues that an organizational shift to the company, especially in an area as sensitive as innovation, requires not only a common framework for managing the innovation process, but also a shift in operational and strategic performance goals. This is a challenge not only to the organization's structure, but also to its behavioral processes. The OpenXFORM model proposes complementary principles that help shape these new processes as new ideas are explored and transformed to scale.

7.2 The Importance of Forward Momentum

Martin Luther King, Jr., in a speech at Spelman College, said, "If you can't fly, run; if you can't run, walk; if you can't walk, crawl; but by all means keep moving."[2] Dr. King often implored those in the American civil rights movement to focus on their common goals, even when faced with seeming impossibilities and insurmountable odds. His words inspired multitudes in the fight against racial injustice and continue to help many persevere in the ongoing struggle. It makes good sense: why worry about what you can't fully accomplish in an instant? Instead, focus on what can be done right now, in the moment.

Finding ways to maintain stamina and a positive perspective comes through incrementalism. This is a natural tendency for many when we must tackle imposing and important problems, especially when they require a great determination of purpose. Becoming too distracted or frustrated with obstacles along the way can be deeply discouraging, and incrementalism is an approach that helps keep us tuned to our greater purpose. Especially in our professional work, this sense of incrementalism, in which small steps rather than giant leaps are the best option, provides flexibility and adaptability for often too-fast-moving initiatives. Furthermore, simple and gradual changes serve to reduce risk, uncertainty, and even internal conflict with our collaborators when our greatest ideas begin to meet material reality.

---

[2] King, Martin Luther, Jr. (1960). "If You Can't Fly, Then Run." Literary Devices. Retrieved August 28, 2016, from http://literarydevices.net/if-you-cant-fly-then-run/.

But, let's not wave our hands around and believe that Martin Luther King, Jr., somehow preferred incrementalism to the right and proper outcome of equality. Rather, he was seeking to mitigate the dangers of lost motivation, infighting, violent expression, the diminishing of faith, and the existential hopelessness one must feel when fighting for their own human dignity. Truly, incrementalism as a corporate strategy is not nearly so inspired, and perhaps there is nothing less inspiring than incremental innovation. It's worth a closer look.

7.2.1 Stop, Look, and Listen

In a 1985 article in the *Harvard Business Review*, James Bryan Quinn, PhD, who later authored the book *Intelligent Enterprise*, mapped out his theories about the relationships among technology, strategic planning, and innovation, writing that managing innovation is a lot like playing a game of stud poker over several hands: "A player has some idea of the likely size of the pot at the beginning, knows the general but not the sure route to winning, buys one card (a project) at a time to gain information about probabilities and the size of the pot, closes hands as they become discouraging, and risks more only late in the hand as knowledge increases."[3] Thankfully sparing us the worse analogy of strip poker, Quinn goes so far as to fully assert that innovation itself is an *inherently* incremental process. He evidenced this, in part, by pointing out the long-time horizons from invention to production—after all, we didn't launch a rocket to the moon overnight.

It also seems intuitive that carving up work strategically in a sort of "take smaller bites and chew thoroughly" approach provides the flexibility and the space to adjust to new learnings, both anticipated and totally unexpected. It should be no surprise that this incrementalism has become an encompassing preoccupation for many who tout a strict adherence to phased approaches, scheduled intervals, and organized increments as the only way forward. But are they wrong? These individuals point to the ease with which their strategy spares us from the two perils of innovative projects:

1. It helps us break down an audacious goal into something doable.
2. It gets the team pointed in the right direction, gets things working, motivates, and increases the chances of getting work done.

---

[3] Quinn, James Brian (1985). "Managing Innovation: Controlled Chaos." *Harvard Business Review* [online]. Retrieved September 4, 2016, from https://hbr.org/1985/05/managing-innovation-controlled-chaos.

Furthermore, because of the way that today's consumer markets shift so quickly, the only way to perform to economic demands is to constantly reconnect with customers and their needs. Disruptive innovation is risky, because even when new markets can be reached, consumer patience for early underperforming is very small. Why not leave the unknowable markets to the *two guys in a garage* and buy them up later? Incrementalism works: if played well, a firm should be able to carefully listen to its customers and then satisfy their predicted needs.

Sure, there may be some troubling implications to eschewing strategic investment for incremental cherry-picking (sometimes called *trials* or *pilots*), but as a principle, it strips great swathes of uncertainty from corporate performance by instilling hope that costly long-term problems will emerge early, when they can be addressed on the cheap. And further, the notion that achieving something, no matter how small or non-representative of the broader reality, is a way of communicating a vision and nearly always seems better than doing nothing.

Incrementalism has become a driving framework that shows up in many ways—as gradualism, fractionalization, continuous improvement, "breaking it down," cherry-picking, and even formal production methodologies such as Agile. But as a process, incrementalism is best captured by the crawl-walk-run (CWR) methodology as a natural approach to learning. Moreover, this is an adoption framework that can be found in nearly every technology and marketing company.

The CWR strategy asserts that it is best to start small and easy when introducing a new process by choosing a small project that will likely work well (cherry-picking) with low probability of failure the first time out and a few

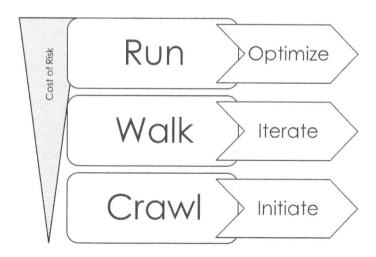

Figure 7.1   Start at the bottom to contain the impact and costs of risk to the firm.

rudimentary metrics. Then momentum can be built over time to the point of massive success (or flying). As described in Figure 7.1, we all walked before we ran; if a company really doesn't know what it's doing with a new initiative, doesn't know its direction or how to measure success, then perhaps it's best to just slow down and contain the costs of risk to the firm. This is a logical, rational, and reasonable way to constrain capital costs on a potential fool's errand.

In fact, the CWR methodology is so pervasive in today's organizations that it's worth exploring further. One typical view is the so-called "bottom up" Agile. Agilists who want to bring this methodology to their companies, or at the very least their teams, often make two basic arguments: (1) It's efficient. (2) It's what the best engineers do anyway. Today's CWRers tend to call themselves *agilists,* comparing their move-slow-and-learn method to the iterative development approach. Some agilists will even phrase their approach with this nomenclature.

Agile, in fact, builds incrementalism directly into its processes, in which software can be built and delivered in parts, where each piece is a subset of a growing body of refinements that will eventually make up the whole. Mike Cohn, a seasoned Agile expert, compares Agile development increments that are delivered in iterative stages to the art of carving. He writes of a sculptor who, after selecting his stone, ". . . carves the general shape from the stone. At this point, one can perhaps distinguish the head and torso, and discern that the finished work will be of a human body rather than a bird. . . . However, the sculptor is unlikely to look on any one area as complete until the entire work is complete."[4] Thus, while Agile practitioners strive to deliver working bits throughout the project, it is not that they don't plan for a final achievement, they plan instead to make adjustments along the way.

The following are key arguments made on behalf of incremental strategy, founded in the idea that parsing out deeply focused efforts into small, manageable stages results in a flexible and adaptive environment that saves money, the health of the project team, and maybe even the project:

- **Efficiency Benefits.** Save time and money by failing fast. Instead of waiting for a massive integration scenario way down the line to expose a fundamental flaw, find it early, fix it fast.
- **Improved Ability to Execute.** Because of the sense of immediacy and transparency inherent in close-in goals, it is easier, faster, and cheaper to collaborate as needed. Collaboration improves enthusiasm and motivation to complete the required work.

---

[4] Cohn, Mike (2014). "Agile Needs to Be Both Iterative and Incremental." Retrieved August 27, 2016, from https://www.mountaingoatsoftware.com/blog/agile-needs-to-be-both-iterative-and-incremental.

- **Quality Is Inherent in the Process.** Because teams are focused on building on progress met, it is in their interest to work to a higher quality. Quality gets built in as a matter of self-interest and the transparency of small projects with quick-hit demonstrations and metrics.

Every incremental framework has its own flavor, with the Agile methodology perhaps being the most modern expression of its methods. Iterative and incremental development (IID) can make the chaotic seem easier, keep everyone engaged and grounded, and still scale dramatically well and successfully in the realm of software development—not just in the venturesome startup, but in private industry and government efforts since the mid-1950s. As Craig Larman and Victor R. Basili note in their brief history of the practices in software engineering, "IID concepts have been and are a recommended practice by prominent software-engineering thought leaders of each decade, associated with many successful large projects, and recommended by standards boards."[5]

7.2.2 Should We Stay Forever?

Admittedly, customers are living in beta, but that doesn't seem like a bad move. In the early days of the online world, soon-to-be massively successful online products, such as Google's Gmail, ran for years under the banner of "beta." Beta even defines some company cultures, and it is characteristic of the "move fast" mentality that customers want to be your partner in fixing your glitchy, nonfunctional products. And as a driving concept, it continues to grow and morph.

Beta used to mean that the products were early and might be buggy, but a customer bug report made them one of the team. Yet it is also inherent in the Agile concept of "release early, release often," or RERO—deploy faster, users benefit faster and stay engaged, and developers don't feel rushed to force features. Open-source advocate Tim O'Reilly even once positively described the movement as being in "perpetual beta."[6] But if you are pointing to a beta success such as Gmail, you may be thinking that one of Google's greatest innovations was held together with just enough tissue paper and spit. That's a misconception. Instead, for Google, "beta" was just the word that defined the starting point

---

5 Larman, Craig and Basili, Victor R. (2003). "Iterative and Incremental Developments. A Brief History." *Computer,* vol. 36, issue 6, pp. 47–56. DOI:10.1109/MC.2003.1204375.

6 Lapidos, Juliet (2009). "Why Did It Take Google So Long to Take Gmail Out of Beta?" Retrieved September 24, 2016, from http://www.slate.com/articles/news_and_politics/recycled/2009/07/why_did_it_take_google_so_long_to_take_gmail_out_of_beta.html.

of one of Google's greatest innovations. Beta may be the way that some new ideas are tweaked (very effectively) to life, but in this case, it wasn't the creative impulse that brought it to life, it was the way the impulse was shaped.

Instead, Google has a *mindset,* and it's about striving to work on projects that are 10x: ten times better than what anyone else is thinking about. 10x has been behind self-driving cars, floating balloons with internet capabilities, Google street view, and even disease-fighting magnetic nanoparticulates. But it was also how a simple mail client came into being: ". . . the 10x mentality also ushered in now established products like Gmail—which initially gave users 100 times more storage than any other product out there and was seen as a crazy digression by people who only thought of Google as a search company. . . ."[7] In 2016, that crazy digression had one billion users.[8] And its strategic value to the ad-serving company? Priceless.

Still, for those who think more expansively, "incrementalism-as-a-strategy" has a downside. As a construct, incrementalism is reactionary (to customers) and, in its very goal of efficiency, metes out resources in a manner that creates a lack of space or time necessary for expansive or strategic thought. In a solely incremental framework, even the incentive for innovation falls away, because the solutions that are most valuable are those that are relatively insignificant in scope and breadth. Visible progress is the only metric that really matters. And if incrementalism becomes the strategy of the company, is there ever an end to the groundhog day of iteration? If one is not convinced that the innovative process fits in an incremental world, then where does it fit?

7.3 Finding the Innovation Sweet Spot

We don't have to reject IID to agree that it doesn't have to codify our every move. Every tool has its sweet spot, and engineering practices have been proven in many instances to be the right place for IID, most often as expressed through the Agile methodology. At the same time, expressing that something is iterative (under any name) doesn't make it the methodological equivalent of fairy dust. Even if there may be applicable tools found within IID—especially as relates to quality—it simply does not mean that, as a rule, IID practices don't have obvious boundaries and limitations. Unfortunately, IID is too often applied without

---

[7] D'Onfro, Jillian (2015). "The Dark Side of Google's Focus on Massive World-Changing Projects." Business Insider. Retrieved September 24, 2016, from http://www.businessinsider.com/the-dark-side-of-google-10x-2015-7.

[8] Smith, Craig (2016). "By the Numbers: 15 Amazing Gmail Statistics." Retrieved September 24, 2016, from http://expandedramblings.com/index.php/gmail-statistics/.

skills and knowledge, which allows it to be wielded in an inappropriate and even dehumanizing manner, treating participants in the process as substitutable.

Liz Ryan, progenitor of the Human Workplace, has long been fighting against the dehumanization of the modern-day worker. She writes in *Forbes* about the perils of excessive box-ticking and evaluation: "Measurement requires stopping the action, getting outside of it and holding it up against a yardstick, exactly the opposite of the activity that would create products or ship them, make customers happy or move our business forward in any way. Most of the time in the business world, goals come down from on high, and the appropriate measuring devices, rubrics or protocols come with them."[9] By design, OpenXFORM works to make room for reflection that defies such a rubric by asserting that the process of innovation can be directed, but that overwrought authoritarian control or administration is the wrong impulse. But even this doesn't have to imply anarchy.

Ironically, it was the early agilists who resisted command-style institutional thinking, complaining that it failed the creative process. They proposed a way to help nearly any organization shift its thinking in a way that wasn't completely unmooring for corporate stakeholders, because they promised increased effectiveness. So why, many agilists have begun to ask, can't we embed strategy and innovative development processes that could be ingrained into the everyday business of execution? After all, top-down strategic planning cannot succeed without the execution of that strategy to adjust and get it right. In many ways, it seems that strategic planning would be greatly improved by incremental thinking, to test hunches in small and limited ways. But this isn't always helpful.

"Agile everywhere" is a philosophy best suited to shorter-term commercialization goals, rather than strategic innovation imperatives. The approach just does not provide an adequate opportunity for big ideas to gain a foothold. Instead, it smacks of a pure risk-aversion strategy, which is likely a side effect of the desire to mimic the entrepreneurial, venture-funded startup that has its exit in mind before the ink is dry on the incorporation papers. Jealously watching the big wins in the startup world, many more traditional corporate stakeholders seem to be seeking incrementalism as a mechanism for risk reduction.

In such a framework, idea origination sinks to the bottom of the murky pond of execution focus. Worse, even traditionally innovative companies are losing their mandate within the business, instead participating in "confirmatory experiments" or "early pilots" that have much shorter long-term impact. In previous generations, small, fast-moving teams lurked in experimental laboratories

---

[9] Ryan, Liz (2014). "'If You Can't Measure It, You Can't Manage It': Not True." Retrieved September 11, 2016, from http://www.forbes.com/sites/lizryan/2014/02/10/if-you-cant-measure-it-you-cant-manage-it-is-bs/#7bb915e43fae.

that ran independently and were designed to create revolutionary impact. As inspiring as Silicon Valley companies like Netflix may be when they say they are so innovative that they don't even have to talk about it anymore, the idea of plugging fast work back in as an input to the next phase of innovation limits the context of innovation to one with rigidly testable assumptions and ideas.[10] Surely, we don't have to mythologize the process of innovation to embrace new ways of thinking, but we also don't have to drip the blood of every creative heartbeat into a facilitated process of information exchange.

As Walter Isaacson reminds us in his book *The Innovators,* about the beginnings of the digital revolution, that while many individuals were involved, the really interesting narrative is about how these thinker/doers collaborated to become even more creative. Their process of innovation was really the mastery of the skill of teamwork. He writes, "The collaboration that created the digital age was not just among peers but also between generations. Ideas were handed off from one cohort of innovators to the next."[11] This reminds us of the importance of understanding the way in which those with great imaginations collaborate.

Unfortunately, even in Silicon Valley, small teams of loosely coupled thinkers may often be isolated and powerless, especially when an organization is structured into diverse groups with myriad functional goals, metrics, and key performance goals that require budgeting, staffing, and the ever-dreaded performance review period. In these environments, there are few shared objectives that would even begin to take advantage of the benefits that incremental thinking brings to the table, unless they are focused on the process of co-creation. And that has to be a lot more than words expressed in a mission statement.

7.4 When We Learn the Wrong Lessons

One hypothesis for the failure of corporate innovation is that disruptive innovation processes that challenge the foundations of the traditional business structure are stymied by a fear of risk taking. This corporation frustrates those who wish to innovate by arguing that a deliberate pace of advancement (at least from

---

[10] Kaplan, Soren (2014). "Tap Into the 7 Secrets of Silicon Valley's Innovation Culture." Co.Design | business + design. Retrieved September 24, 2016, from https://www.fastcodesign.com/3026220/tap-into-the-7-secrets-of-silicon-valleys-innovation-culture.

[11] Isaacson, Walter (2014). "How Innovation Happens in the Digital Age," excerpt from *The Innovators.* Science Friday. Retrieved September 24, 2016, from http://live-science friday.pantheonsite.io/articles/how-innovation-happens-in-the-digital-age/.

20,000 feet) is less dangerous than the risk of the competition's moving more quickly. Coherent process is the recommended way to dispense with these fears. Gary P. Pisano, a professor and member of the U.S. Competitiveness Project at Harvard Business School, describes an innovation system as a "coherent set of interdependent processes and structures that dictates how the company searches for novel problems and solutions, synthesizes ideas into a business concept and product designs, and selects which projects get funded."[12] This sounds rational, but a careful reading of it shows the pervasive press to focus on managing the output of the innovative process from a problem-driven perspective—that is, there is a belief that there's a basket of well-known problems, and thus it's a matter of bubbling up the right solutions.

Many a one-time pioneer has fallen into such faltering beliefs decades before they became painfully aware that they had lost their edge, including Sears, Yahoo, Toys "R" Us, and even Microsoft. The uncontested example of the innovator-lost-in-the-desert is Kodak. Founded by George Eastman in 1888, Kodak found itself filing for bankruptcy protection in 2012 after a storied existence that stretched over a century, with the invention and introduction of breakthrough still and video camera technology. Ironically, the most innovative photography technology company ever suffered its worst pains at the hands of breakthrough imaging technology. Disruptive digital photography was a reality the company chose to ignore—remarkably, as the inventor of the digital camera, Steve Sasson, worked for Kodak itself.

They even had more than the technology itself, with a digital technology adoption forecast marking the pace to come. Vince Barabba, who was head of marketing intelligence in 1981, presented a startlingly prescient assessment of the emergence of digital photography ten years in advance of the digital crossover, giving Kodak the opportunity to master and benefit from the new wave in imaging technology. They didn't. Barabba lamented, "Kodak management not only presided over the creation technological breakthroughs but was also presented with an accurate market assessment about the risks and opportunities of such capabilities. Yet Kodak failed in making the right strategic choices."[13]

How could they miss the digital opportunity? Even with the first digital camera in their own laboratory, one could conclude that Kodak management was afraid that their own innovation would hurt them in the film business,

---

[12] Pisano, Gary P. (2015). "You Need an Innovation Strategy." *Harvard Business Review* [online]. Retrieved August 30, 2016, from https://hbr.org/2015/06/you-need-an-innovation-strategy.

[13] Newman, Rick (2010). "10 Great Companies That Lost Their Edge." *U.S. News.* Retrieved from http://money.usnews.com/money/blogs/flowchart/2010/08/19/10-great-companies-that-lost-their-edge.

so they avoided the outcome of cannibalization. The brand was strong, they thought, and their consumers were unlikely to invest in the cables and cards and new devices necessary to participate with digital. However, another conclusion can be equally drawn: the company was itself no longer atmospherically suited for innovation. Sadly, the company that brought the world a lifetime of "Kodak moments" had—to their own peril—simply stopped embracing a spirit of invention. And the breakdown of the social and cultural forces of teamwork and collaboration were the harbinger of the day in 2012 that they were delisted from the New York Stock Exchange.

For the sake of the story, it is worth noting that in a moment of painful irony, the company was able to sell millions of dollars in intellectual property to companies such as Apple, Google, and Facebook, bringing Kodak out of bankruptcy in 2013 with an imaging technologies business that only footnotes its historic leadership in photography. Living in denial, as Kodak clearly did, represents a form of fear-based organizational thinking reminiscent of the heliophobic who fears the sun, preferring to sit in a dark room rather than wander into the light of the sun that, despite its most pleasant properties of warmth and light, they fear will give them cancer.

7.5 The Innovation Hunt

Contrary to the common mythology of the legendary wolf, these remarkable animals are not advanced collaborators, yet neither are they blind, instinctual, fuzzy rule-driven, robot-like beasts. They are a deeply principled predator, just not in the way we typically think about principles. They exercise what behaviorists term *byproduct mutualism*, in which individuals cooperate to improve fitness or the likelihood of survival.

A group of Georgia Tech students at the Robot Lab set out to incorporate what was known about wolf behaviors into a system of robots, with the aim of introducing beneficial collaborative behavior. Their project, conducted in Yellowstone and reported on in 2010, dispelled the popular myth that wolves deploy strategies and teamwork during the hunt. Not only do wolves appear not to do any coordinated planning, they also communicate very little—if at all—while hunting. This seems especially remarkable, because they hunt in packs over a wide range of conditions and seek a variety of prey, from small rodents to elk and moose. The key to the study was observing how the wolves moved through the stages of the hunting process and then examining the behavior of each individual wolf toward the others (see Figure 7.2). The members drew the following as an important learning for their project: ". . . wolves hunting the same herd do not make transitions between states together (i.e., one may find

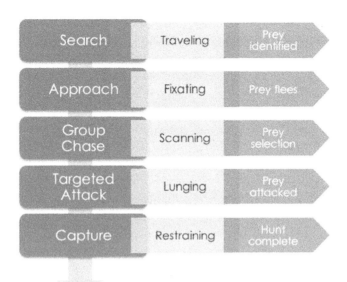

Figure 7.2   States of activity experienced by a wolf in pack hunting scenario. [Author's own work, derived from Georgia Tech. (2009). HUNT Project.]

a weak prey and transition to attack that individual while the others remain in an attack group). The disparity in these transitions goes so far as to see one wolf having killed an animal and begin eating it while the others persist [to attack]."[14]

The most surprising findings were that, by studying the interactions between wolves and their prey, they discovered that there was actually no advantage to the pack in developing a sophisticated attack strategy. This is because there was so much chaos and so many unknowns involved in the hunt states, as described in Figure 7.2, that any strategies would quickly fail. Instead, the wolf pack adapts based on simple and general rules that allow them to react with precision and speed based on a response to the behavior of the prey and not of the others in the pack.[15] Later studies suggested that just two simple heuristics were in play—first to stay close but safe from the prey during tracking (a kick to the face

[14] Georgia Tech. (2009). HUNT Project. Retrieved September 11, 2016, from http://www.cc.gatech.edu/ai/robot-lab/hunt/wolfProject.html.

[15] Madden, John D., Arkin, Ronald C., and MacNulty, Daniel R. (n.d.). Multi-Robot System Based on Model of Wolf Hunting Behavior to Emulate Wolf and Elk Interactions. Georgia Tech. Retrieved August 28, 2016, from http://www.cc.gatech.edu/ai/robot-lab/online-publications/MaddenROBIO2010.pdf.

could mean the end of life), then once the prey is selected to move away from other wolves during a targeted attack.[16]

As the wolves seem to instinctively know, outcomes do not necessarily improve by the *imposition* of coordination among a distributed team and may even cause a process to fall apart out of sheer complexity. However, a strong sense of mission and a sense of how to effectively manage oneself in a group can improve the outcome of the mission for all. As for the wolves, a successful hunt meant that each member of the pack held their appropriate position, allowing them to safely flex, respond, and adapt to completing their mission. When considering how best to work not only in distributed environments, but also in those in which information, data, content, and even our peers may exist on the other side of a gossamer wall—perhaps thousands of miles away, in another culture, speaking another language—understanding the importance of mission over cumbersome process cannot be overstated.

7.5.1 Wolf-Like Thinking

Although it's not clear if early open-source adherents studied wolf behavior, the same instincts seemed to be at play. Sheen S. Levine of Columbia University and Michael J. Prietula of Emory University, who examined the principles of open collaboration distinctive to open-source production (and the organizations they have spawned), observed an emergent organizational form that harkens back to the flex and response of the hunt. They write that the collaborative success of the open-source ecosystem suggests that for "any system of innovation or production that relies on goal-oriented yet loosely coordinated participants who interact to create a product (or service) of economic value, which they make available to contributors and non-contributors alike."[17]

And here's the good news for the firm. If what Levine and Prietula observed is correct, it is possible to focus on the collaboration itself as a means of production. But it also implies two other potential realities: firstly, that collaboration is goal-oriented; and secondly, that contributors are somehow rationally benefitting from that collaboration, including in how their collaboration may inform

---

[16] Muro, C., Escobedo, R., Spector, L., and Coppinger, R. P. (2011). "Wolf-pack (*Canis lupus*) Hunting Strategies Emerge from Simple Rules in Computational Simulations. *Behavioural Processes,* vol. 88, issue 3, pp. 192–197. http://doi.org/10.1016/j.beproc.2011.09.006.

[17] Levine, Sheen S. and Prietula, Michael J. (2014). "Open Collaboration for Innovation: Principles and Performance." *Organization Science,* vol. 25, issue 5, pp. 1414–1433. Available at http://doi.org/10.1287/orsc.2013.0872.

their own private process of creativity, increase their skill and knowledge (and thus their marketability), or perhaps even because it is just fun.

7.6 In OpenXFORM, Collaboration Is Principled

The principles of OpenXFORM draw from many sources of inspiration—including the ideas of Agile, design thinking, peer production, open innovation, and open collaboration—but in large part from the practices of land management philosophies that focus on biological diversity. There is a reason for this: Diverse ecosystems are inherently efficient, but only within certain limitations or boundaries. Furthermore, as we recognize the impacts of our anthropogenic activities on the biosphere, the management of our living resources must necessarily be balanced with other demanding drivers, including economic development and cultural and societal needs, which may sometimes seem irreconcilable.

In our early discussions in Chapter 4, the broad OpenXFORM ecosystem was described as including the commons, which is made of the open resources of data, content, and information. As a reminder, any ecosystem, whether it be forest, grassland, desert, tundra, or marine, represents a rich tapestry of interactions among the living organisms and nonliving features within it. As previously discussed, science classifies the two major components of an ecosystem as *biotic* and *abiotic.* Biotic features are the plants and animals within the community of the ecosystem, and abiotic features include the non-living parts of the environment that affect the functioning of the biotic components in the ecosystem, especially in terms of growth, maintenance, and reproduction. Abiotic resources include water, sunlight, temperature, soil, humidity, the quality of the atmospheric chemistry, and even pressure and sound waves in a marine ecosystem.

Throughout the first part of this book, innovation has been defined solely as a process, not an outcome, and certainly not an environment. However, to discover the opportunities for efficiency, we work to identify and define the sort of ecosystem that supports a balanced innovation process. We can compare this efficiency to natural processes within a healthy ecological space that involve the transfer of energy from one system to the next, as well as the resultant chemical cycling that keeps an ecosystem churning. A good example is a plant's self-nourishment process, which transfers energy through the interaction of photosynthesis, using the abiotic resources of water, sunlight, and carbon dioxide. As that plant reaches the end of its life, a series of physical and biochemical reactions occur that carry the components of the biotic plant into the realm of the abiotic.

In a balanced and sustainable ecosystem, this is a very efficient process that encompasses a variety of "conversions" that interplay. Indeed, it is quite simple to calculate mathematically the efficiency within an ecosystem by factoring various forms of resource utilization that measure how energy travels through trophic levels (often referred to as the *food chain*). This is called *net production efficiency* (NPE), and it is a measurement of how efficiently energy moves through the food chain.[18] In general, scientists want to understand the relationship between how well food is ingested and assimilated and the extent to which such "resources" are ultimately converted into organic matter through decomposition. The more diversity within an ecosystem, the more complicated the trophic pathways through the chain.

There are three kinds of organisms in an ecosystem (shown in Figure 7.3), which deploy various strategies in the coordination of their energetic exchange through so-called "trophic levels," of which up to six can generally be supported within a single system:

- **Producers.** Plants and algae are nourished from abiotic sources through processes such as photosynthesis.
- **Consumers.** Consumers eat the primary producers and are either herbivores that eat plants, carnivores that eat other animals, or omnivores who will not let scruples stand between their mouths and a square meal.
- **Decomposers.** Decomposers are those who feed on dead animal and plant material, and through their feeding cycle dump nutrients back into the environment to feed producers.

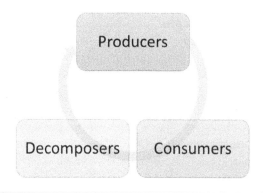

Figure 7.3 Energetic transfer between ecosystem participants in a healthy ecosystem.

---

[18] Boundless (2016). "Transferring of Energy between Trophic Levels." Boundless.com. Retrieved August 28, 2016, from https://www.boundless.com/biology/textbooks/boundless-biology-textbook/ecosystems-46/energy-flow-through-ecosystems-257/transferring-of-energy-between-trophic-levels-953-12213/.

One of the most challenging things about quantifying ecological efficiency is that such calculations always reside somewhat within the realm of an educated guess. Why? Because the measurements required to perform the calculation include such things as deep knowledge of a system to understand how much food has been consumed in an ecosystem, the caloric content of that food, and other tough-to-measure variables such as prey production and other values related to metabolic, respiration, and activity rates.

Despite popular myth, ecosystems are really not all that efficient, at least in strict economic terms. A general rule of thumb is to assume that about 10% of the energy available will pass to the next trophic level.[19] And despite the best efforts of some cattle and livestock producers (which have low NPE values because they use energy to breathe and heat their bodies), because energy decreases as it moves up the food chain, if efficiencies are to be gained it will not be from making a cow that breathes less; instead of supporting systems to raise livestock to feed humans, efficiencies will be gained by asking the consumers of livestock (typically human beings) to eat less meat and dairy.

The important point of this discussion is to understand that if one really wanted to squeeze out every efficiency from an ecosystem, it would be best to keep the *exchanges of energy* from one level to the next at a minimum and the NPE high. In the world of economics, we call this *economies of flow*. In the world of collaboration, we achieve this by seeking effective communications.

7.6.1 The Problem of Scale

Economies of scale is the classic reason for looking for cost advantages where output will increase as fixed costs are spread out across more units. This theory is especially useful when all other factors are equal, in that increased scale will naturally create cost advantages, even as applied to production issues of a human scale; for instance, we missed our software delivery deadline, we need to hire more engineers and we will achieve a linear improvement. [For opposing thoughts on this, please reference Brook's law, which states that "adding manpower to a late software project makes it later."[20]]

We know intuitively that there are very clear limits to this form of growth, although it is perhaps most convincingly argued when a services-oriented company tries to manage unit costs and finds that they are left holding a paradoxical

---

[19] Regents of the University of Michigan (2005). "The Flow of Energy: Higher Trophic Levels." Retrieved September 11, 2016, from http://www.globalchange.umich.edu/globalchange1/current/lectures/kling/energyflow/highertrophic/trophic2.html.

[20] Wikipedia (n.d.). Retrieved August 28, 2016, from https://en.wikipedia.org/wiki/Brooks_law.

bag of increasing overall costs. This is the result of a phenomenon named *failure demand*. This is when demand for a service increases because of a failure to do the right thing for the customer in the beginning. A classic example of failure demand was first identified by John Seddon, British occupational psychologist and author, who found that when telephone work was moved to call centers from local bank branches, the total number of calls soared. Why? Because people weren't getting their problems solved the first time, as they were when they engaged directly with the local bank branch. Thus, in the end, the quest for efficiency drove up overall costs.[21]

To confound the problem for the typical neoliberally trained company director, individuals accustomed to handling widgets are asked to "be innovative," but then must justify their innovation plans through traditional economic exercises. These individuals must answer to accounting departments that are steeped in traditional notions about measuring return on investment in order to ensure that corporate dollars are well spent. For example, we know how to measure if we hit a deadline, but we're not good at measuring the conditions that created the conditions for our success or failure. Seddon encouraged organizations struggling with these issues to break away from seeking efficiencies through economies of scale and instead begin looking at what he called *economies of flow*.

Economies of flow is a way of looking at optimization that diverts the focus from the volume of transactions (or whatever is being counted) and instead looks at ways to streamline the flow of a process to the point of interaction between the customer and the provider, or in our ecosystem example, the transfer of energy. While an economies-of-scale perspective demands standardizations that, as a side effect, increase the amount of fragmentation in a process, economies of flow eliminate waste by absorbing unique requirements or perspectives, limiting overall complexity, and reducing rework and duplication of effort (which is inherent in failure demand). For example, what if instead of having to access six highly-trained specialized medical doctors, each having to study a patient record at great expense, stress, and with coordination strain, we trained a single doctor to focus on the sick patient who knew how and when to access the specialist? That's flow.

Quite salient to the design of OpenXFORM, Seddon further advocates a local level of engagement in optimizing flow, noting that when participants in the system are able to enjoy their immediate environment, their behavior becomes more positive and they eschew indifference by increased awareness and engagement in the effort at hand.[22]

---

[21] Seddon, John (2010). "Economy Is in Flow, Not Scale." *ResPublic*. Retrieved December 10, 2014, from http://demingcollaboration.com/systems-review-2/.

[22] Stimmel, Carol (2015). *Building Smart Cities: Analytics, ITC, and Design Thinking*. Auerbach Publications. DOI: 10.1201/b18827-3.

7.7 Ready, Mindset, Go!

Bringing organizational shift to a company, especially in an area as sensitive as innovation, does not just draw on the common frameworks of change management, but may also shift operational and strategic performance goals, and surely challenges the organization to consider its existing behavioral processes. The actual process that a company prefers to employ is somewhat neutral; as long as there is a clear rationale for change, the organizational stakeholders are genuinely convinced that innovation processes must be improved, and there is a widespread sense of acceptance within stakeholder teams for exploring new approaches to collaboration and communication, learning, and the ability to get comfortable with discovering and implementing metrics that create a healthy ecosystem for a nascent innovation process.

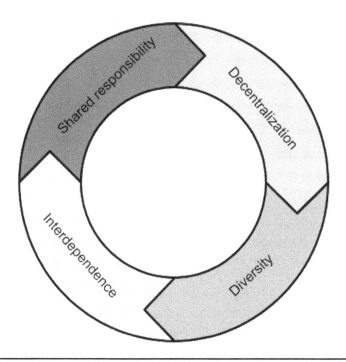

Figure 7.4 Exercising the living principles of OpenXFORM produces a natural efficiency.

Figure 7.4 and Table 7.1 describe the four principles of a living OpenXFORM ecosystem that is required to support an innovation process in all of its stages. These principles have been greatly influenced by those enumerated by the

Convention on Biological Diversity and adapted to this context.[23] These stages are complementary and are linked with each other in a manner of sequencing (think flow) that helps define how the acts of ideation, exploration, and transformation of a new idea to scaled production can be achieved. As with all systems that bring together both regulated (biotic) innovation teams and unregulated (abiotic) resources such as open information, data, and content, the unexpected is sure to happen.

At its best, a principled environment will be inviting of surprise, resilient and adaptive as the powerful wolf. At its worst, humans will assert principles as rules, will use them to disrupt and distract, and in the end, will find their products starve.

Table 7.1 The Principles of the OpenXFORM Ecosystem

OpenXFORM Principles	
Principle 1: Decentralization	Embracing a decentralized organizational structure and system increases efficiency and the ability to balance the forces within the network of the innovation ecosystem, whether they involve the collaboration of people with each other, people with their systems, or even systems as they relate to other systems through machine interfaces. This decreases energy loss as interests shift throughout the life of the project.
Principle 2: Diversity	Diversity of people, ideas, and information creates flexibility and resiliency. If an environment is over-managed or over-measured, the ability to adapt positively to stress will be impacted. Disturbance of a balanced ecosystem must be carefully considered and involve all participants.
Principle 3: Interdependence	While each functional group within an ecosystem may maintain unique relations among themselves and with other members and resources, every group must be protected within the ecosystem to protect the system from negative distortions and perverse incentives, especially for members or groups with low net production efficiency.
Principle: Shared Responsibility	Even members in a decentralized organizational system operate within boundaries that include both temporal and special features. These boundaries should be appropriate to the objectives and eschew favorable short-term, intermediate gains that distract from the long-term balance and protection of the innovation ecosystem.

---

[23] Convention on Biological Diversity (1995). "Ecosystem Approach: Principles." Retrieved September 11, 2016, from https://www.cbd.int/ecosystem/principles.shtml.

Chapter Eight

OpenXFORM:Ideate

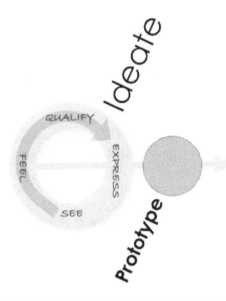

Ideation is the first step in a successful innovation process that appreciates the context of the users, the ability of the designers to communicate well, the capabilities of the company, and the goals of the project.

8.1 Chapter Theme

The OpenXFORM model proposes complementary principles that help shape innovation processes to drive new ideas that can be transformed to scale. This chapter focuses on the theory, motivations, and practices of ideation. Through examples and case studies, we explore the notion of collaborating openly to develop new innovations, in the context of open data, information, content, and collaboration. Often, as organizations attempt to reorganize their innovation processes to be more entrepreneurial, they seek structural and sometimes physical solutions to motivate and empower. However, what is really most useful in encouraging innovative imagination is a simple and uncomplicated approach, even when the social dynamics can be challenging.

8.2 Structured Wonderment

This is an idea book, and while it could be used prescriptively, it doesn't have to be. If this book is opened, leafed through, and perused and stimulates a new sense about how to take concrete steps to improve the innovation processes of your team, your company, or your class project, breaking down the emotional, psychological, and arbitrary structural barriers that dilute the innovation process and hamper creative progress, then it will have served a worthwhile purpose.

The model described as OpenXFORM is less an attempt to conjure up some newfangled process that requires a certification to manage, than an effort to disentangle and reconstruct the conflated and confusing policies and approaches to organized ideation and development. There are no OpenXFORM:Ideation matrices, tests, or flashcards, but instead materials that help in foraging for useful patterns for thinking about open forms of collaboration/information and a process of naming what we already intuitively or tacitly know about solving problems and creating new solutions. However, we must also address the elephant in the boardroom: while out-of-bounds collaboration may bring directly measurable advantage to a firm, it also threatens the concept of scarce intellectual property driving value upon which so many corporations tenuously cling.

An artificial system to begin with, the open movement—beginning with open-source software—is structuring and promoting the creation of intellectual assets and knowledge that is neither proprietary nor a meal ticket for a patent litigator. Like open data and open scholarship, in the realm of future tech, corporations and companies must abandon rigidity, especially when it comes to holding back important proprietary artifacts and encumbering employees, and instead refocus their processes of innovation away from solving a diminishing set of private problems to the sea of opportunities that a more public collaboration brings. There is no guarantee that this won't be difficult, but it does guarantee that organizations won't be left behind because they didn't understand that creating impediments to progress will sooner or later inhibit their own growth. Or worse, that the suppression of advanced ideas such as cancer treatments or clean energy collectively punishes society through the loss of a common benefit. At least one of today's great thinkers gets that: on the day that Elon Musk opened up Tesla's patents, he wrote, "Our true competition is not the small trickle of non-Tesla electric cars being produced, but rather the enormous flood of gasoline cars pouring out of the world's factories every day."[1] The benefits of ideation, exploration, and transformation grow greater when the barriers to enrichment by the commons are removed and the process of closed innovation must be either adapted or completely abandoned.

It is likely that the patterns of work that we already know will continue to exist in their own forms with or without any effort to name them here in the context of OpenXFORM or elsewhere. However, the importance of naming these systems of work is not to cynically measure them to improve output (although that is a running theme in this book) to squeeze out every drop of efficiency, but to rough out the work so that the jagged edges can be shaped into something more useful, perhaps even something that is more beautiful and enjoyable.

8.3 Naming Our Work

Think for a moment about how we name things that have special meaning to us, especially when it comes to our children (furry or otherwise). Choosing a name can be a very special act for parents, because it's about establishing a clear connection and creating a vision for that child's life. For most new parents, it is part of inculcating or own dreams, solidifying a meaningful lineage or a remembrance of someone and proffering it to your child—a material link to a future that will outlast you. Most of us also name our companion animals and our prized possessions, such as homes and cars. The act of naming expresses the existence of, or a desire for, a personal relationship.

In the relatively short formalized life of Agile, many have worked to make the process their own: consider Extreme Programming (XP), Scrum, Feature Driven Development (FDD), Lean Software Development, Agile Unified Process (AUP), Kanban, and variants of the Toyota Production System (TPS)—and this is a markedly truncated list. Depending on one's perspective,

---

[1] Musk, Elon (2014). "All Our Patent Are Belong to You." Tesla. Retrieved November 6, 2016, from https://www.tesla.com/blog/all-our-patent-are-belong-you.

the balkanization of Agile has been a boon for those who have capitalized on their preferred approaches by consulting or building wildly expensive tools to manage it, usually on an open-source platform. Design thinking is similarly rendered, as its users adapt the process to its core values and mission; and this is encouraged by the progenitors of design thinking as an expression of the process of learning that is inherent in the process itself. We call this "divergent thinking," "user-centered design," "Lean startup-up thinking," "Industrial empathy," and the well-worn "brainstorming." So-called "open collaborators" name themselves "peer producers," "human attractors," "crowdsourcers," "co-creators," and "open innovators."

But none of these capture the full stack of efforts required to identify, render, and transform an idea to a product; some are methodologies, some are tools, others are techniques. And while it is not useful to replace one fetish with another, it is important to recognize that brainstorming, being a good communicator, and feeling good at the end of the day is not what innovation is about—it's about implementing a process that will meet an organization's strategic goals, inspire employees, and provide a scalable and unified approach to ordering the chaos that emerges when trying to meet customer needs and deliver on a strategic vision.

David Kelley, the founder of IDEO and the Stanford d.school, describes his inspiration for naming that thing designers do when they intentionally create something—he named it *design thinking*. He lets us all in on the secret: "I'm not a words person," Kelley says, "but in my life, [design thinking is] the most powerful moment that words or labeling ever made. Because then it all made sense. Now I'm an expert at methodology rather than a guy who designs a new chair or car."[2] As Kelley reminds us, too often ideation in the role of corporate innovation is seen as mystical whitewashing and hand-waving, when it is really the product of investment—in time, people, effort, and structure. And while public companies pay lip service to this phantasm, pointing to their new product pipeline, their research and development efforts, and their speed to market, serious long-term investors are looking beyond the quarterly dog and pony show and searching for long-term value. It can be rough out there—for every time a corporate CEO is asked why their company isn't more like Apple, Apple is slammed for not being innovative enough.

Apple has always been an excellent case study for corporate inventiveness, going from near-bankruptcy to progenitor of massive, disruptive innovation time and time again. Still, investment advisors are already forecasting a decline

---

[2] Tischler, Linda (2009). "Ideo's David Kelley on Design Thinking." Retrieved October 20, 2016, from https://www.fastcodesign.com/1139331/ideos-david-kelley-design-thinking.

for the creative greatness of the company by pointing to its anemic R&D budget, which bottomed out in 2012 (Steve Jobs died in 2011) even though it has ramped quickly since then. Michael Boyd warns investors about denying the problems of reclaiming Apple's storied innovative flair, writing in the financial journal *Seeking Alpha,* "Just as throwing money at problems in your personal life rarely works, it also rarely works in the business world as well . . . To get products to market quickly, weak projects need to be culled early, so focus can be directed where it could be most beneficial."[3] Adding that a rapid change in R&D spending policies can be even more confusing to company strategy and motivation, Boyd draws a straight and existential line between innovation and corporate wasting disease without even touching on an even more troubling problem—money doesn't always buy the best talent. The free talent that lined up to help Linus Torvalds develop Linux proved that.

If we hope for our organizations to embrace a more open innovative process, in which we can learn to embrace non-traditional partnerships, relationships, techniques, and perspectives, then it is of crucial importance that we be able to give conscious meaning (naming) to the linkages among these. For many of us, those linkages are already there and work, but they are very rarely a concrete part of the organizational framework for many reasons, including trade secrets, private ownership, perceived competitive advantage, and the demand for loyalty. Those individuals, teams, and organizations who are willing to explore new and somewhat uncomfortable ways of collaborating are asked to bring their most personal selves forward in a way that allows the best ideas to emerge from their own design and development processes. The names we choose describe not only the structures and relationships within our processes, but also our vision for where they might take us. And the notion of ideation is among the murkiest of all.

OpenXFORM is a way to point at the methods for innovation that already happen in so many ways, typically without any strategic directive except to "do something innovative," and too often with avoidance for how using open information, data, and content is the key accelerant to achieving the goals of many future tech endeavors. Among the most successful corporate innovators—Apple, SpaceX, Tesla Motors, Salesforce, Regeneron, Incyte, Under Armour, Unilever, Amazon, and Netflix—there are many commonalities, but only on one shared strand of DNA: the awareness that a single great idea is luck, but that a deliberate focus on structured innovation programs with focused investment in new idea generation and design *is the mission.* Nothing else works. Every

---

[3] Boyd, Michael (2016). "Apple: Throwing Money at The Innovation Problem Won't Fix It." *Seeking Alpha*[α]. Retrieved November 6, 2016, from http://seekingalpha.com/article/3976797-apple-throwing-money-innovation-problem-fix.

innovative company that invests in perfecting the art of collaboration may have begun with a specific goal in mind but endures because they link the memory of that process to their ongoing efforts.

8.4 Why the Time for Open Ideation Is Here

No one wants to make a recommendation for radical change that may be dangerous to the health of a firm. After all, being a "fast follower" is a very reasonable corporate philosophy for letting the upstarts stress the system while you keep doing what you do best—filing patents, building competitive walls, protecting investors. And "open" breaks everything we know about free market economics, which depends on coherence for faster and better growth. We've already pointed out that the digital economy is a post-scarcity world, but there is other evidence that market equilibria are being disturbed.

For example, let's evaluate how this is playing out for advanced biotech players (also known as *the pharmaceuticals*) using an age-old strategy of funding new research through so-called "hurricane pricing" on drugs that are nearing the end of their patented life. In 2015, Turing Pharmaceuticals played this game by purchasing an aging (nearly 30-year-old) toxoplasmosis treatment and subsequently raising the price of the drug daraprim from $13.50 USD to $750 USD per pill (an approximate 5,000% increase). The cost to treat a patient under the new pricing scheme hovered around half a million dollars for treatment of common food-borne diseases most dangerous to those with weakened immune systems, such as those with HIV AIDS. The public response was fierce and unforgiving. The company, alleged to be engaged in flagrant price-gouging, was defended by a spokesperson for the company, who said, "The company needed to raise prices in order to fund its research work on toxoplasmosis, along with new education programs for the disease." This rationale is certainly nothing new and nothing short of bizarre if one considers the implied assumption that research for *new* lifesaving drugs means squeezing out customers who can no longer afford their *current* regime of lifesaving drugs.

After Martin Shkreli (the detested biopharmaceutical entrepreneur who'd hiked the prices to "fund research") had insulted nearly every journalist and observer he could, the fact that he was doing exactly what had been done time and time again in the industry was lost in the swirl. But in this case, the smirking "pharma bro" demonstrated that there is a ceiling on the price that society is willing to pay for "advancement." Not one serious observer of the biopharmaceutical market seemed shocked that a medical company was blinded by profit, because it is a competitive business replete with the trappings of intellectual property, a mission to drive down government regulation, and the imperative to charge customers whatever the market will bear. This is how the free market operates, and it is precisely why other pharmaceutical executives were measured in their response—not for what Shkreli did but for his lack of decorum and his unbalanced approach.[4]

8.4.1 New Approaches to Innovation

The problem that Martin Shkreli characterized so well is one of the reasons that advanced medical research is increasingly orientating to translational research. Translational research is an interdisciplinary approach to medical science that focuses on all sorts of knowledge—from clinical observations, to charts, to data and laboratory research—to accelerate approaches to enhancing human health. And it is an excellent model for how new forms of collaboration and information sharing can begin to change something as complex as the medical industry. Translational researchers rule out very little in their process of discovery, including community best practices and cost-effectiveness of certain strategies.[5] This sort of research is criticized for its supposed scientific irreproducibility, but it is not without pragmatic success.

The Cancer Institute in New South Wales, Australia, funds the Translational Research Centres and Units. They use a model for their research program that focuses on improving the translation of health research to service delivery as described through a series of transitions (or translations). They classify the stages of their research as described in Figure 8.1, which is an interpretation of the translational pipeline model:

T1: Translation to Humans. This is the interface between basic research and new knowledge into a clinical setting to help observe, trial, and document in a controlled manner.

T2: Translation to Patients. This is the stage in which new clinically relevant science and knowledge makes it into health services' provision to drive practice and decision making. These practices help translate practice guidelines and policy. Furthermore, the findings in T2 can begin to inform new research.

---

[4] Sanneh, Kelefa (2016). "Everyone Hates Martin Shkreli. Everyone Is Missing the Point." *The New Yorker*. Retrieved November 6, 2016, from http://www.newyorker.com/culture/cultural-comment/everyone-hates-martin-shkreli-everyone-is-missing-the-point.

[5] Woolf, Stephen H. (2008). "The Meaning of Translational Research and Why It Matters." *Journal of the American Medical Association*, vol. 299, issue 2, pp. 211–213. http://doi.org/10.1001/jama.2007.26.

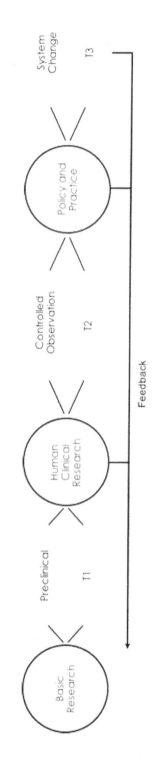

Figure 8.1 Translational model expedites bringing new research to a clinical setting.

T3: Translation to Practice. At this stage, with the benefit of practice-based research and evidence from patient use, the new practice is disseminated and implemented throughout the healthcare system.[6]

A primary example for the use of translational research is found in the story of the development of bortezomib, a cancer drug designed to treat multiple myeloma, which was "discovered" through the course of a program of systematic translational research that brought the drug from discovery to the market in an expedited timeframe. Harvard academicians discovered the drug in 1992, it was in clinical trials by 1997, and by 2003 it was approved by the US Food and Drug Administration (FDA). This was record time for knowledge transfer from lab to market, and it was due primarily to a new form of relationship not just between academia and industry, but among public institutions, private investors, and pubic advocates.

The relationship was unique because it was bi-directional—a feedback loop from industry to the academy helped displace blocking issues of incentive that are brought to bear by the profit drivers of the pharmaceuticals. Ibis Sánchez-Serrano provides an extensive description of the case study, in which he describes the richness of the collaboration as the primary marker of success. He writes, "Academia [consolidates] the scientific ideas and the work of people from different backgrounds, cultures, ethnicities and countries . . . that allows for rapid interchange of information among people from all over the world. This constant flow of people and ideas enriches scientific research and promotes progress. In other words, economic and social progress is achieved via a trade of assets and knowledge."[7]

It is a core case study for researchers who are seeking ways to break down the barriers between the academy, the pharmaceutical industry, and the public without trading on innovative outcomes. This is not in any way to malign pure research, as anyone with even a remote sense of curiosity understands that the pursuit of knowledge outside of the confines of application has a very important role in scientific development. Surely, many creative people oil their mental engines (or procrastinate on their mundane tasks) by reading about how we might be living in a matrix universe or hologram. But, translational research shortens the distance one has to travel between the deep blue sky and the

---

[6] Cancer Institute NSW (2012). "Translational Research—Defining the Ts." Retrieved November 6, 2016, from http://www.tcrn.unsw.edu.au/translational-research-definitions.

[7] Sánchez-Serrano, I. (2006). "Success in Translational Research: Lessons from the Development of Bortezomib." *Nature Reviews Drug Discovery*, vol. 5, issue 2, pp. 107–114. Accessed November 6, 2016, from http://doi.org/10.1038/nrd1959.

customer in advancing cutting-edge technological pursuits. Apple's Steve Jobs brought the problem to earth this way, saying, "Creativity is just connecting things. When you ask creative people how they did something, they feel a little guilty because they didn't really do it, they just saw something. It seemed obvious to them after a while. That's because they were able to connect experiences they've had and synthesize new things."[8] To make compelling connections, we require collaboration between communities of people and freely available material assets of information, content, and ideas. And even more importantly, it means finding ways to make those connections fruitful through dialogue, friendly rivalry among solution-makers, and synthesis.

8.5 Climbing the Ideation Peak

If we do believe that the strength of our collaboration and access to openly available assets is the key to accelerating our most innovative ideas to market, then organizations can no longer explicitly choose to disregard their innovation anemia. The question then becomes, how can the organization become innovation literate in an open world with difficult-to-discern borders? As in any type of ecosystem, there are animals that travel between communities, some species that are restricted to one side of the border or the other, and even some that only live between the edges. Human activity can also create edges to certain ecosystems through our development and agricultural efforts, and as in nature, the construction and behaviors of our organizations also create edge effects.

As described in Figure 8.2, with OpenXFORM:Ideate, our corporate edges can merge with our open communities in which the relationships may be defined through open data, information, content, and collaboration. It is these relationships that enrich and fortify us during our climb to the peaks of inspiration. But it is in the pursuit for a meaningful solution when the creative forces of our organizations are brought to bear. Meaning begins to emerge as we bring forth our organizational experiences, talents, skills, and endowments; the swathes of undistinguished bits of information and data that float around us as "problems" are brought down to earth as the compositions of our own innovative solutions. In some processes, this is the stage in which we "ideate," "brainstorm," or, simply, "design." Yet, falling from the cliffs of inspiration to meaning can be deadly.

---

[8] Jobs, Steve (n.d.). BrainyQuote.com. Retrieved October 22, 2016, https://www.brainyquote.com/quotes/quotes/s/stevejobs416925.html.

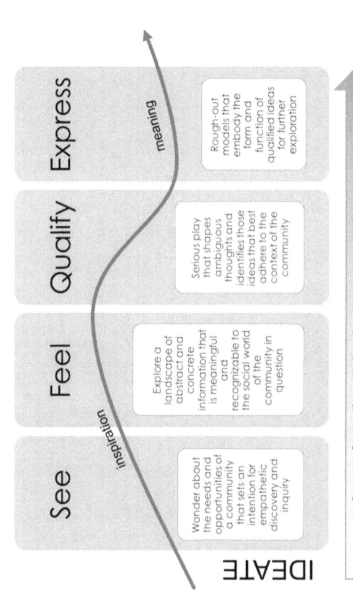

Figure 8.2 Climbing the ideation peak.

Table 8.1 The Motivations of Ideate as Applied to the Problem of Sanitation

IDEATE		
See	The entry point to the ideation process, refers to the notion of "seeing" a solution to a problem in the mind's eye, as an inspiration, a spark of a new idea, or the viewing of a problem with new eyes.	Chapin's team didn't show up in Cambodia to solve the sanitation problem. Instead, they had a specific goal of creating an affordable latrine that not only would improve sanitation outcomes, but would be adopted by the villagers and adapt to the realities of the local economy and capabilities.
Feel	This is a technique that brings imagination to the act of discovery and refers to the conscious manipulation of the mental lens. Methods can be applied to aid in thinking about the contours of the idea and imagining it at work within a context, without details or opposition, from the user's perspective.	Because the team was focused on a specific goal, they had a point of view toward the problem and, therefore, a way to begin communicating with the villagers in order to learn more about their experiences with clean latrines. By speaking with the villagers, they learned how they built up their homes in an additive way to improve as they could, and the team imagined that if they could design a latrine that could be improved over time, the villagers would resonate with the idea.
Qualify	This is the time to start a conversation about the idea and elicit enough feedback to begin to arrive at how it may be concretely expressed to others. The qualification stage allows the formulation of a research question or hypothesis based on working assumptions that are oriented toward establishing the value of an idea to its users.	First the team designed a large flowchart with pictures that show how a barebones latrine could be acquired and then added to over time. Chapin noted that he was faced with a room full of "blank stares" to this idea. This was because the linear nature of the chart didn't actually map well to the idea of how they build their homes. Next, they took the same images and instead layered them one on top of the other using transparencies. With this approach, the team was able to gather creative feedback from the villagers on the idea.
Express	This is the moment of arrival at the proverbial "drawing board." At this time, it should be possible to express a lightweight representation of the idea. It doesn't have to be a computer design, or even a physical object. It could be a dramatic endeavor or a poster. The most important aspect to the prototype is that it is clear enough to garner specific feedback. If the idea cannot be expressed, then the idea is not testable and has no means to progress.	At this point the team realized that their prototype would hardly be unique; it was the simplest of toilet systems that could be built around, from upgraded tile floors to the latrine housing and decorations. What needed to be tested was how this design could be locally sourced and marketed. Similarly, with their handwashing stations, the design that was most successful had very little to do with the features of the system, but to where it would be placed in the home. Virtually all of the villagers expressed that with access to only a single handwashing station, they would place it in the kitchen where it would have the greatest chance of decreasing the spread of disease among the family members by giving them an opportunity to clean their hands.

8.5.1 The Steps of the Journey

Interestingly, the notion of collaborating openly to develop new innovations is often defined as an expression of resistance to corporate pressures to hold information tightly. For example, as organizations attempt to reorganize their innovation processes to be more entrepreneurial, they will often work to provide their employees with a motivating work environment and empower them to share opinions and solutions openly and without judgment. This perspective begs for a strict methodology, but what is really useful is often a simple and uncomplicated approach, even when the social dynamics can be challenging.

In early chapters of this book, the motivations for each step in the model were explored with a glimpse of high-level techniques. Table 8.1 reminds us of the motivations of the pieces that make up OpenXFORM:Ideate, which we'll continue to explore in the next few chapters. For now, we'll focus on a well-known case study from Jeff Chapin, IDEO executive, that he shared in a popular TED talk in 2011 about latrine and handwashing projects in Cambodia.[9]

Chapin's team wanted to help solve sanitation problems in Southeast Asia, specifically in Cambodia and Vietnam. Sanitation is a real-world problem, in which access to clean toilets and hand-washing stations is problematic, and nearly all toileting is traditionally done in open areas. This lack of basic resources results in the spread of infectious diseases such as cholera, typhoid, hepatitis, polio, and cryptosporidiosis. It's not that rural villagers don't have the knowledge or can't acquire the materials to build a latrine, the issue is the cost-effectiveness and degree of difficulty required for those who make just a few hundred dollars a month and are unable to transport supplies. How then could a team of product designers possibly hope to create sanitation solutions that could be adopted by the villagers in a way that was affordable and could be embedded in the indigenous economy through local sourcing, manufacturing, and distribution?

Given this example, many will pick up this book and try to shake out some real techniques. After all, Chapin was a trained professional from IDEO, and perhaps we can shortcut this process by downloading and implementing his execution model. Maybe, but what Chapin really wants us to learn in his TEDTalk is that the design team was most successful when they remained closely attentive to finding successful ways of communicating their ideas with the villagers (don't give a flowchart to someone who has never been trained in linear modeling), built their solution upon an analogous practice (noticing how they added to their homes), and then followed the wisdom of the community when it came to developing their idea (we want to do this ourselves).

---

[9] *Jeff Chapin: Sanitation in Cambodia TedXChange* from UH Center for SE Asian Studies. Retrieved on November 25, 2016, from https://vimeo.com/67542403.

Chapin and his team demonstrate that coming up with innovative ideas that might be adopted by the intended users is best served by drawing directly on their experiences and creating designs that make sense in the context of their lives. It turned out that the real innovation in the case of the sanitation problem was not providing a really great latrine, it was leveraging the basic plumbing of every toilet in the world and embedding it in a way that it could be adopted. Remember that the innovation process is not prescriptive, it's more descriptive and perhaps a bit diagnostic. It is premised upon the idea that a *successful innovation process requires an appreciation for the context of the users, the ability of the designers to communicate well, the capabilities of the company, and the goals of the project.*

Tim Malbon, co-founder of Made by Many, says it this way: "In reality, when you return from a trip to Brainstorm Island you probably won't have done any real innovation—at least, not the sort that's going to transform the fortunes of your business. This is because [the Design Thinking framework] often underestimates the strategic context of how specific industries and markets really work. Truth is, it's easy to come up with beautiful, clever ideas without the burden of understanding constraints—but this is where the genuinely transformational stuff is probably hiding."[10]

8.5.2 Some Thoughts about Inspiration

For some, inspiration might be some random explosion of stars, but when we're on technology-enabled problem solving, we are usually looking to find a novel way to express the requirement to adapt. For example, Tesla is helping us adapt to anthropogenic climate change, while Elysium is developing biologicals to treat aging, Microsoft's HoloLens seeks to break down barriers of location between people, Mint developed a breathalyzer for the smartphone, and many transportation innovations are breaking into the realm of possibility, such as the hyperloop and the myriad bicycle schemes that include self-correcting designs and incline management. Not all emerging technologies are gadgets; guided bullets, drone warfare, self-driving trucks, and automation robots are primed to change the specter of work, whether we are soldiers or nurses. And with access to 3D printing, there has never been such a good time to be inspired.

But as Malbon implied, moving from the dopamine high of a great brainstorming session to the duress of extracting an opportunity to take a new idea to

---

[10] Malbon, Tim (2016). "The Problem with Design Thinking." Made by Many. Retrieved November 6, 2016, from https://medium.com/the-many/the-problem-with-design-thinking-988b88f1d696#.wxb23nnxk.

market requires a rigorous ability to look for opportunities that fit not just within a vision, but within disruption and shift. Sustaining innovation is not the goal in future tech; scientists, academics, and research-and-development–oriented companies are working to actively recognize disturbance, the tectonic shifts that are detectable enough that they can be described and defined. Consider ultrasonic-powered haptic technology as an example. Haptic tech allows us to feel virtual reality instead of just see it—and it didn't just emerge like an anomalous worm in the dirt. It arose because there are problems that can be solved by the enabling of digital gestures, be it in medicine, our homes, or our cars. And it is pursued because of the technology advancements that came before it that created its own possibilities. Today, it is an example of an opportunity that has been recognized but is not yet well articulated in the science of a design or even in the imagination of market participants.

Haptic technology is the sort of technology that enables other advanced products and is precisely the kind of advancement that could launch companies that develop unimagined products, algorithms, or other optimizations once its operations are well understood. However, to be part of a solution for a particular market, it must first solve a real-world problem, not just a fascination. And such is the goal of a focused and structured ideation process. An organization could choose design thinking, or some other systematic way to capture, cultivate, and prototype a possible solution, but there must be a structured process to move through a collection of ideas and solutions that can be not only articulated, but conceptualized and tested—and repeated. Without a process for ideation, it is very difficult to discover the value sought by the organization, even with the most advanced research and development organizations; there is too much competition, it moves too quickly, and for those companies that are locked out of the communities of open collaboration, it leaves an immense amount of value on the table.

No matter the techniques deployed by the team or organization—it is key to remain human-centric. The idea of "feeling" the way through a problem is quite literally a way to maintain an awareness and discernment about the potential value of a solution. Some designers describe their need to maintain an emotional connection or even attempt to adopt the point of view of their focused user. Lest an engineer, business stakeholder, or policy wonk feel lost in the process, the notion of "feeling" is primarily about brainstorming techniques that can help shape the team's primary reflections during the process so that they stay anchored in consideration of the user needs. Remember that the goal is to provide a treatment for the benefit of some person or process—a problem that is causing disruption, strife, or a poor experience.

Thus, as we build inspiration and develop a greater pool of candidate ideas, we stay grounded in the knowledge of a theory that we can ultimately test and confirm. Although the admonishment of "no bad ideas" at first seems to counter that view, it is still important to appreciate the notion that a greenfield will still die with too much water. But what does it mean to "stay with" the user? How is it possible to simultaneously empathize with those we are inspired to help, but not wander off into irrelevance? Most in future tech disciplines are scientists and engineers, trained to solve problems with the scientific method. This doesn't mean that people aren't part of the theory, but the method is overly rigid for this part of the innovation process.

8.6 Problem Solvers Need Goals

The following example was originally described by the author in her 2015 work *Building Smart Cities: Analytics, ICT, and Design Thinking*,[11] providing a useful variation on the typical question-hypothesis-experiment approach that we so often rely on in developing a credible solution; it is the sort of skill we learn from the very beginnings of our learning life. But it isn't always useful to eschew practical empiricism for the order of doing things properly. Here are two ways to look at the problem of the chronic issue of the lost car keys, as a *scientist* or as a *designer*:

The Scientific Approach. When a problem involves observable phenomena—when something can be tested by observable, empirical, or measurable means—the scientific method is reliable and indisputably useful in solving the conundrum. That's because we are most comfortable believing that the truth can ultimately be verified.

Question: Where are my car keys? I swear, I am always losing my car keys!

Hypothesis: Well, my car is in the driveway. My house keys are on the same keychain as my car keys, and I obviously unlocked the front door because I'm standing in my kitchen. I put away all the groceries, took out the trash, and hung up my jacket at some point after I returned home. My first hypothesis is that they are in my jacket pocket; my second hypothesis is that I put them in the freezer with the ice cream; my third is that I accidentally threw them away when I took out the garbage.

---

[11] Stimmel, Carol (2015). *Building Smart Cities: Analytics, ICT, and Design Thinking.* Auerbach Publications (CRC Press). https://www.crcpress.com/Building-Smart-Cities-Analytics-ICT-and-Design-Thinking/Stimmel/p/book/9781498702768. ISBN 9781498702768.

Prediction: If I search in my jacket, in the refrigerator, and in the trash, I'll find my car keys.

Experiment: I searched in my jacket pockets and the keys weren't there; I looked in the freezer and there were no car keys; finally, I dug through the garbage and they weren't there either. But there they were on the floor next to the trashcan.

Analysis: I lost my keys somewhere in my house, yet the experiment showed that my keys were not in any of the places hypothesized. Rather, they had dropped out of my jacket while I was throwing away the trash and were neither in my jacket nor in the trash. None of my hypotheses were correct, but by being flexible enough to keep looking when my experiment failed, I was able to move forward toward the solution even with the theories I had until the real facts of the situation emerged.

But did I really fail?

Technically, I'd have to go back to the drawing board, and with a lot of time and patience (or luck), it is feasible that with a very good reworking of the hypothesis, I could get very close to defining a useful key-finding algorithm.

But what happens if we tweak our thinking and instead try to solve for a goal (i.e., I want to solve the problem of losing my keys) or solve an even more ambiguous problem? I will likely need to define and redefine my initial understanding of the issues, and it is unlikely that I will be able to test my hypothesis adequately. Then what? What would a design team do to solve this problem? And what if that design team was hired solely to help me solve my problem?

The Designer Approach. In eschewing the scientific method, a structured process of design can be quite helpful. The characteristics of many stylized design-thinking processes are held in common and they include:

- An empathetic viewpoint
- A creative ideation process
- A rational approach that moves us toward execution

So, we start looking at the lost keys problem with a design-thinking approach, focusing not on finding the keys, but on *reducing the impact and frequency of losing them in the first place.*

Empathize: In this early phase of the design process, a challenge is identified for some user or particular group of users. In our very simple example, I repeatedly lose my car keys, it makes me anxious, I run late, and I get upset when they're lost.

Define (or Interpret): In this phase, we start to develop a meaningful understanding of the problem, one that gives shape to the challenge. It's nearly always the case for me, that when I'm lost in thought, I'm not thinking about putting things back where they can easily be found; I'm rushing and things get misplaced or lost. Already in a high state of distraction, I'm not always even sure where to begin looking when I invariably misplace my keys.

Idea: Here we begin to transition from problem definitions to solutions. Tools like brainstorming, sketching, and mind-mapping can bring shape to ideas. What if I could feel confident that I could always find my keys, even if I dropped them in the driveway? Maybe I could put some sort of retractable string on my keys that would tether them to my body, or somehow activate a clicker on my key ring (the way I call a misplaced phone), or a strobe light, maybe a sensor. We finally settled on exploring a wireless device that interfaces with my iPhone, which is usually in my pocket (and for which I already have a process to locate if I misplace it). I wasn't sure how another gadget would solve my already bungling approach to maintaining my gadget inventory, but I stuck it out.

Prototype: This is the experimental gadget stage, in which a mock-up is produced that enabled us to gain feedback from our target user (me). My design team cut out a small square and taped it to my key ring. Then, they mocked up a smartphone application that mimicked the behavior of a wireless sensor attached to my keys. The location of my keys is always being updated on the phone, and the sensor plays the game of cold, warm, hot as I get close to my keys. In addition, I can find the keys by asking the app to play an audible tone on the sensor. I was able to imagine how useful this would be and I was enthusiastic about the idea.

Test: Like most projects, our key-finder initiative was a highly iterative and evolving process. The team made a sensor based on my initial feedback and hung it from my keychain. When I lost my keys, I used the app to play a tone, but at first it wasn't loud enough, so they fixed that. Then I asked them to add a map to the app in case I dropped my keys while on a hike. That way, I'd be able to go back and find them. Turns out, I liked the solution so much, I put a sensor in my backpack and my wallet, and even hung one from my dog's collar.

Though the scientific method was very useful in solving the problem of finding my lost keys once, it did nothing for me in terms of solving the conditions that created the problem to begin with, which is absent-mindedly misplacing my keys when I'm busy. Design thinking is not focused on excessive analysis or even on working it all out; instead, design thinking is about human-centered problem solving. The problem began with my being unfocused, rushed, distracted, and stressed out—the perfect recipe for misplacing important items. With the scientific method, we were given a methodology to find the answer to a discrete problem—find my car keys by developing a hypothesis about where they might be—and then test it. With the design-thinking approach, the focus was instead on solution-solving, in which we attempted to develop a way to make it easier to solve the issue the next time I was inevitably faced with searching through the freezer for my keys. In fact, my stress level dropped because I always knew I could find my keys (that is until I dropped the sensor in the water, but that's another design challenge).

So, a quick recap is in order:

We stuck to our goal of *reducing the impact and frequency of losing my car keys,* and an unexpected and useful solution emerged. The designers identified the human experience of distraction and stress and found a way to lower the anxiety related to the *prospect* of misplacing an important item. In ideating, the propensity for technology was accounted for as a guide to potential solutions. Then the designers created a paper prototype to form a basis for discussion about their ideas and how those ideas might work. The team took feedback and went back to ideation and prototyping. Then they delivered a sensor that could serve as a key fob that helped reduce my overall anxiety about losing things and provided a mechanism to easily locate important (and thus tagged) items with a map and a signal.[12]

8.6.1 A Familiar Approach

With that story in mind, now is the right time to revisit the translational medicine practitioners' ideas from the previous figure and recast their ideas with what we've discovered about solving the lost key problem in Figure 8.3. Far away from the boundaries of design thinking, this approach allows us to rewrite the translational model this way:

T1: Translation to Problem Solving. This is the interface between open sources of data, information, content, research, and new knowledge into a structured setting to help brainstorm, explore, suggest, and document new ideas.

T2: Translation to Solution Construction. This is the stage in which relevant knowledge and data helps us qualify our best ideas for fit to the user and our organizational capabilities. Techniques such as "serious play" can help a

---

[12] Modified from and used with permission of Carol L. Stimmel.

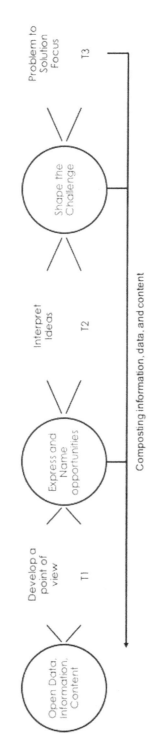

Figure 8.3 Viewing ideation as a translational model from problem to solution focus.

cross-section of participants, such as operational experts, software developers, product managers, and marketing staff, engage in drawing out and explaining ideas in a manner that they could be constructed in a low fidelity prototype. This may be the most sensitive and complex part of the OpenXFORM:Ideate process, and why it was characterized earlier as a dangerous cliff one could fall off between gathering inspiration and extracting meaning. This is a highly material and literal step for many participants and can become personally charged and competitive. Excellent team relationships and mutual respect among members are crucial to the process.

T3: Translation to Designing a Solution. At this stage, with the benefit of the skills and expertise of the team, we can construct a testable prototype of our idea that we hope will help us move forward in finding an innovative solution to our users' problem.

8.6.2 Ready! Set! Prototype!

Now it's time to build something and see how it works, how our target market feels about it, and discover whether it helps us achieve our goals. However, functional prototypes can be quite challenging. The car design industry hasn't forgotten this important reality. Clay modeling for car prototypes began early in the life of the car industry when, in the 1930s, the head of the General Motors' styling studio, Harley Earl (the father of the tail fin), began using industrial plasticine to allow designers to visualize their products in clay. In a 2003 interview, Alan D. Biggs, the North American design modeling manager for the Ford Motor Company, encapsulated the usefulness of prototypes quite succinctly, stating, "No one is willing to sign off on a production car looking at a picture."[13] (And that includes even your prettiest digital image on a large screen.) Models and prototypes can prove or disprove new concepts and reveal where the edges might still be rough. When an executive can walk around a clay model and see its potential to meet the needs of the target market, only then will she risk investment.

Yet prototyping can be tricky and is too often deprived of its intended value when it comes to software designs that look polished and marketable. They can be expensive and time-consuming to construct, and they can snuff out a great idea by not representing it in an understandable way. This is especially true

---

[13] McCosh, Dan (2003). "Driving: Most Cars Are Born as Models of Clay." *New York Times*. Retrieved November 23, 2014, from http://www.nytimes.com/2003/03/07/travel/driving-most-cars-are-born-as-models-of-clay.html.

when a prototype is unfamiliar, like the one Henry Ford probably presented to his buddies when he first sketched up his horseless carriage. Prototypes also may inspire new and better ideas, and the cycle of ideation and implementation may enter a phase of rinse and repeat. This can be a frustrating and lengthy process, but it deserves patience and trust in the right team.

Ultimately, what goes into production will more likely meet the initial goals of the project and even provide valuable insight into the marketing and communications strategies that emerge from the design process itself. By beginning with empathy and inspiration, the team understands the people and their unmet needs that your new product, organization, park, building, policy, or even traffic sign will fulfill. It's obvious how the up-front investment in human-centered design creates better outcomes not only from a social perspective but from an economic investment perspective as well, as many ideas are produced in the service of a greater goal.

8.7 Expectations and Perceptions

There is a vitality, a life force, that is translated to you into action, and because there is only one of you in all time, this expression is unique. And if you block it, it will never exist through any other medium, and will be lost.

—Martha Graham

In the previous chapter, we discussed the importance of setting organizational intention for innovation through adjusting our mindset, and we identified the principles described:

- Decentralization
- Diversity
- Interdependence
- Shared responsibility

Those are guiding principles, and they represent both personal and organizational expression. We often hear that any new project endeavor "must have a high-level stakeholder." That is undoubtedly important if one has to shake out money and time to get new initiatives off the ground, but when it comes to innovation, it is even more crucial to determine if your stakeholder is going to have to do more than pitch ideas. Meaning, is the organizational ground fertile for disruption? What is the temperament for organization? What does it feel like to be a creative thinker in your organization?

There are many ways that organizations "test" their employees, most especially with the Meyers-Briggs Type Indicator (MBTI) or the Predictive Index

(PI). Without remarking on the usefulness of a well-researched behavioral assessment and an understanding of what makes your team members "tick," it is a rare event indeed when an employee has a moment to assess their company's drives and motivations. Too often, that comes from a Power Point deck at the annual company meeting, or the email that finally shows up when the company went off the rails months ago, or hours after the last poorly-managed layoff. Most employees have a sense for the organizational temperament, but there is much to be learned by taking a moment to think about how well organizational behaviors align with a propensity for employees to recognize and cultivate their own power toward ideation. If we are individuals that work in teams and in companies, then it is helpful to be cognizant of how the pieces are working together.

In that spirit, the following is a casually formulated set of questions that are offered solely as a tool to think about the presented principles of OpenXFORM. These questions are intended to create an opportunity for reflection about the opportunities for innovation afforded by your work environment.

Specifically, think about how you respond to the principles and then how your company responds. This is not a skills assessment, nor will there be an opportunity to count up your score with a grade proffered. A mark on the scale indicating your personal propensity measured against your organization's will provide a visual meter of alignment. What is revealed is a sense of how your preferred modes of expression and work align with the behaviors and principles supported by your organization, especially where they show a propensity for taking measured risks toward open innovation.

Place a mark on the scale for each characteristic that describes each principle, then in the following table, do the same to describe how your organizational culture reflects these principles in their actions and policies. See what you see. Are you in a company that supports your approach to innovation? If not, are they somehow complementary in the tension that is created by your varying styles with the corporate philosophy? Do you believe that you are part of an organization that is disciplined and poised enough to capture innovation opportunity outcomes?

Personal Inventory

Decentralization			
Aspiration	I only take action if it aligns with my desired goals.		I take risks unconstrained by the need to adhere to rigid goals.
Determination	I prefer to act on problems that are clearly defined.		I enjoy complex, unclear challenges.
Diversity			
Challenges	I am most often satisfied with the obvious solution when faced with a problem.		I am willing to force a disruptive solution to solve a problem.
Criticism	I prefer formal feedback from my peers.		I enjoy impromptu feedback from my peers.
Interdependence			
Self-Assessment	I often check to ensure that I'm meeting established goals.		I rely on my instincts to keep me on track.
Success of Others	I believe that a peer's performance is a reflection of my own performance.		I never let the actions of others impact my independent thinking about my own performance.
Shared Responsibility			
Disappointment	I always take personal responsibility for failure.		I embrace failure as the cost of doing business without further introspection.
Achievement	I aim to finish projects early.		Project timelines are a yoke upon my ability to be innovative.

Organizational Inventory

Decentralization			
Aspiration	We seek to take an action only if it aligns with our desired outcomes.	●———————●	Our employees take risks unconstrained by rigid adherence to goals.
Determination	No one wastes our resources with poorly defined efforts.	●———————●	It's in the company DNA to deal with complex, unclear challenges.
Diversity			
Challenges	Our solutions are optimal, expedient, and efficient.	●———————●	New solutions to everyday problems are tolerated.
Criticism	Structured peer reviews are important to our culture.	●———————●	We expect our employees to provide continuous feedback to each other.
Interdependence			
Self-Assessment	We expect our employees to track to their established goals.	●———————●	Our employees typically rely on their instincts to stay on track.
Success of Others	Our high-performing team members push each other to their best for maximum achievement of our goals.	●———————●	Our most high-performing teams are those that accommodate members with different styles for achieving goals.
Shared Responsibility			
Disappointment	Every person is accountable for failure and we work for individual improvement.	●———————●	We embrace failure as the cost of doing business and find retrospection to be of little value.
Achievement	We proudly finish our projects right on time and often under budget.	●———————●	We believe that rigid timelines degrade our ability to flex quickly to market demands.

Chapter Nine

OpenXFORM:Explore

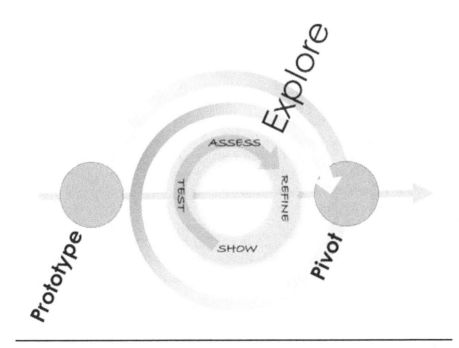

OpenXFORM:Explore is a spiraling process that carries a prototype that has emerged from the ideation phase and tests, assesses, and refines it based on the goals and limits established for the project.

9.1 Chapter Theme

Building on the concepts in the previous chapter describing OpenXFORM: Ideate, this chapter examines the process of exploration named OpenXFORM: Explore. Focusing on theory, motivations, and the practices of exploration, real-world examples demonstrate how a structured approach to testing, assessing, and refining ideation prototypes works to challenge the assumptions bound up in our design with confirmable research outputs. These challenges are given not as an opportunity to defend our ideas, but to provide an ample chance to validate, improve, and refine our prototypes to effectively adhere to the demands of user value while tending to the realities of technical feasibility and business investment.

9.2 The Exploring Mindset

Margaret Bourke-White, the pioneering American photographer, arctic traveler, and the first US woman war correspondent, developed and deployed innovative techniques to capture harshly lit industrial scenes. Raised by a father who was a naturalist and initially consumed with herpetology, her work shows a patterned beauty of things and people even in the grittiest conditions. Her most famous works show holocaust survivors staring from behind a fence; Gandhi with his spinning wheel; everyday objects such as spoons, towels, spools of thread, shoes, and speakers; and recurring natural configurations found in clouds, seashell designs, swirling water, and the windblown desert.

Yet she was repelled by repetition in her own life, writing in her autobiography, "The element of discovery is very important. I don't repeat myself well. I want and need that stimulus of walking forward from one new world to another."[1] Like many people who stretch one life to its limits, she reminded us of a common impulse that seems to run through so many of the most creative and imaginative explorers among us—an insatiable quest for understanding. She witnessed the extremes of both human joy and suffering, including images of harsh conditions in the Soviet Union, strikingly difficult industrial images, the American Great Depression, Nazi concentration camps, and famine conditions.

Her work is iconic, beautiful, and of profound historical importance, yet it is difficult to fully appreciate given the often dehumanizing environment of her

---

[1] Bourke-White, Margaret (n.d.). Retrieved on December 21, 2016, from http://www.goodreads.com/quotes/259762-the-element-of-discovery-is-very-important-i-don-t-repeat.

subjects. Despite this, she maintained a personal perspective that allowed her to remain above despair: "The very secret of life for me, I believed, was to maintain in the midst of rushing events an inner tranquility . . . I needed an inner serenity as a kind of balance."[2] She had trained her mind to be flexible and tolerant in the way that is required if one is to discover things that were never thought or seen before and capture a precise, yet universally symbolic moment. Her success as an explorer was set first by the state of her mind, then by external events.

Bourke-White demonstrated the mindset that we call on for our explorations—*trusting our skill and knowledge developed in the exercise and repetition of our practice*—to move with confidence to tell and test the story of our embryonic innovative product. Like the ever-forward-looking photographer with her serene mind, we must find the willingness to allow our subjects to guide the narrative and allow their voices to be fully rendered in our creations. Indeed, Bourke-White's need for balance in the face of extreme external pressure is an essential skill for designers and inventors in navigating feedback; one must be detached from the very subject of their affection. As a photographer imbued with deep skill for her art, Bourke-White instructed, "Saturate yourself with your subject, and your camera will all but take you by the hand."[3]

9.2.1 Going 'Round in Circles

A spiral wends its way in a continuous and ever expanding or tightening curve; in either direction, it can be both dramatic and quietly persistent. Nature seems to be fascinated with the spiral, or gyre, and once observed, it seems to be omnipresent—in poetry, mathematics, natural systems, man-made designs, and even in conspiracy theories and spiritual mythology. With a quick survey of radial patterns, one will find at least dozens of different ways of gazing upon and designing with the spiral—in mathematical problems, data visualization, art, spiritual iconography, architecture, bicycle racks; in natural systems and materials; and even in audio and physical effects, like the winglet spinning in the vortices of a flying aircraft. What they all hold in common is their predictable path and process, as an adjustment of angle or magnitude creates its patterned linkages.

Figure 9.1 shows a Fibonacci spiral, also called the *golden spiral,* which is an example of a logarithmic spiral that gets wider by a factor of φ for every

---

[2] Bourke-White, Margaret (1992). *Written by Herself: Autobiographies of American Women*. Vintage Books, p. 440.

[3] Bourke-White, Margaret (n.d.). Retrieved January 3, 2017, from https://www. brainyquote.com/quotes/quotes/m/margaretbo133423.html

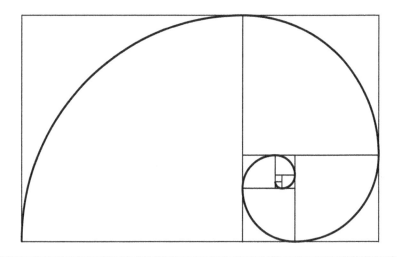

Figure 9.1   An example of the Fibonacci spiral, also called the golden spiral.[4]

quarter turn it makes. Golden spirals are found all over the natural world, most recognizably in the nautilus shells that allow an organism to grow without changing shape.

Adopting this metaphor, in Chapter 6 we compared the exploration phase of the OpenXFORM model to the propulsive function of an insect, structurally represented by the thorax of the animal and by a spiral of forward progress marked by a repetition of activities. The thorax is the "engine room" of the insect, and in OpenXFORM it is the region that represents a spiraling process that carries a prototype that has emerged from the ideation phase and tests, assesses, and refines it based on the goals and limits established for the project (see Table 9.1).

When we show our prototype for testing, we hope that it conveys what we plan to build. But that is a very small part of OpenXFORM:Explore's purpose. The breadth of what is being tested is the designers' assumptions reified by the prototype. Explicit or not, the prototype itself contains our ideals, values, and biases; when we explore our creation, our ultimate innovative product or idea validates not just form and function but also a concrete representation of our company's self-perceived place in the market.

---

[4] By User:Dicklyon (Own work using: Inkscape) [Public domain], via Wikimedia Commons. Retrieved on January 12, 2017, from https://commons.wikimedia.org/wiki/File:Fibonacci_spiral_34.svg.

**Table 9.1 A Prototype Begins the Phase of Exploration
and Exits with a Pivot**

PROTOTYPE
The research question is posed, the prototype shows a design that might answer that question, and it is clearly identified through the prototype that we want to test.

OpenXFORM:EXPLORE	
Show	This is a team effort now, and that team includes those who will be served by the idea. Showing the prototype to users is communicating the idea through a conveyance that is specific and concrete enough to be understandable.
Test	Testing the viability of the idea represented by the prototype means being open to feedback. Test every prototype extensively enough to inform the next prototype or to agree that it is complete. Testing at the exploratory stage should be focused mainly on the user's experience and reaction to the design, and not on being "right."
Assess	When assessing the feedback from the prototype, the open-minded team will look not only for ways to refi ne their prototype, but also for an understanding of whether the problem was framed correctly. A complete testing effort will likely expose unexpected insights in the form of additional unmet needs among users.
Refine	At this stage, the team is ready not only to reconstruct the prototype, but to tune the research question to better reflect context. Since this is an iterative and not a top-down process, such a refinement doesn't mean that the effort has failed, only that there is an additional opportunity to invalidate poor solutions and improve the overall likelihood of adjusting the product to more appropriately meet the user's needs. If the assumptions were wrong, reject them and try again.

PIVOT
We have validated our idea with a design to the extent that we know the form or structure that the idea should take. The pivot is the opportunity to tweak the outcome of the exploratory phase to allow it to simultaneously meet company strategic goals and satisfy the needs of the actual market of consumers represented in user-feedback testing.

9.3 It's What's Inside That Counts

The organization Design Thinking for Mobility (www.designthinkingfor mobility.org) is a process, advice, and tools group that provides materials to help communities create customer-centered approaches to innovating transportation offerings. The group provides many valuable materials to help local stakeholders leverage the design-thinking process in their work; their approach is a testament to the fact that customer-centric product design can reduce risk dramatically in solving complicated problems (like transportation networks) by first understanding its value to those who will benefit most.

The group encourages the use of prototypes as a reality check to test the assumptions of an idea's concepts, and our model takes inspiration from their simple approach, if not from the particulars of their methodology. While their stated aim is to increase the probability of a successful implementation, their approach reveals something even more important for the design process—rooting out bias. The team designed a set of worksheets that help identify and articulate those assumptions, and to test their correctness. OpenXFORM adopts a similar approach.

The realm of future tech is especially challenging in that there is a propensity for unexpected adaptation by users and consequent rapid iteration. These demands greatly accelerate the process of innovation and validation, especially with emerging cultural influences and connectedness. Advanced technologies have even forced changes in the way we express ourselves; notice the way in which space-limited media (such as SMS or Twitter) has influenced "standard" language usage—LOL, RT, SMH. Furthermore, when we search for information in Google, we use "Googlish," with simple syntax and sometimes even with "incorrectly on purpose" queries designed to provoke a particular response. At the Googleplex, one can see these oddly formed queries streaming by on a monitor in the waiting area as they are excitedly peered upon by lingering sales professionals, engineers, linguists, journalists, and big-data analysts who hope to understand what people "out there" want to know.

All serious product designers have been taught that the hallmark of great design is that it holds value for its intended beneficiary (named variously the customer, the consumer, the user, etc.). But too often—especially in the age of big-data validation—we overlook how the success or failure of an innovation rests just as profoundly in its technical feasibility and fitness for mission to the business. This doesn't mean that an innovation can't disrupt an entire industry or technology, just that we must be utterly conscious about this. One may remember the example of Kodak and its rejection of the digital camera. If it had better understood its own biases in assessing the technology, it might have made a very different decision about how to cope with digital photography and not left a generation of photography enthusiasts (not to mention their shareholders) agape at its flame-out.

When we have validated our theories with a design to the extent that we know the form or structure that the idea should take, then we can see how we hope to meet company strategic goals and satisfy the needs of the actual market of consumers. Specifically, the exploratory phase of the innovation process provides the opportunity to overcome our faulty assumptions and mold our ideas toward expressing a powerfully innovative outcome. Understanding the assumptions lurking within the innovative cycle is important, not to overly restrict the process, but to understand its impact and to better increase its chances of success through refinement and an honest evaluation of both the viability of the concept and the parameters of investment. Some prototype research will challenge existing corporate perceptions of the market. As we discuss in the *pivot* moment, this is where things can get very dodgy.

9.3.1 The Domains of Our Assuming

When we first came up with our idea and worked to give our flash of insight meaning, it was borne of inspiration and imagined in a particular context. Even if you've designed a helium balloon to float alone in space, it has materiality and a place (or a virtual materiality defined in a place of bits and bytes). It is our concept within that context that we must test and judge if we have a foundation upon which to build. While in OpenXFORM:Ideate, as described in Chapter 8, we focused on translating our inspiration to a solution construction, yet in that moment we have little concern about how our target market feels about it, nor do we consciously visit the question of whether it helps us achieve our business goals. While models and prototypes can be revealing, they have very rough edges, and only as we smooth them over may we discover the cracks and pits that lurk under the surface and, finally, the real potential of our innovation.

This is also the point in the process to explore the viability of the concept, not to prove that it is out-of-the-box correct—if anything, this is an excellent time to be proven *wrong* and offered the rare and valuable opportunity to inform our insight into meaningfully inspired action with the help of real data and real people. Please remember that a "negative result" to a research question does not imply an exit from the innovation process, although it certainly could. This is where the explorer's mindset becomes so important: trust the process to show a way forward, but don't insist that the team skip, run, or walk backwards on that road. In the spirit of the principles of diversity and openness, collaborating with others both inside and outside of the organization can be most enriching.

9.3.2 Surveying the Landscape of Co-Creation

Our partnerships in the domains of prototype testing are those of co-creation, but not just with our users, which in future tech might be a non-human target.

Remember the principle of diversity, too. Broader testing might show that your idea is perfect for someone or something you never considered, and engineers, marketers and business stakeholders also have unique perspectives. Truthfully, this part of the process requires patience, practice, and a steady hand. Also, it is an opportunity for the practices of adaptation and information decomposition described earlier in the book, where one can borrow liberally from the ever-expanding world of open resources while also providing value back to the commons. As the process itself instructs in this stage of development, there may be little direct proprietary value, unless the corporate strategy is to lock up information through patenting or a similar strategy. This book has vehemently argued against deleterious hoarding as a viable long-term strategy, but to be fair, there are still choices to be made in the process of innovation regarding the goals of profit and fitness towards those goals.

Table 9.2 describes the domains of user testing and their linkage to the OpenXFORM:Explore facets represented as a forward-moving spiral toward concept refinement. The research goals defined are universal to every idea that has a goal of user adoption and utility and that requires resources to develop, implement, and scale. Figure 9.2 renders the spiral of exploration of our domains of inquiry describing the facets of that process. This figure is a touchstone, showing how a prototype spirals forward outside the boundaries of time (there are no constraints on how long it takes to test an assumption), progressing and improving its demonstrated viability, to find its way to its ultimate transformation as an innovative product or service.

Table 9.2 The Domains of Assumption Testing

Domain	Facet	Research Goal
User Values	Test	Learn if the concept appeals to the customer. Is it desirable? What is its utility?
Technical Feasibility	Assess	Understand what it will take from a technology perspective to implement the concept. Is there existing technology to implement the concept?
Business Viability	Refine	Reveal how the concept fits into the business strategy. Is the idea aligned with the mission of the organization? How will it be funded and how is value returned to the organization?

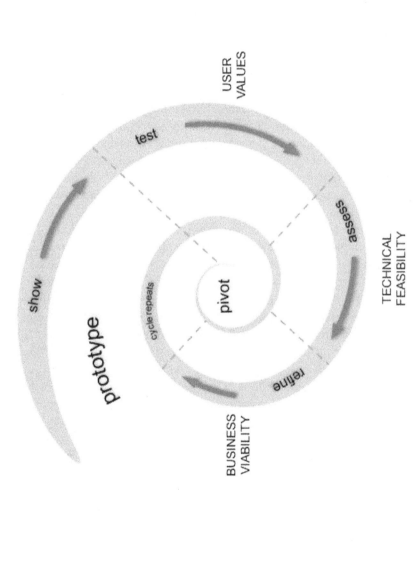

Figure 9.2 OpenXFORM:Explore challenges assumptions across the domains of user values, technical feasibility, and business viability to guide the process of prototype refinement.

9.4 Sightseeing Among Our Assumptions

You can use an eraser on the drafting table or a sledge hammer on the construction site.

— Frank Lloyd Wright[5]

The assumptions brought to the table by the innovation team are wrought deeply into the working prototype and re-manifest themselves at every loop around the exploration circuit. Our goal is to take stock of these assumptions, validate their fitness and utility, and accept or reject them in our final rendering. Every prototype is a testable model that will become more refined as more is learned about the aptness and workability of the concept. While prototypes are simple, they still must be concrete enough to spark conversation and interaction and to enable the collection of feedback to extract an improvement to the next instantiation of the concept in a new form. Most especially, prototypes are indefensible, as in, they should never be defended. If the goal is to show up with the perfect idea, then what is required is to convene a princely court of reliable enthusiasts. The concept prototype, instead, is best viewed as a container of assumptions that need to be validated and endorsed.

Following are several worksheets that can be used as templates to help explore assumptions throughout the cycle using an example project and expressed in the form of challenges in each domain of the user, technology, and the business. Suggesting a concept of a mobile app for EV charging, the following provides insight into how a rough prototype can move to a validated hypothesis, wherein the form and structure of an idea can ultimately meet an actual market of consumers in unity with strategic company goals and capabilities. In the process, the company goals become better understood or augmented. Much is left out of this illustration, except the bones and some interstitial tissue, but it is proffered only as a sketch for how to expose the best and cull the worst of our suppositions.

9.4.1 Concept: Integrated EV Charging Station Mobile App

There is widespread consensus among experts who study electric vehicle (EV) adoption that a lack of public charging stations holds the market back. This is expressed in what has been called *range anxiety*, meaning that prospective EV drivers are concerned that they will run out of charge and become stranded

---

[5] Lloyd Wright, Frank. *Quotes on Design*. Retrieved on December 29, 2016, from https://quotesondesign.com/frank-lloyd-wright/.

without access to services that will allow them to get back on the road in the same way they would if they ran out of gas. Helping EV drivers reliably and easily find the most affordable charge at the best price when needed will propel the market forward.

Since our company is a charging network provider (we provision charging stations and sell charging service plans to customers) whose mission is to usher in a zero-carbon transportation world, our growing business depends on the vitality of the EV market.

The product must serve the customer in three distinct ways, by helping them:

1. Understand **when** to charge for the cheapest rate.
2. Support the technical factors related to EV charging and help the consumer understand **how** to manage those factors to meet their individual requirements.
3. Provide real-time access to information as to **what** infrastructure resources are available to meet individual customer requirements for charging.

To address these issues, our team is designing a mobile app that provides the EV customer with a live map of active charging sites, availability, price for the required connector type, and supported network service provider. Despite our competitive stand in relation to other service providers, we will agnostically provide information for all providers to the extent that it can be gathered from open-data sources; this is because our mission is focused on improving the market overall, and range anxiety is holding the entire market back. We believe that with this service foundation we can provide myriad enhanced services and integrations that will make this nervousness an emotion of the past, massively improve the EV market, and ultimately drive consumers to subscribe to our company for their EV needs.

Initial Cycle: Rough Prototype

The initial prototype is a cardboard cellphone with a few hand-drawn screen mockups that can demonstrate a sense of the interface that is sufficient to collect early feedback in the design process, is inexpensive, and doesn't waste time or resources with a poorly executed digital rendering.

For each circuit around OpenXFORM:Explore, a more refined prototype will emerge, and each will provoke a new set of assumptions. The challenge at each stage is to examine user value, technical feasibility, and business viability and to assess the significance of each identified assumption with an *importance measure* (e.g., an assumption is so important to the innovation that if it fails, the entire notion is infeasible). Over time, with each turn of the spiral, there are fewer and fewer new issues to test and overcome.

Rigorously testing prototype assumptions is by far the most overlooked and undervalued task in new product development. Neglecting this step has caused many companies to either develop a fear of moving forward after multiple innovation failures, or the opposite and equally suicidal impulse to move forward on every big idea without sufficient attention to the nuances of cultural and societal biases within their new products. It is yet to be shown how any product team can avoid expressing their own discursive and unexamined preconceptions about the nature of "their" users and who we imagine them to be.

This is especially true in the realm of advanced technologies, where engineers are often masters of a tiny domain and have trouble transposing their internal narrative (no matter how interesting) to the market. Still, trusting the marketing team is perilous, as marketing is too often tied to sales, which creates a tendency to define a product that can be quickly sold and converted into revenues and paycheck bonuses at the risk of conscious innovation. The risk, then, is that an innovative product is designed in a bubble that ultimately cannot be translated to business stakeholders, where it remains on the shelf to later become a case study for failed innovation (sorry, Kodak). Thus, by bringing the technology and business stakeholders closer to the user-validation process, conversations are compelled that force a deeper understanding of the correctness of the problem framing, the sustainability of the solution, and an explicit recognition of the context for the innovation and how it might be adapted in the future.

9.5 Testing Assumptions

As mentioned, for each cycle of the explore process (which will be completed at least once), a refined prototype will emerge, and each will provoke a new set of assumptions and related questions. It is helpful to remember that we are not trying to pass/fail the concept prototype; rather, we hope to dispense with unproven ideas about the innovation, its users, its feasibility, and its business prospects. The process is designed to collect information that can help us make an effective assessment as to the viability of the idea and whether there is sufficient optimism for it. Avoid a false sense of reassurance and confidence by inculcating this process with an excessive sense of rigor.

Thus, the process is represented as a spiral and in a sequence of concerns from user, technology, and business. If an important user assumption fails and the prototype can't be tweaked, why bother expending resources on an extensive technology feasibility study or dragging in business stakeholders and involving them in assessing a knowingly broken prototype? It is absolutely fair to adjust and tweak as the team progresses through the testing, again reminding us that we are eschewing the scientific method, even as it is important to use vetted and appropriate research methodologies for user studies and data gathering.

The following steps describe the testing procedure:

1. Create a quick but complete list of questions that show how the design expresses its internal concept of user value.
2. Take note of the assumption inherent in each question, in the form of an affirmative statement, for consistency. It is possible that one question may expose more than one assumption. In that case, use separate lines as the process is designed to test the assumptions, not the questions *per se*.
3. One a scale of 1, 3, 5, where 5 is of highest weight, understand the importance that an assumption brings to the viability of the concept.
4. Indicate the approach to testing this assumption.

9.5.1 Test Assumptions for User Values

Top-Level Goal. Determine if, *from a user's perspective*, the concept meets expectations for value, specifically for usability, desirability, and utility. The team will ultimately learn what it will take to move the concept from a nascent idea to something with form and structure that can be specified and built (see Worksheet Example Challenge: Test Assumptions for User Values).

Worksheet Example Challenge: Test Assumptions for User Values

Question	Assumption	Importance	Approach
Will every one of our subscribers be able to design their journey online?	All drivers have the capability to design their journeys online.	5	Conduct a user survey that establishes the level of internet connectivity, ability, and propensity to use an online service.
Will every user understand the charging requirements of their vehicle to select the right station?	All EV owners are educated on the requirements for charging their vehicle.	3	Test mass-market customers who are first-time owners of EVs to learn about their experience in transitioning from gasoline to electric.
add additional questions and assumptions as necessary			

9.5.2 Test Assumptions for Technical Feasibility

Top-Level Goal. Determine if, *from the perspective of technical feasibility*, it is possible to implement and build the product. It is not necessary to address questions of scale at this point, nor is it yet important to address business viability.

If a new technological approach or material is required, denote that and its weighted importance. Specifically, the team will understand what the technical requirements will be to provide materiality to the proposed form and structure of the prototype. Most importantly, continuously evaluate how open information, data, and content can accelerate your efforts, and identify the sources where it can be found, their reliability, and the cost of including or adapting such resources (see Worksheet Example Challenge: Assess Technical Feasibility).

Worksheet Example Challenge: Assess Technical Feasibility

Question	Assumption	Importance	Approach
Will the company be able to support drivers in every nation?	Drivers will be able to access this service wherever they choose to drive.	3	Investigate various mapping data sources, including open data, and understand their quality and reliability.
Will the company have adequate resources for up-to-date geographic information resources?	The company will be able to leverage accurate mapping information that is fast, secure, and reliable.	5	Investigate open source mapping data sources for the world and compare the licensing impacts, reliability, and security of varying mapping products.
add additional questions and assumptions as necessary			

9.5.3 Test Assumptions for Business Viability

Top-Level Goal. Determine if, *from the perspective of the business*, it is within the purview and the mission to implement and build the service. Consult and collaborate with stakeholders from across the company to explore issues of strategic investment, requirements for return on investment, and impact to brand. Again, questions of scale and business viability are not important at this point. If a new business capability is required, determine its criticality to the concept (see Worksheet Example Challenge: Refine Prototype for Business Viability).

9.5.4 Fully-Realized Concept: Refined Prototype

At the end of the process, the team is satisfied that they have tested, sorted, validated, and gotten quite specific about the assumptions of their concept and of what has been consciously discarded and generated along the way. Choices have been made, and the story has been told and retold. In hand is an innovative

Worksheet Example Challenge: Refine Prototype for Business Viability

Question	Assumption	Weight	How to Test
Will the idea generate immediate revenue for the company?	The company requires the ability to forecast reliably on new products.	3	Produce a "back-of the envelope" model with business stakeholders who are skilled in new product development. Assess for fitness against goals.
Will the new product risk the brand of reliability and quality that the company promotes?	The company spends millions of dollars every year saying they are the most reliable in class, and this product will not damage that reputation.	5	Compare the proposed features of the concept with the predominant branding features for the company. Assess for consistency and impact on the brand image.
add additional questions and assumptions as necessary			

concept that holds a story within it, one of who needs it, when and where it will be available, and why it must exist.

The final prototype is a digital sketch-up of linked, designed screens with gesture and transition support to achieve the look and feel of an app that would run on a mobile device, such as an iPhone, Android device, or smart watch. It includes the structure and functionality of all the required features.

9.6 The Pivot

The word pivot is a dangerous one in the entrepreneurial world. A "pivot" usually means that the business model or the flagship product is not performing as expected, and the CEO desperately changes direction (most likely just before or after an investor meeting).

But what if a pivot means that a company is willing to reinvent itself based on new information or a disruptive innovation? If the validated and closely studied behavior discovered in the OpenXFORM:Explore phase tells us something new and important, then ignoring it because it doesn't fit the dominant storyline of the company means that growth opportunities (perhaps even risking corporate viability) will surely be missed.

Here's a pivot that wasn't missed: Twitter. The platform that has dramatically changed the political climate across the entire globe is the result of such a shift in focus, from serving as the communication underpinnings of Arab Spring to arguably electing the 45th president of the United States. Twitter was begun as a network called *Odeo,* in which people could find and subscribe to podcasts. Then Apple's iTunes started doing the same thing, and not only was its user base bigger, the service was well integrated into the Apple ecosystem. Odeo was going to die over it. At that point, the company gave its employees two weeks to come up with a new idea, which Jack Dorsey and Biz Stone did—a status-updating platform. Odeo pivoted, and became the undeniably disruptive Twitter.[6]

In exploring insect morphology in earlier chapters, it was described how the connective tissue between the regions binds the structures of the creature together. These are metaphors for the design and verification gateways between the structural and functional specialties of the innovation process. Specifically, in OpenXFORM, we connect with prototypes and pivots. Leaving the "head" of the process through ideation, we are in possession of a material prototype, no matter how rough its edges might be. As we began our exploration phase, we knew some things about our ideas, which we described with a low-fidelity prototype, and that was the beginning of our quest to learn more about how that idea could better fit the needs of our users with appropriate technology for the benefit of the business. At the end of OpenXFORM:Explore, the innovation team has validated their proposition, tested it for user efficacy, assessed its technology feasibility and business viability, finally producing a high-fidelity exemplar that can be brought with confidence to the process of rigorous specification.

---

6   Nazar, Jason (2013). "14 Famous Business Pivots." Retrieved December 29, 2016, from http://www.forbes.com/sites/jasonnazar/2013/10/08/14-famous-business-pivots/#542a6bf1fb94.

Chapter Ten

OpenXFORM:Transform

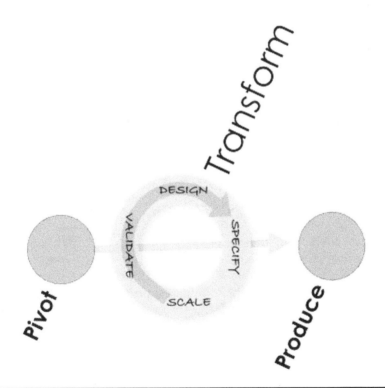

OpenXFORM:Transform explores the issues related to vetting and specifying a refined and ready prototype that gives the development team its best chance of succeeding.

10.1 Chapter Theme

Building on the concepts in the previous chapter describing OpenXFORM: Explore, this chapter discusses the phase of achieving development readiness through the process of *Transform*. The strategies considered in this chapter reflect the challenges of the increased system uncertainties and increasingly rising decision stakes in the domain of advanced and future technology. Furthermore, we explore both the theoretical perspectives and the practical approaches to reducing those risks.

10.2 Making Innovation Work

The discussion of transformation within the context of the OpenXFORM model does not promote a production methodology; instead, this chapter explores readiness issues related to vetting and preparing specifications for a refined prototype. This is quite intentional. By popular measure, this phase of innovation should be the easiest. After all, a refined and perhaps even seemingly functional prototype is in hand, the business likes it, the users want it, and a high-level technology approach is identified. Yet the exit strategy from the world of the prototype to a true development project is notoriously difficult to navigate, to the point at which a well-conceived concept can easily fall prey to a "squeezing out" of proper design and specification construction because the prototype, in fact, was just too good.

In 1999, the author documented a series of patterns for the Pattern Languages of Programming (PLoP 1999) conference that described how engineers and managers who created concept prototypes, using the then-just-emerging rapid-development tools, were pushing prototypes over to their Agile development teams, anticipating that the iterative process would resolve any shortcomings in design. The paper sought to assess the problem of ". . . an increasing emphasis on quick product turn-around and fast-to-market pressures, [where] concept prototypes feed the illusion that development cycles can be drastically shortened." This problem was caused by a prototype looking so visually complete, thanks to new tools, that it created a perception that all that was left to do was "wire it up." This misconception continues to cause many product development failures, from satellite launches to online retail operations.

Although prototypes are useful for the engineering team, managers, clients, and even venture capitalists, their value is too often overstretched by a misinterpretation of purpose. Although the paper was a short exploration of an intuitive sense as to why so many projects were failing, it was obvious that *prototypes had become a proxy for requirements gathering,* and that this was due in large part to the influence of the Agile methodology. In some ways, proto-types became totem objects in the quest for efficiency that the Agile process claimed. Thus, any document or meeting that appeared too rigid or formulaic was rejected outright. This is one reason why Agile methods were long rejected in any domain in which there is a requirement for strong governance, and why the paper suggested that, "In architecture, clients may purchase the services of an architect based on preliminary plans of the structure they want built. A com-petent builder, on the other hand, will wait for plans with actual measurements before breaking ground." But with Agile, taking risks is often preferable to the perception of superfluous requirements.[1]

In many ways, the problem of prototype-to-delivery has only gotten worse, as a visual prototype of convincing complexity can be created in a weekend, the competition for funds and projects has increased, and a feature-rich proto-type that looks production-ready is the way to achieve stakeholder buy-in and cement a project. It's also worth noting that Agile methodologies are almost entirely expressive of those same ethical principles and values that underpin FOSS development projects (and why open and Agile often appear in the same cultural context), open ideas, content, and data: build software that works for its users, blend design and implementation, work in groups, collaborate, and put people first. This unconscious alliance only increases the pressure to avoid formal specifying artifacts (think: "Don't worry, if there's a problem it will be fixed by the team, not our problem"), embracing the fact that nothing is ever perfect in the beginning while actively denying the fact that expedient choices today become the support team's nightmare tomorrow.

But ironically, the constant downward pressure to be resilient and efficient has been tragically rigid in its insistence on not being rigid. There is absolutely nothing in the principles of the Agile methodology that claims that products should not be well designed, just that we must be willing to acknowledge that we know less about the development of the product at the very beginning than we do when we deliver; learning is the essence of adaptability. Therefore, the focus of OpenXFORM:Transform is not on product development per se, but on what can be done to reach confidence in the readiness to build. So, what are the features of an innovation process that explicitly stages a prototype for success? In an increasingly uncertain and risky world, clearly stated objectives, appropri-ate risk analysis, communication conventions, and the adoption of reasonable

---

[1] Stimmel, Carol L. (1999). "Hold Me, Thrill Me, Kiss Me, Kill Me: Patterns for Developing Effective Concept Prototypes." *Proceedings of the 1999 Pattern Languages of Programming (PLoP'1999) Conference.* Available at http://hillside.net/plop/plop99/ proceedings/stimmel/HoldMeThrillMeKissMeKillMe1.PDF.

specifications are, in fact, important ways to improve and expedite the engineering lifecycle—even an incremental one.

10.2.1 The Danger of Ritual Enforcement

Lest one treat the admonition for clarity and reasonable specification as a permission slip to swing the heavy maul of process, this exercise is not an opportunity to generate artificial intellectual assets to gain proprietary advantage. Such efforts rarely lead to breakthrough results and are typically of advantage only to the patent law firm and the CFO who values them on the books. Don't count on a patent strategy to build competitive advantage or customer relationships or to be a ready stream of innovation.

In many ways, OpenXFORM frames a resistance to corporate innovation programs that seek a disingenuous or ill-informed bolt-on process producing theoretical value, inspired in many ways by the central impulses of Agile. The 2001 Agile Manifesto sparked a bonfire in its attempt to show that breaking down process-heavy management while lifting up the knowledge worker as the center actor in the creation process would improve software development outcomes. Jim Highsmith wrote that delivering good products to customers has much to do with how the process of creation is carried out in an atmosphere "that does more than talk about 'people as our most important asset' but actually 'acts' as if people were the most important, and lose the word 'asset' (or 'human resources,' 'human capital,' etc.). So, in the final analysis, the meteoric rise of interest in—and sometimes tremendous criticism of—Agile methodologies is about the mushy stuff of values and culture."[2] These origins of Agile sentimentality are important to remember, as the Agile methodology itself has become over-engineered and cultish, just as systematized innovation threatens to abandon its roots in discovery. This is not because of Agile; it is instead a management tendency to seek indirect forms of control, which is a real reason why an authentic open-source/ideation/collaboration/innovation strategy is so threatening.

Authors Don Olson in 1995 and James Shore in 2008 raised a similar flag of warning about illusory practices. Olson described an organizational anti-pattern called "Cargo Cult," while Shore pointed to a methodological problem with "Cargo Cult Agile." During World War II, American troops flew onto a remote island in Melanesia, bringing with them technologies and goods that had never even been imagined by the islanders. Prosperity and comfort came on

---

[2] Highsmith, Jim (2001). "History: The Agile Manifesto." Retrieved January 4, 2017, from http://agilemanifesto.org/history.html.

those airplanes, first from the sky, then to the airstrip, controlled by men with headphones who directed the metal birds from the sky. After the war, the birds stopped arriving on the island, and decades later, researchers who returned to the island observed a remarkable scene—the islanders had developed a religion that involved a ceremony on a ritual airstrip, where the chief would climb a bamboo platform, his head decorated with coconut headphones, and cry to the heavens for the birds to return.

At first the alliterative Cargo Cult may seem humorous, but then the destructive power of fundamental misunderstanding becomes quite apparent. It's really quite a tragic tale. Both Olson's and Shore's warnings of fruitless and enforced rituals of organizational collaboration and measurement that violate the very spirit of innovation and creativity have come to pass in many companies, including the hottest Silicon Valley startups. At this point, it's anyone's guess as to the size of the Agile marketplace of charts and gadgets, consultancies, books, and companies focused solely on the practice. While this is an inevitability of its widespread adoption, it also a sign of misunderstanding that trades one form of wastage for another. Shore wrote, "The tragedy of the cargo cult is its adherence to the superficial, outward signs of some idea combined with ignorance of how that idea actually works. In the story, the islanders replicated all the elements of cargo drops—the airstrip, the controller, the headphones—but didn't understand where the airplanes actually came from."[3,4] Precisely.

10.3 Avoiding Prototype Fetishism

Corporations and companies must abandon their cargo cult mentality, especially when that mentality impedes ideas and creativity from emerging under the pressure and force of proprietary rituals. Ironically, even the well-intended impulse to "loosen things up" can bring burdensome mandates, directives, and decrees that are meant to define what a more relaxed system ought to look like. Even the de-systematization of innovation, such is in the case of Ford's company-wide program, carries its own weight.

In December of 2016, Ford announced that it had been granted double the number of patents than it had been granted just two years earlier. There are a few issues that belie this success, specifically related to their approach to

---

[3] Olson, Don (1995, last edited 2011). "Cargo Cult." Retrieved January 12, 2016, from http://wiki.c2.com/?CargoCult.

[4] Shore, James (2008, May 18). "Cargo Cult Agile." The Art of Agile (blog). Retrieved December 30, 2016, from http://www.jamesshore.com/Blog/Cargo-Cult-Agile.html.

stimulating a *culture of invention*. The company directly asserts that an investment in innovation pays long-term dividends, yet their measure of success is the number of patents filed. This metric is also expressed in their innovation vetting process, which apparently has become too much for the company to keep up with; another mark for the achievements of the program.

In an interview with Ford Global Technologies chief executive Bill Coughlin by the *Washington Post*'s Innovations Blog team, Coughlin boasted that the company wasn't simply targeting an uptick in the number of inventions, but an "increase in Ford inventors." Coughlin says this excites employees, "Once you start thinking like an inventor, you cannot turn that off. Problems become opportunities, and it's a fun game that you can play in your mind on how to solve this a new and different way."[5] There is nothing obvious to be upset about here; not only are employees getting to participate in new ways, Ford gives them a chance to work in a maker space that helps them prototype their ideas and fix problems that weren't obvious at first. Because a prototype is often functioning at some level, says Coughlin, the program has also improved the ability of management to pursue a new idea. This sounds like an important step in the right direction.

However, if we scratch the surface a bit more, we see that while Ford wants to benefit from an investment in long-term innovation—which is required for a company to thrive into the future (and perhaps in their short-term stock price)—they have chosen to anchor their program in the production of discrete artifacts without making a core change to their business culture. While the notion of providing Ford employees the opportunity to build out their ideas to a prototype is a dramatic step in the right direction, it is their system of metrics that tells the real story. As discussed extensively in this book, while there is much evidence that a patent strategy can positively impact a major company's valuation, there is no evidence that there is a direct relationship between the number of patents and the achievement of innovation in a marketplace. And if it is a gambit to hit on a disruptive idea, that is an expensive bet.

Money is playing a big role in the Ford program, not just in a variety of financial incentives for company inventors, but also in the manner that they manage their innovation pipeline. Coughlin stated that there are so many entries for new products and ideas that a "vetting and quality assurance" process is required, and ultimately, "Ideas are reviewed by a panel of engineers who determine which ones are worth patent protection and might be pursued

---

[5] Overly, Steven (2016, December 14). "How Ford Turned Thousands of Employees into Inventors." *The Washington Post.* Retrieved January 2, 2017, from https://www.washingtonpost.com/news/innovations/wp/2016/12/14/how-ford-turned-thousands-of-employees-into-inventors/?utm_term=.b6e8a74065ff.

commercially."[6] This raises even more troubling problems of who sits on the panel, what their organizational role might be, their influence over corporate resources, and the mandate.

Compare the notion of a systematized program of innovation, such as described in the case of Ford, with how Apple claims they manage to stay in front of nearly ever curve, seemingly ready to capitalize on any new wave of their choosing. Steve Jobs specifically attributed this readiness to a *non-systematized* sense of individual cross-pollination that has been described as *interdisciplinary design,* and which is imbued with the idea that innovation is expansive and should be the constant focus of the way work gets done, and certainly not an external, bolt-on process. When introducing the iPad 2 in 2011, Jobs said, "It is in Apple's DNA that technology alone is not enough—it's technology married with liberal arts, married with the humanities, that yields us the results that make our heart sing."[7] This doesn't mean that Apple plunges ahead mindlessly at every fad; in fact, that is entirely the wrong conclusion. What it does have is an innovative mindset that is pervasive and allows it better visibility into the next groundswell of consumer adoption.

Don't feel like the CEO of Nokia, who, in tears, announced the acquisition of his company by Microsoft in 2013, saying, "We didn't do anything wrong, but somehow, we lost."[8] Doing things the way they've always been done—even if they are executed perfectly—is no longer a predictor for future success.

10.4 Stop Being Normal

As companies like Apple and Ford come closer together at a digital intersection, the difference between them becomes much smaller. But, what is still very different is how they manage risk, embodied in how they value the benefits and costs of innovation. Innovation has always been challenging, but advanced technology especially challenges our notion that innovation (much like science) is value-neutral, apart from class, culture, and society. This is a fairly new recognition, and not one that is enjoyed by all. The idea was first captured in the notion

---

[6] *Ibid.*

[7] Lehrer, Jonah (2011). "Steve Jobs: 'Technology Alone Is Not Enough.'" *The New Yorker.* Retrieved January 3, 2017, from http://www.newyorker.com/news/news-desk/steve-jobs-technology-alone-is-not-enough.

[8] Gupta, Rahul (2016). "Nokia CEO Ended His Speech Saying This . . . 'We didn't do anything wrong, but somehow we lost.'" Retrieved January 4, 2017, from https://www.linkedin.com/pulse/nokia-ceo-ended-his-speech-saying-we-didnt-do-anything-rahul-gupta.

of postnormal science (PNS), which was forwarded by British philosopher of science Jerome Ravetz and Argentinean mathematician Silvio Funtowicz in the early-1990s. In working on problems of risk, it became obvious to the team that sound empirical data and rational scientific conclusions were not guaranteed to compel a complementary political outcome. The authors also claimed that we now live in such an interconnected world that even revolutionary science has no domain of its own. Instead, we live in a world of accommodation, in which solving complex problems is less about what is most effective in the laboratory and more about what is possible in the face of multiple legitimate perspectives; and therefore, the PNS mantra is "facts uncertain, values in dispute, stakes high, and decisions urgent."[9]

So, what is normal? Consider briefly the classic example of a paradigmatic scientific shift as described in 1957 by Thomas Kuhn in *The Copernican Revolution: Planetary Astronomy in the Development of Western Thought*,[10] which describes the traditional relationship of science and society. Kuhn's ideas are summarized here:

- **The Rules Are Debated (normal science).** In the 16th century, Copernicus posits, based on a geometric model, that the sun is the center of the solar system. His theory is so outside of the then-current rules of thought, that he is largely ignored, causing only mild controversy.
- **The Rules Are Questioned (shifting perspectives).** Sixty years later, Galileo champions Copernicanism, and soon a decree is issued against him by the Pope for his defense of Copernicus. He is forthwith convicted of heresy against the Holy Scriptures and is placed under house arrest for the rest of his life. His real crime was pushing on the laws of science, and thereby the systematized rules of society.
- **Making New Rules (the new normal).** By the early 17th century, a revolution in cosmology occurred, and various mathematicians, philosophers, and scientists provided convincing evidence that the sun was indeed the center of the universe, and political ideology began to bend. And with that, both the rules of cosmology and society shifted.

---

[9] Ravetz, Jerry (2002). "The Post-Normal Science of Precaution." NUSAP.net. Retrieved January 2, 2017, from www.nusap.net/downloads/articles/pnsprecaution.pdf.

[10] Kuhn, Thomas S. (1957). *The Copernican Revolution: Planetary Astronomy in the Development of Western Thought*. Cambridge, MA: Harvard University Press. ISBN: 9780674171039.

This example describes the comfortable, familiar trajectory of scientific thought (although sometimes old rules seem to re-emerge under all sorts of doctrinaire and somewhat paranoid conditions). In the normal system, research science convincingly solves a puzzle, and sooner or later the conclusions are accepted and built into new social policy. But we have come far from the problems of Galileo, as postnormal theorists have observed, and much slips into the gaps between normal and revolutionary breakthrough, bringing their own cognitive and political discontinuities.

As these gaps of inquiry become more complex, we find that our problem/solution pairs have lost their deterministic nature and instead comprise a network of sub-systems, including institutions, human beings, and the natural world. It is of no surprise, then, that our most advanced innovations continue to become more deeply embedded in the human experience, as demonstrated quite dramatically in the case of issue-driven sciences. For example, in debates about environmental degradation and sustainability, core facts are disputed in an ideological context, values are in play, the stakes are enormous, and the decision-making horizon is urgent. About this problem specifically, Funtowicz examines sustainability from the perspective of postnormal science, writing, "Anyone trying to comprehend the problems of 'the environment' might well be bewildered by their number, variety and complication. There is a natural temptation to try to reduce them to simpler, more manageable elements, as with mathematical models and computer simulations . . . But environmental problems have features which prevent reductionist approaches from having any, but the most limited useful effect."[11]

Funtowicz seems to be pointing out that we can no longer usefully reduce a problem to pure science outside of some artificial systems of analysis, nor can we deny the myriad legitimate perspectives on the issue of the environment, especially considering the relationship of economic institutions and jobs to the health of the planet. Ideal solutions just do not exist when there is an intricate complex of stakeholders. As frustrating as this perspective is for those of a certain fact-based bent—especially when it comes to the illogical fallacies in much anti-environment ideological reasoning—this sociopolitical reality is hard to deny.

Perhaps we shouldn't be surprised; advanced science itself has led to profound shifts in the nature of scientific thought itself, where paradoxical states more easily coexist. Nick Knisely, the thirteenth and current diocesan bishop

---

[11] Funtowicz, Silvio and Ravetz, Jerry (n.d.). "Post-Normal Science—Environmental Policy under Conditions of Complexity." NUSAP.net. Available at http://www.nusap.net/sections.php?op=viewarticle&artid=13.

of the Episcopal Diocese of Rhode Island, calls them *entangled states,* in which we recognize in the duality of phenomena such as particle/wave theory or the notion of gravity as an emergent force. Knisely writes, "For a long time philosophers and scientists assumed that this inherent duality was an artifact caused by imperfect understanding. But the more we look at the situation, the more stubbornly the data indicates that it's not an approximation of reality. It is reality. We may not be able to completely conceive it. But it's what *is*."[12] That is, reality is inscrutable, a puzzle, enigmatic, and paradoxical.

In part as a response to this, the conclusions of science have become more difficult to assert as a rational resource for developing policy. It also seems to be true that any company working to innovate within the area of advanced technology will find itself dealing with many complex phenomena within a network of asymmetric systems and subsystems. At play are often natural systems, organisms, social institutions, and profound hierarchies of function. Furthermore, the increasing rate of change across these networks creates massive uncertainty with very high stakes, and there is a marked loss of space and time to act with the kind of confidence that business, engineering, and science stakeholders find comfortable in the system of "normal." Furthermore, within the course of casting new rules, it has become increasingly difficult to efficaciously resolve contradictory perspectives, especially with the growing impact of many viewpoints on the process. It is very difficult to make comfortable assumptions about science and how it should be used to treat societal problems.

As stated at the beginning of this chapter, many believe that moving a prototype to delivery is a slam dunk. In a postnormal world, even a refined and seemingly perfect prototype—one which the business likes, the users want, and in which a high-level technology approach is identified—isn't just a pass through to scaling to market. The exit strategy from the world of the prototype to a true development project is particularly difficult because a well-conceived concept guarantees much less than it used to in a deterministic world.

10.5 Complementary Construction

While perhaps not first contemplated by PNS theorists, social media and its role in the trajectory of world events has increased uncertainty, and undoubtedly the stakes have become higher and higher, especially for the most vulnerable

---

[12] Knisely, Nick (2010, May 24). "Can Two Opposing Ideas Be True at The Same Time? Science Seems to Say 'Yes' Once Again." Entangled States (Twitter). Retrieved January 3, 2017, from https://entangledstates.org/2010/05/24/can-two-opposing-ideas-be-true-at-the-same-time-science-seems-to-say-yes-once-again/.

populations. And while many people have come to distrust scientists, there is no lack of dependence on pharmaceuticals, agricultural products, industrial automation, advanced service and commercial tools and products, and of course consumer products such as cell phones and the ubiquitous modes of digitally mediated communication. This raises the importance for postnormal construction of solutions that shifts our problem-solving strategies to account for more than just growth in technological capability, but in reckoning with the stakeholders of humanity, the natural world, and social and cultural institutions as well.

PNS casts itself as a complementary strategy to identify effective approaches to cope with various levels of uncertainty and risk. In Figure 10.1, the so-called *quadrant-rainbow* is drawn with three zones that rest on the axes of system uncertainty and decision stakes. When the stakes and system uncertainty are low, we are in a normal *applied science* space, in which typical forms of expertise are completely effective; as the stakes and uncertainty climb, we find that science is dependent on skills not held within the realm of applied sciences, and consultants such as design engineers or neurosurgeons are required. This realm is called *professional consultancy* and is where much innovation occurs,

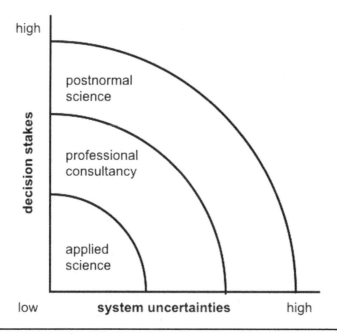

Figure 10.1 The Postnormal Science (PNS) Model. (*Source:* By the author, adapted from FrancoisDM—Own work, CC BY-SA 3.0. Retrieved January 2, 2016, from https://commons.wikimedia.org/w/index.php?curid=16042041.)

propelled forward by the academy and brought to bear by the skill of those with realistic judgment. Finally, when uncertainty is peaking and the decision stakes are highest, it is in the realm of the *postnormal* that the essential role of science becomes contested by both the natural and the social world.

PNS exposes the inadequacies of our standard approaches to science and, in the case of our discussion, innovation. It is important to state that there is no intended attack on applied science or on the role professional consultancy, only the confirming observation that people's values (as discordant as they may be) must be brought into the conversation, *and that to fail to rigorously explore the range of viewpoints across the network of influential subsystems can profoundly increase uncertainty and the decision stakes from the earliest stages of innovation.* This creates a distinct requirement for leaders to develop skills that help them cope with both the difficult forces of consensus where "everyone gets a say" and identifying the opinions and positions that add value to the process. While this conversation may at first seem stultifying to innovation, a rush to progress is never the solution.

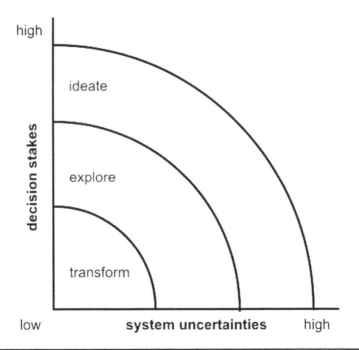

Figure 10.2 OpenXFORM represented in a postnormal science (PNS) framework.

When considerations of society, the natural environment, and human beings are eschewed, as Ravitz observed in a 2002 article entitled *The Post-Normal Science of Precaution*, "In the rush to 'progress,' the problems of safety and ethics are unloaded onto national regulatory bodies, with the warning that there are always less restrictive locations to which the research could run away. [Biomedicine] increasingly invades the domains of the private and the sacred. Public compassion for the sick is regularly enlisted in the service of corporate imperatives."[13] One can then conclude that the way innovation is brought to bear must consciously traverse the interfaces between user value, technology feasibility, and business viability or risk, driving greater uncertainty and dispute in the market itself. This is why OpenXFORM:Transform is designed explicitly to drive down the decision stakes and system uncertainties prior to pushing an innovative idea to production and construction.[14]

In Figure 10.2, this idea is demonstrated by overlaying the phases of OpenXFORM on the PNS framework. In this model, the stakes and uncertainties are highest during the phase of ideation and decrease as more information is known and prototypes are refined. This figure is not intended to demonstrate a linear progression, only to show how advancement of an innovative idea within the context of OpenXFORM accounts for risk and uncertainty. This is especially important when we attach our innovative attempts to the ecosystem of open data, ideas, and content, where open systems of collaboration, access to shared data sources, and the strengthening of judgment informed by the extended peer community brings forth essential value that can drive up confidence by accounting for confusing factors that may jeopardize success.

10.6 From Inputs to Outcomes

Very few in the future tech industry have an appetite for another do-over of their production process, often because of institutional requirements, resource constraints, or simply because governance and regulation (as in bioscience) mandate how a company brings an innovative idea to the market. And there is certainly little room on the bookstore shelf for yet another regurgitation of software development "principles" that admonish managers/leaders for their heartlessness, a new Machiavellian tome, or a hippie chapbook written by a resentful creative thinker looking to be recognized for his specialness and thus achieve

---

[13] Ravetz, Jerry (2002). "The Post-Normal Science of Precaution." NUSAP.net. Retrieved January 2, 2017, from http://www.nusap.net/downloads/articles/pnsprecaution.pdf.
[14] *Ibid.*

a high salary and the right to be left alone. With OpenXFORM, the goal is to observe, capture, and recommend a process of innovation that interrupts the rubric of exceptionalism for all involved in the process. Instead, innovation is perceived as neither a mystical act nor one that may be fulfilled by a cast of automatons under strict directorial control, but a uniquely human endeavor.

Putting an end to the fears of FOSS, open data, free and available content, and open ideation is part of cracking open the world of innovation, as it is this very "openness" that makes it possible to adapt the fertile resources in the world of knowledge to solving high-value problems that produce tangible value. Data, information, and content are quickly becoming universally accessible, and competitive advantage will soon be more closely tied to the application and adaptation of information into delivered knowledge in the form of a product, process, service, or even experience than in a patent portfolio or basket of secret databases.

There is interesting evidence that the way an organization integrates openness to help mitigate rapidly shifting external conditions can lead to an improved sense of organizational mindfulness. This mindfulness contributes to a focus on outcomes, while recognizing that inputs still matter. Diana Oblinger, president and CEO of EDUCAUSE, a non-profit association that promotes information technology in higher education, makes an interesting observation about how institutions with access to open sources of information shift their focus from educational resources to knowledge acquisition. She says, "The shift is from inputs, or a focus on content, to more of a focus on outcomes and how you assess those outcomes. The shift from the inputs to outcomes is a positive shift and a very important one. However, it is a challenging one because it's hard to think about competencies and how you measure them."[15]

This importance of focusing on outcomes is that it requires tying execution to the innovation process, but without embedding special operations into the creative act. Yet, this is a difficult balance, as we require more rigor and predictability than expressed by Picasso, who said, "The chief enemy of creativity is good sense."[16] OpenXFORM explicitly embraces the uncertain nature of creativity without accepting that it must be chaotic; instead, innovation is best served by a good *system* of innovation, directly tied to organizational intent and a focus on how the mission of the organization depends on innovative success.

---

[15] Mandell, Alan and Travers, Nan L. (2013). "Learning in a World of Perishable Knowledge: An Interview with Diana Oblinger." *PLA Inside Out: An International Journal on Theory, Research and Practice in Prior Learning Assessment*, vol. 2, issue 1. Available at http://www.plaio.org/index.php/home/article/view/49.

[16] Picasso, Pablo (n.d.). BrainyQuote.com. Retrieved January 2, 2017, from https://www.brainyquote.com/quotes/quotes/p/pablopicas110182.html.

Unfortunately, without a system, more ideas die on a napkin than ever make it to market. The reason for this is not because the napkin is stained with a lunchtime martini, but because there is a lack of understanding of how to effectively invest in testing and refining big ideas early. Instead, many companies execute within a hardened system that is remarkably anti-innovation, while others attempt to wring out untapped potential without making the necessary cultural changes required to promote a truly innovative mindset.

10.7 The Ants Are Still Marching

In Chapter 6 we revealed insect morphology as the bioempathetic inspiration for OpenXFORM and explored how the three major body regions—the head, the thorax, and the abdomen—could help us understand the functions and characteristics of the proposed model. The *head* is designed for sensory input and food ingestion, the thorax anchors the legs (and wings, if they exist) and manages other systems that are specifically designed to propel the insect, and the *abdomen* digests, reproduces, excretes, and sometimes even defends (most of us have been stung by an angry bee at least once in our lives). OpenXFORM:Transform corresponds to the activities of the abdomen. Tables 10.1 and 10.2 remind us of the characteristics of an ant's abdomen that help describe the organizing principles of transformation. The abdomen begins the expression of the creative potential of the ideation and explore processes and represents the single turning process that takes a confirmed and refined prototype (the *pivot*) that has emerged from the OpenXFORM:Explore phase to envision the innovation at scale, where it is ultimately handed off to production experts (in *produce*).

Table 10.1 Comparison of Functions of Output in Insect and Innovation Morphology

FUNCTION	STRUCTURAL REGION		CHARACTERISTICS	
	Insect	*Innovation*	*Insect*	*Innovation*
Output	Abdomen	Transform	Digestion Excretion Reproduction Defense	Scaling Validating Designing Specifying

Table 10.2 The Phases of OpenXFORM:Transform

PIVOT
We have validated our idea with a design to the extent that we know the form or structure that the idea should take. The pivot is the opportunity to tweak the outcome of the exploratory phase to allow it to simultaneously meet company strategic goals and satisfy the needs of the actual market of consumers represented in user-feedback testing.

REGION #3: TRANSFORM	
Scale	What's it going to take for the company to deliver this product to the customer? What are the channels, types of infrastructure, or marketing capabilities required? Much of this information may have been loosely acquired in the exploratory phase, especially if other teams have been included during the exploratory phase. Scaling efforts also focus on developing customer personas as artifacts that will serve the progressive product development effort.
Validate	Are the designers, developers, and product managers all on the same page? What are the priorities for the company in supporting this idea? This is the time to flesh out the assumptions built into the refined design; to document technical, business, and user requirements; and to validate business goals, objectives, and capabilities.
Design	Design steps may be unique to every team, but every design should reflect enough detail to build a complete story for the customer that in turn builds on the raw information from the exploration phase. This should include designing toward specific success metrics.
Specify	The proper specification depends on the idea itself and the fact that every successful team has created its own way to develop requirements. However, any specification must represent the authentic experiences and plans drawn out during discovery, or something entirely different will be built that drives the value of the very process asunder.

PRODUCE
Stay connected to the user experience of the product, system, or experience. It is important to continuously test, incrementally improve, verify, and seek to understand the resulting context of an idea as it is built and released, especially as a way to harvest new solutions to emerging problems.

10.7.1 Envisioning Development

In Chapter 4, we discussed at some length the advantages and shortcomings of incremental development, be it Agile, Lean, Toyota Production System (TPS), or any variation within. Yet, while it is not our concern here to further argue execution models, there is something to be said about how best to prepare in general for production readiness. All production methodologies have some unit of work. It is that thing, whatever it is, that allows the flow of production to be measured. No business can operate without some visibility into its product development timeline. In any sort of continuous model of production, the best model for value creation is one in which customers get their needs met with a minimal expenditure of resources—be they time, materials, or human effort; or more succinctly, *stop wasting time with no-value-added activities.* The hope is that by reducing counterproductive activities customer value naturally increases, and while open to interpretation in practice, it is this principle that drives quality, speed to delivery, and a better product.

Incremental production methodologies—properly implemented—provide a solid system of focused efficiencies. And while customer acceptance is considered a core tenet, when it comes to building a product, the time of addressing the question of "why" the product is right for the customer must be answered before production begins. This is true even when the development team will find that they must adapt and revise to bring the idea to life. In good practice, development methodologies prescribe "how" to build the product, represented by a concept prototype appropriate for all stakeholders involved. It is when we foist questions of "why" onto the development team that things can go so wrong and why OpenXFORM:Transform demands that we pound the stake of "why" in the ground, if for no other reason than to give the development team a unified and fair start.

10.7.2 Agile Modeling Still Works

In OpenXFORM:Explore, much was made of the importance of flushing out user, technical, and business assumptions. This provides a measure of confidence and agreement about how the innovation will take shape in development. And hard pressed to find any other methodology that allows such low marginal costs in delivery, the general practices of Agile are still preferred. Agile Modeling (AM) is one such approach that has been well documented by Scott Ambler, software engineer and prolific author in the field of unified process and Agile software development. His site, agilemodeling.com, is one of the most comprehensive resources available to learn disciplined modeling approaches; many of the ideas recommended here as possible outputs are explained at great length on Ambler's site and in his books.

While there are many participants, many of these tasks will be shepherded by a product owner, or team of product owners (who typically serve as the proxy for the customer); the intent is not to produce a notebook of documents, but to

Table 10.3 Illustrative Table of Outputs

Domain	Facet	Goal	Outputs
Initiate	Scale	Formalize the user, technical, and business assumptions reflected in the refined prototype accepted during the PIVOT.	• Statement of the mission • Description of the desired result • Accounting of the features and functionality required to produce the result
Technical Strategy	Validate	Understand the practical implications of the assumptions built into the refined prototype.	• Technology stack • User interface models • Entity relationship diagrams • Functional requirements • Non-functional requirements
Priority Stack	Design	Provide the detail necessary to initiate product development.	• Identified stakeholders • Initial product backlog • High-level options and alternatives to potential challenges
Requirements Stack	Specify	Communicate what happens next.	• Sketches • Collaboration tools • Post-It notes • Estimating tools

provide a level of credible detail that can be cast as priorities during the forthcoming development cycles. There are crucial questions related to the scope of the project that must be explicitly answered so that the correct resources and budgets are brought to bear. In this phase of transformation, we are seeking a reasonable understanding of the actors involved in the project, the relationships among them, and how the built system will enable those relationships. We had a reason we wanted to get this done, so we must insist on a credible representation of the actions, events, and interactions that must occur within the system, among the humans and other systems required to realize the concept.

In Table 10.3, we explore the possible outputs that a product manager will produce to brief the team on what is being built, why it has been designed in a particular way, what it means to the business, and what the return on investment is expected to be. Ultimately, the product owner will shepherd the product through its delivery evolution, and the development team must trust that the owners are advocating effectively. The product owner(s) had best not be shooting from the hip. When they do, it shows. Distilled down to its very basics, the following must be identified and documented in the way deemed most useful to the goals of the product development team. The goal is to transform the vision to a baseline with:

1. A coherent scope of the project
2. A priorities stack
3. An architectural perspective

Even with this relatively light level of detail, it is important to exert some control for quality and to prevent excessive waste in the creation of a working product or experience. Addressing the practical implications of the scale and design of even a well-refined prototype will go far to fully engage those with whom you collaborate to bring your innovative solution to life.

Chapter Eleven

Practicing Innovation

Bees are insects with a complex social colony complete with a queen, nurses, foragers, and laborers. Since 2006, honeybees have been dying off at rapid rate; yet for all the measures being explored to help save these critical populations from becoming extinct, scientists stress that it is fundamentally important to first improve collaboration and information sharing among cropgrowers and beekeepers before any intervention is attempted.

[1] Unknown (1984). *Popular Science Monthly*, vol. 45. Public domain. Retrieved January 5, 2017, from https://commons.wikimedia.org/w/index.php?curid=13313250.

11.1 The Art of Provocation

As the 21st century is now nearly two decades in, the landscape of ideas and methodologies for driving innovation into the organization has taken a surprising swing. After many companies found themselves being pummeled in the market over the last 20 years for not bringing enough "new" products and services to the market, experts and industry observers began to reflexively blame heavy-handed bureaucratic organizations for stifling innovation. Large organizations especially found themselves surprised by the technologies and products that were emerging from entrepreneurs and small businesses. Books and articles continue to be written by the ream on the subject, providing opinions and suggesting interventions to answer the question of "how can we become more innovative?" Indeed, this book will sit on the virtual shelves among them. And major companies will continue to spend huge sums of money and time trying to mimic the agility that comes so easily to the disrupters, even if that sense of agility is an optical illusion. A brief history may clarify how this came to be the case.

While every major company adopted comprehensive techniques to deal with uncertainty and the typical forms of chaos inherent in complex and fast-moving team projects, innovation wasn't the result, even if order and predictability were. Because one of the most common themes to start-up success was *incrementalism*, organizational researchers quickly ascertained that detailed planning was the culprit and not the solution to innovation woes. In fact, the story goes, planning was squeezing out creativity. Thus, more interactivity, smaller and more frequent goal setting, and highly interactive and collaborative processes were the obvious keys to achieving the nirvana of *disruptive innovation*.

Yet, it wasn't long before leading management scholars began to point out that even if successful organizations were learning to accept chaos as part and parcel of doing business, they weren't adequately appreciating it. It seemed to many, including James Brian Quinn, author of *Intelligent Enterprise*,[2] that, "Only highly committed entrepreneurs can tolerate (and even enjoy) this chaos. They adopt solutions wherever they can be found, unencumbered by formal plans or PERT charts that would limit the range of their imaginations. When the odds of success are low, the participation and interaction of many motivated players increase the chance that one will succeed."[3] In essence, chaos was fuel and highly correlative with breakthrough success.

---

[2] Quinn, James Brian (1992). *Intelligent Enterprise*. Free Press. ISBN-10: 0029256151, ISBN-1313: 978-0029256152.
[3] Quinn, James Brian (1985). "Managing Innovation: Controlled Chaos." *Harvard Business Review*. Retrieved January 5, 2017, from https://hbr.org/1985/05/managing-innovation-controlled-chaos.

The idea of breaking away from linear, deterministic organizational methods became extremely popular, not only in the business world, but also in the world of warfare, about which Steven Mann, diplomat and author, wrote *Chaos Theory and Strategic Thought* for the US Army War College Quarterly in 1992.[4] This short piece described the use of the science of *chaos theory*, which presented a paradigm of a world doomed to chaos, but one that always ultimately created opportunity. He wrote, ". . . each actor in politically critical systems possesses conflict energy, an active force that instigates change in the status quo, thus contributing to the formation of the critical state. In our international system, this energy derives from the motivations, values, and capabilities of the specific actors, whether governments, political or religious movements, or individuals." Mann went on to describe how it is that these actors contribute to a shift in the status quo that may be violent, but that pushes a system toward what he called an "inevitable cataclysmic reordering." In short, the role of conflict in instigating chaos is a tool that, if used properly and to one's advantage, is a very good one. A quick read of the morning paper further establishes the idea of chaos as a disruptive tool.

To business consultants, the management approach of "controlled chaos" has until recently continued to serve as a popular management strategy. In 1999, Dee Hock, founder and former CEO of the VISA corporation, conceived of *chaordia,* a portmanteau of chaos+order, to describe the harmonious coexistence of the states of chaos and order that give dominance to neither a strong bureaucracy or a state of anarchy. To this day, the tenets of chaordia are still appreciated, perhaps ironically, by those who work within peer-to-peer (P2P) groups, in which teams stress a robust set of principles that include shared purpose, self-organization, equity of power and responsibility, restraint of overt command and control on the project, and, most revealing, a practice that is "compatible with the human spirit and the biosphere"[5] (words you are unlikely to hear in any multinational boardroom). Including the P2P Foundation, many organizations still enjoy the conscious implementation of a chaordic strategy, though perhaps with differing motivations.

But there is a problem with the poetical whimsy of controlled chaos, especially when it comes to the quest for disruption. For one thing, the reactive stance of "controlled chaos" does nothing specifically helpful to improve a firm's ability to integrate a process of innovation. Anthony H. Cordesman, the Arleigh A. Burk

---

[4] Mann, Steven R. (1992). "Chaos Theory and Strategic Thought." *Parameters (US Army War College Quarterly)*, vol. XXII, Autumn, pp. 54–68. Retrieved January 4, 2017, from http://www.dtic.mil/cgi-bin/GetTRDoc?AD=ADA528321.

[5] P2P Foundation Wiki (n.d.). "Chaordic Organizations – Characteristics." Retrieved January 5, 2017, from http://wiki.p2pfoundation.net/Chaordic_Organizations_-_Characteristics.

Chair in Strategy at the Center for Strategic & International Studies (CSIS) described it this way: "The world is suddenly far more complex, sometimes to the point where no effort in dealing with complex theory can really help."[6] Likewise, in business, it is difficult to cash in on unexpected problems (unless you are disaster consultant) and still manage and plan to a standardized process required by Wall Street. This is why it often seems that innovation efforts bounce behind a company like a dinghy tied to a yacht, and are not seriously pursued in a manner that might stimulate fundamental cultural change in the organization. The experience can be jarring.

Russell Raath from Kotter International describes innovation whiplash this way: "Management decides that they need to innovate. Individuals and teams form a working group, establish a charter, and set out to work on innovation improvement initiatives. The results are usually a rehash of something they are already doing, perhaps with some improvements on the margins, all complicated by Gantt charts, red-yellow-green dashboards and issue logs."[7] Or in Agile organizations, Kanban boards, roadmaps, user stories, the backlog, which all must be managed and kept up to date. With every foundering project, innovation teams can rarely afford to be honest about their failures and difficulties, because that certainly wouldn't be practical in terms of achieving corporate honorariums and spiffs. And even when the drive for innovation to increase profits is disappointing, chaos is still embraced.

11.2 The Hammer of Chaos

Since the mid-2010s, theories of controlled chaos have been upgraded to something akin to a spiritual practice, something that is an inspirational and powerful accelerant for business growth. In the face of the inability to contain chaos, business thinkers sought to unleash it. Today's business pundits now promote chaos less as something to be understood and molded than as a defining feature of an actively creative organization. To some, it isn't enough to redefine chaos; instead, chaos itself has become a blunt instrument that is perfectly shaped in weight and size to slam down on the heads of a team, if only to create urgency and stress that surreptitiously increases performance.

---

[6] Cordesman, Anthony H. (2015). "America's Failed Approach to Chaos Strategy." Center for Strategic & International Studies (CSIS). Retrieved January 5, 2017, from https://www.csis.org/analysis/america's-failed-approach-chaos-theory.

[7] Raath, Russell (2012). "When Innovation Fails." *Forbes*. Retrieved January 5, 2017, from http://www.forbes.com/sites/johnkotter/2012/06/28/the-leaders-path-to-innovation-less-control-more-chaos/#7f4227027daf.

The path to this thinking has been something of a broken dialectic, in which chaos has simply been reframed from something that is generated from within to something that comes from without. That chaos is after all, they say, not a side effect of the collaborative process, but a thing that, wielded properly, will drive teams to peak performance and unleash innovation. With breathy enthusiasm, professional texts name chaos as an imperative, a paradox to be unleashed. Authors Ori Brafman and Judah Pollack, in their book *The Chaos Imperative: How Chance and Disruption Increase Innovation Effectiveness and Success,* even draw on extreme examples such as the Black Plague in Europe, noting pragmatically that even in the face of the demise of an estimated 25 million people, the pandemic actually "turned out to be the crucible in which the modern Western world was forged . . . It may seem magical and bizarre that the Renaissance came about so quickly after the plague."[8] While this notion seems to take the concept of "seeing the bright side of things" to absurd levels, it defines a common and distinct attitude that binds the requirement for chaos to innovation.

11.2.1 Kick Out the Ladder

Corporate refugee-turned-graffiti-artist-turned-corporate-thought-leader Erik Wahl, in his book *Unthink: Rediscover Your Creative Genius,*[9] tells us that the future belongs to the provocateurs. As an example, he describes Soichiro Honda, the founder of the car company bearing his name, who observed how panic situations seemed to improve outcomes and bring about better results than ever intended. He came to the point where he would invoke stress by manufacturing a false catalyst in a practice he called "kick out the ladder." Wahl explains, "Just as a team neared completion on a project, he would create a crisis that seemed to threaten everything. He would then shorten the deadline. Each time he kicked the ladder out from under his people, they were forced to improvise." The active theory was that they worked harder and more ingeniously under the threat of failure.

---

[8] Walter, Ekaterina (2013). "The Chaos Imperative: How Provocation Breeds Innovation." *Forbes.* Retrieved January 5, 2017, from http://www.forbes.com/sites/ekaterinawalter/2013/11/05/the-chaos-imperative-how-provocation-breeds-innovation/.

[9] Wahl, Erik (2013). *Unthink: Rediscover Your Creative Genius.* Crown Business. Download available at https://s3.amazonaws.com/saveas36/unthink rediscover your creative genius erik wahl.pdf. p. 69.

In a nutshell, Honda and others who practice similar techniques coerce their teams into a state of overstimulation, where it is believed they will enter a state of heightened creativity that cannot be achieved through an act of individual will. That is, it just can't be mustered on demand. In 2010, Honda declared the months of October and November as "Kick out the Ladder Week," during which Honda inspired others use similar tactics in "setting ambitious goals and then refusing to settle for anything less than achieving them."[10]

Like Wahl, the management practice of "kick out the ladder" has many advocates, although, frankly, it sounds a bit perilous to employee mental and physical health if used as a regular methodology to inspire greatness. It's startling that some business leaders believe that great things can only be achieved at the expense of grinding down their employees in the service of ambition, because it so clearly avoids the cold business implications of stress-related lost productivity and increased employee absence and presenteeism, never mind the outlay of direct medical expenditures made by companies themselves. The American Psychological Association notes that a feeling of powerlessness (which is directly invoked by Honda's philosophy) is a ". . . is a universal cause of job stress. When you feel powerless, you're prey to depression's traveling companions, helplessness and hopelessness. You don't alter or avoid the situation because you feel nothing can be done."[11] While there may be advantages to performance by invoking critical stress for limited high value, a corporate culture of chronic depression and powerlessness hardly feels like a sustainable incubator within which creativity in the service of the company will thrive.

There is no doubt that the failure to innovate is a major reason for corporate loss in disrupting the marketplace, but surprisingly little been done to study the relationship between the push to innovate and employee happiness and well-being. Admittedly, where there is joy and satisfaction in being part of a breakthrough team, there is sometimes a price to be paid for the time and commitment demanded of company employees who contribute. But, from a holistic perspective, for every profit in dollars ratcheted up in getting to the market first with a new product, what is the cost for lower worker well-being and job satisfaction? It is a question shareholders and venture capitalists rarely ask, but the stress and anxiety of new work methods and processes may be either enriching or intensifying. It seems quite important, then, for any company to deeply consider the costs and benefits of their innovation strategy.

---

[10] Facebook (2010, October 17). "Dream the Impossible: 'Kick Out the Ladder' Week." Retrieved January 5, 2017, from https://www.facebook.com/notes/honda/dream-the-impossible-kick-out-the-ladder-week/163413083686769/.

[11] American Psychological Association (n.d.). "Stress in the Workplace." Retrieved January 5, 2017, from http://www.apa.org/helpcenter/workplace-stress.aspx.

At the end of the decades of "revolutionizing," it seems that many innovation strategies completely fulfill Einstein's definition of insanity: doing the same thing over and over and expecting a different result.[12] And that is why this book has focused entirely on how innovation can be sustainably accelerated yet maintain an internal equilibrium, as inspired by bioempathetic ideals and concepts for collaboration found in the principles of shared responsibility, decentralization, interdependence, and diversity. We don't have to conjure new recipes for innovation fairy dust, when the most successful doctrines for bringing meaning to inspiration are expressed all around us.

11.2.2 Arguing for the Innovation Mindset

In Chapter 1, it was offered that this book would not only raise the question of colliding traditions of property ownership and the use of incentives for efficiency to increase profitability, but suggest a new way of thinking about how to mitigate the stresses brought about by our current system of production and distribution—arguably, the foundations of which are being rocked by the exploding availability of information and knowledge in the connected world. The threat is real for any orthodox corporate entity that cannot face the fact that there is no need for many of the occupations of capitalist trade in a world in which we can simply take what we want. Furthermore, if we persist in our traditional thinking that we achieve power by hoarding information resources, our ability to rapidly innovate will diminish.

The entire first section of the book was dedicated to exploring the evidence for this viewpoint, discussing several perspectives and scrutinizing case studies and anecdotal evidence that might confirm or deny that *traditional business practices will never be effective in overcoming barriers to innovation, because these corporations are by nature focused on generating value by hiding information, data, and content at the cost of other forms of unguarded value.*

During this investigation, three hallmarks of an evolving open innovation ecosystem were identified: that abundance is paradoxical, that ideas and relationships are key enablers to innovation, and that incremental adaptation is a natural and valuable feature of the innovation process. In summary:

- **Abundance Is Paradoxical.** The challenging realm of future tech is described as a collapsing world of economic traditions that use property ownership and incentives for efficiency through technology to increase

---

[12] Einstein, Albert (n.d.). BrainyQuote.com, Xplore Inc. Accessed January 19, 2017, at https://www.brainyquote.com/quotes/quotes/a/alberteins133991.html.

profits. Open data, information, and content are a threat to the orthodox corporate entity.

> Capitalism thrives on the notion of scarcity; where there are digital assets, scarcity is not natural—it must be forced on the system.

While emerging technologies create massive opportunities, including for investors and companies that seek more adaptable forms of economic growth than currently available, value is held in inert dollars by traditions that require containment practices such as with patents or other closed systems. Open data, content, and information may indeed be the key to mass innovation for future technologies, although they bring difficult challenges to private-industry business models that depend on the established ideas of intellectual property. This, as any artist or author knows who has seen the royalty system fail miserably for them as copyright protection grows more Sisyphean by the day, new models for innovation must bring research and innovation into the light, where strategies for identifying problems, breaking them down into the right questions, directing resources in research and development, interpreting results, disseminating information, manufacturing and distributing products, and commercializing enterprises occur in an open environment.

There are profound and potentially significant benefits to applying open thinking and systems to our business in adopting a strategic philosophy toward accessible resources, be they information, data, or content, and the deployment of those in driving innovation.

- **Ideas and Relationships Matter Most.** Counting the number of books, consulting companies, TED Talks, and business and cultural philosophies that focus on it, innovation is an obsession, it's big, and it's glamourous. But, it's just a word. Many of us may experience awe when we see a first flash of inspiration move from whim to reality. But, how do we work to avoid inertia and adopt innovation-oriented processes not only for ourselves, but for our communities and companies, where so much raw creativity hopes to be translated into existence? Through our relationships.

  Traveling the road from insight to marketable innovation requires both the ability to affect rational progress and a culture of collaboration and patience (don't fall into the trap that patience is inefficient). But our first task is to give up buzzwords and avoid the kind of symbolic use of language that dresses up innovation as a sort of mystical path to credibility. Jargon has its place, but it can destroy precision and lock others out of the creative process—people who may not follow along, but who may have an invaluable perspective to lend to an idea. Furthermore, it is a poor reflection on a company to promote how "innovative and open" it is, yet demonstrate a lack of rigor for and understanding of the principles of openness that may provide the kind of acceleration that is required to move quickly and effectively in a world of specialty, where artificial intelligence, human genomic modification, and bioengineering have entered the mainstream culture.

If we want to authentically pursue innovation and open thinking in our work cultures, we need to recognize that concepts don't get the work done—whether it's finding a cure for cancer, colonizing Mars, cloning a pig, or finding a silver bullet to end anthropogenic climate warming. In our guts, we can understand the ideals implied, but they are ideals that require skills development, humility, and truth-telling. And in the age of Wikileaks, #fakenews, and even lawsuits against major companies that have held back information as proprietary that result in negative societal implications, "alternative truth" has become something of a blood sport. Open techniques are not always an easy option for those struggling to do new and creative things in our hierarchical ranks—but, collaborative and open innovation processes that lead to massive breakthrough innovation in future tech calls for messiness, a tolerance for failure, and often a ride on an emotional rollercoaster.

> Innovation teams that understand the fundamental linkages between ideas and relationships will create value networks that are measured by the creative interactions that generate new ideas and solve problems.

These relationships may always require some degree of reciprocity, even when the boundaries among team members are fuzzy and vague. It is a hallmark of open collaboration that social participation is integral to evolving imperfect ideas through testing and refinement.

- **Adaptation Is Natural.** Natural ecosystems provide powerful clues and models for understanding the sort of patience, invention, and collaborative thinking that is required to discover and design within the complex domains of future tech.

> Many inventors have a long history of adapting what is found in nature, and adapting open information, data, and content already serves as a key accelerant in the field of future tech, especially in working toward a sustainable future.

The tools already available, including design thinking, Agile, and peer production methods, are all well suited to this sphere because they make room for both human and human-machine collaboration.

Bioempathy, a softer form of biomimicry, reflects the inspiration found within the structural forms and biomechanical designs of nature. These inspirations help to develop techniques to put materials together and discover new, lighter, more efficient, and even just more beautiful materials. But as we garner more and more ability and insight into how animals, plants, and their ecosystems operate holistically, we also learn how systems are balanced in the natural environment; future tech researchers are finding ways to emulate entire physiological systems by developing a deeper understanding of the complex mechanisms that keep plants and animals alive and adapting in every stage of their lives, from the biochemical to the cellular level. This is a largely untapped reservoir of inspiration for the pursuit of future technologies.

11.3 Why OpenXFORM Matters

It is from these three foundational observations that OpenXFORM (a blending of the words Open and the engineering abbreviation for Transformation) was developed. The intent of the model design is to synthesize an approach to the process of innovation, inspired by natural systems and human-centric design processes. Thus, OpenXFORM describes how an open system of innovation can adapt to the unregulated world of information, data, and content; can decompose its own information to release to the open world; and can discover ways to find the points of synergy among the studied and tested methodologies that put human relationships first.

This approach was identified as a sufficient way to resolve the troubling ideas of profit and the perceived needs for corporations to hoard information for theoretical return or defense. Thus, the idea of a company as a "regulated ecosystem" models how a living (we called it *biotic*) company can benefit greatly by connecting to the opposing unregulated (*abiotic*) resources found in open information, data, and content. Not only can companies benefit from open thinking, collaboration, and innovation, any company may establish a firmer stand in delivering on their strategic goals—whether they are founded in new products or services or not—by focusing on their core strengths rather than pre-creating or re-creating the wheel. When it comes to innovation, the further we can balance our corporate ecosystems with open approaches by pushing into more creative relationships with partners and collaborators, the greater our potential returns.

11.3.1 A Performance Ecosystem

An approach to innovation that is described as an enriching relationship between regulated ecosystems (these are ecotones) encourages creativity and innovation and is recognized by creating new pathways to open sources of data, content, and information that help achieve and realize strategic goals that have previously been out of reach. Bioempathetic designs, especially from the organizational perspective, are an intriguing way for any motivated business entity to achieve these sought-after qualities. Yet, even if it makes good sense to mimic natural forms for innovative new functional designs, such as copying the shape of a whale fin for ergonomic advantage, taking natural systems too literally is counterproductive, especially when we want to transform the way we work to drive peak performance (as author Don S. Olson once noted, a plane doesn't need flapping wings to fly). The OpenXFORM ecosystem works to bridge the uncertain and difficult relationship between open resources and the private world of the innovating company entity.

Stigmergy, one of the most important collaboration principles discussed in Chapter 5, is derived from entomological concepts, which we explored within the context of the ant world. Capturing bioempathetic ideals for self-organization and decentralization, stigmergy defines a mechanism whereby *work done stimulates the work to be done,* and Ant Colony Optimization (ACO) mimics ant food-seeking behaviors for solving problems that involve finding the best way through a graph (represented mathematically as a series of nodes interconnected by vertices), including vehicle routing, scheduling problems, and even image processing. Further human social movements have been analyzed and new ones proposed, in which stigmergy is considered not only a defining characteristic, but a positive framework or set of practices through which to perform complicated, cooperative tasks.

> A powerful and convincing model of stigmergy is found within the open source movement. Often unconsciously applied, a stigmergic model of collaboration exists where the code base itself, rather than a centralized leader, stimulates the next right action of any agent in the project.

For corporations that worry about losing their competitive edge by giving data, information, and content away, it is worth considering that in natural systems, adaptation is a change to an organism that helps it survive in its environment. It is in the adaptation of those open resources that future tech companies are already beginning to realize their greatest value and profit. And it is why companies like Tesla have flung open the doors to their patented systems, recognizing that their job to win in the market is simply to make a more desirable electric vehicle. Similarly, decomposition plays a vital role in the cycle of any ecosystem, because, firstly, death and decay prevent resource scarcity; and secondly, it unleashes nutrients into the system that are crucial for new growth. Like chemical decomposition, information decomposition breaks down the components of a material corpus and dissolves its structural integrity. Chapter 5 provides an in-depth description of how the OpenXFORM ecosystem works to flexibly accommodate the uncertain and difficult relationships between abiotic resources and the biotic world of the innovating company entity. The points of connection between the two are symbiotic and generally described as the functions of adaptation and information decomposition.

11.3.2 Structure Is Not the Enemy

In Chapter 6, we discussed the morphology of the model, not just to exploit the bioempathetic perspective, but to explore how the system of OpenXFORM can thrive sustainably within an organization, and in some organizations even represent the whole. An explicit innovation process is required to treat organizational problems—in this case, how a breakthrough idea can be moved through a process that encourages innovative thinkers to test their assumptions, validate their hypotheses, and tune and tweak their ideas, not only to drive solutions for users but also to meet the strategic goals of their companies. The anatomy of innovation through OpenXFORM contains the process for moving ideas from a flight of fancy to an explicit concept that is ready to produce.

But explicit doesn't mean overbearing. Collaboration and innovation are not corporate departments (well, they are lots of places, but they aren't recommended here), and such rigid stances help us little in our efforts to revolutionize future technologies, not only for material success, but for the advancement of society in medicine, energy, artificial intelligence, robotics, nanotechnology, space exploration, and every aspect of our built and natural environments. Innovative models of design that are implemented for their external benefits, optics, measurability, or ease of communicating up the chain are insufficient. There is a reason that Apple and Google have always had relatively little to say about why, how, and when they innovate, because it is what they are always doing.

When one reads extensively about how a system of innovation was mandated and introduced under the auspices of change management, it is too often not a natural fit for the company culture and will stumble. When an innovation process relies on downward pressure and chaotic surprises, it becomes sour and short-lasting. Further, companies that want to drive innovation in an open world are well served to deeply consider that traditional systems of innovation and production that rely on fixed measures are broken. To improve requires stepping into the disorganized world of human relationships, and employing less rigid systems of motivation and patterns of communication and collaboration. At the very least, we must attempt to capture and amplify the new perspectives that successful innovation in the open world demands.

In the attempt to extract a meaningful bioempathetic approach from natural systems of adaptation to the process of innovation, it is worth remembering that the data, information, and content that live in the commons only become something of value when placed in the context of a unique idea. Otherwise, we are only staring at puddles of regurgitated fact, figures, and disembodied pieces of information that signify nothing. Data and evidence should not be confused with truth; there is nothing inherently valuable in a stream of numbers, nor does even a clever analysis make one complete in one's knowledge. Open data, information, and content become valuable only when they are given meaning within the boundaries of specific design goals.

Make them valuable.

Section Two

Review of Themes and Concepts

Chapter Seven: Setting Organizational Intention

Maintaining Forward Momentum

There are documented benefits to incrementalism, including improved efficiency, greater collaboration capabilities, and enhanced quality. However, serious questions remain about applying the principles of incrementalism as a corporate strategy toward improving the processes of innovation within the firm. Incrementalism plays a role in problem management, helping designers break down problems, and prevents overinvestment in the wrong solution. Chapter 7 discusses the sensitive organizational shifts required that help create a common framework for managing the innovation process, in alignment with operational and strategic goals. This is a challenge not only to the organization's structure, but also to its behavioral processes.

Key Concepts

- Incrementalism defined by small steps rather than giant leaps can be a strong option, providing flexibility and adaptability for fast-moving initiatives. Furthermore, simple and gradual changes serve to reduce risk, uncertainty, and internal conflict among collaborators.

- Incrementalism is a driving framework in today's organizations that show up in many ways—as gradualism, fractionalization, continuous improvement, "breaking it down," cherry-picking, and in formal production methodologies such as Agile. Fundamentally, it is the idea of crawl, walk, then run (CWR).
- With the Agile methodology perhaps being the most modern expression of incrementalism, users look for improved ability to execute, better quality, and greater efficiency. This form of iterative and incremental development (IID) can make the chaotic seem easier, keep everyone engaged and grounded, and still scale dramatically well and successfully in the realm of software development. Unfortunately, IID has also become the subject of misuse and abuse, as it is wielded as just another tool by poorly informed executives and managers.
- IID also represents a mindset for collaboration, which is goal-oriented; with it, contributors rationally benefit from work with others, because strong collaboration will inform their own private process of creativity, increase their skill and knowledge (and thus their marketability), or even enhance fun and work pleasure.

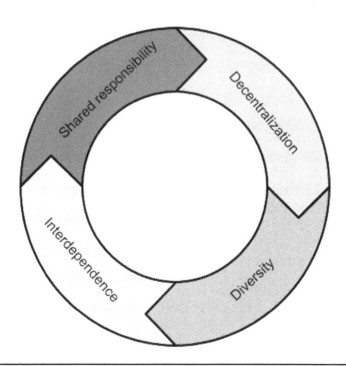

Figure 1 Exercising the living principles of OpenXFORM produces a natural efficiency.

- Economies of Flow is introduced as a way of encouraging streamlined collaboration among stakeholders that values a fluid process over the number and volume of interactions.
- Figure 7.4 in Chapter 7, shown here as Figure 1, describes the four principles of a living OpenXFORM ecosystem that are required to support an innovation process in all its stages. These stages are complementary and are linked with each other in a manner that defines how the acts of ideation, exploration, and transformation of a new concept may be scaled to production levels.

Chapter Eight: OpenXFORM:Ideate

Driving New Ideas Forward

The OpenXFORM model proposes complementary principles that help to shape innovation processes to drive new ideas that can be transformed to scale. This chapter focuses on the theory, motivations, and practices of *ideation*. Through examples and case studies, we explore the notion of collaborating openly to develop new innovations in the context of resistance to the corporate pressures to hold information tightly. Often, as organizations attempt to reorganize their innovation processes to be more entrepreneurial, they seek structural and sometimes physical solutions to motivate and empower. However, what is most useful in encouraging innovative imagination is a simple and uncomplicated approach, even when the social dynamics are challenging.

Key Concepts

- The model described as OpenXFORM is less an attempt to conjure up some newfangled process that requires a certification to manage, than an effort to disentangle and reconstruct what has emerged as conflated and confusing policies and approaches to organized ideation and development.
- Many of the identified methods for innovation already happen in so many ways, but often without a strategic directive except to "do something innovative." OpenXFORM explicitly identifies many of these methods.
- Translational research is an interdisciplinary approach to medical science that focuses on all sorts of knowledge—from clinical observations, to charts, to data and laboratory research—to accelerate approaches to enhancing human health. And it is an excellent demonstration of how new forms of collaboration and information sharing are changing something as complex as the medical industry.

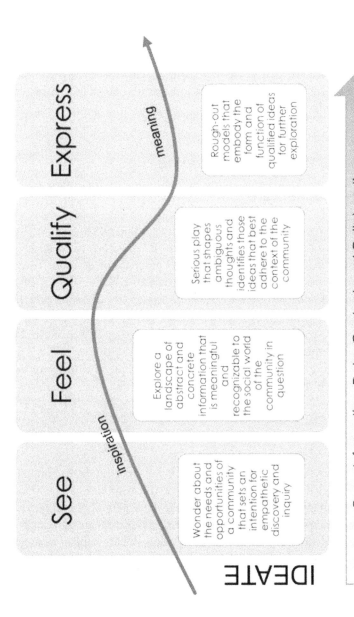

Figure 2 Climbing the ideation peak.

- *Meaning* (see Figure 2, Figure 8.2 in Chapter 8) in the ideation phase begins to emerge as we bring forth our organizational experiences, talents, skills, and endowments; the swathes of undistinguished bits of information and data that float around us as "problems" are brought down to earth in the compositions of our own innovative solutions. In some processes, this is the stage in which we "ideate," "brainstorm," or, simply, "design." Be warned, that falling from the cliffs of inspiration in an effort to find meaning can be deadly to a project.
- No matter the techniques deployed by the team or organization—it is key to remain human-centric. The idea of "feeling" the way through a problem is quite literally a way to maintain an awareness and discernment about the potential value of a solution. Some designers describe their need to maintain an emotional connection or even attempt to adopt the point of view of their focused user.
- Engineers, business stakeholders, and policy wonks may quickly feel lost in this process. Remember that the notion of "feeling" describes brainstorming techniques that help participants stay anchored in user needs. The goal is to provide a treatment that will benefit some person or improve a process—typically those that are causing disruption, strife, or a poor experience.

Chapter Nine: OpenXFORM:Explore

Exploring Our Assumptions

Building on the concepts in the previous chapter describing OpenXFORM: Ideate, this chapter examines the process of exploration named OpenXFORM: Explore. Focusing on theory, motivations, and the practices of exploration, real-world examples demonstrate how a structured approach to testing, assessing, and refining ideation prototypes challenge the assumptions bound up in our work with confirmable research outputs. These challenges are given not as an opportunity to defend our ideas, but to provide an ample chance to validate, improve, and refine our prototypes to effectively adhere to the demands of user value from the viewpoints of technical feasibility and business investment.

Key Concepts

- This is the time when an explorer's mindset becomes so important: trust the process to show a way forward, but don't insist that the team skip, run, or walk backwards on that road. The way the process is executed is less important than treatment of the issues.

- At this point in the process of innovation, it is invaluable to be proven wrong. This is the rare and valuable opportunity to meaningfully inform early ideas with the help of data and people. Remember that a "negative result" to a research question does not imply an exit from the innovation process, although it certainly could.
- Table 1 (Table 9.2 in Chapter 9) describes the domains of user testing and their linkage to the OpenXFORM:Explore facets represented as a forward-moving spiral toward concept refinement. The research goals defined are universal to every idea that has a goal of user adoption and utility, and that requires resources to develop, implement, and scale.

Table 1 The Domains of Assumption Testing

Domain	Facet	Research Goal
User Values	Test	Learn if the concept appeals to the customer. Is it desirable? What is its utility?
Technical Feasibility	Assess	Understand what it will take from a technology perspective to implement the concept. Is there existing technology to implement the concept?
Business Viability	Refine	Reveal how the concept fits into the business strategy. Is the idea aligned with the mission of the organization? How will it be funded and how is value returned to the organization?

- Figure 3 (Figure 9.2 in Chapter 9) renders the spiral of exploration, describing the facets of that process. This figure is a touchstone, showing how a prototype spirals forward outside the boundaries of time (there are no constraints on how long it takes to test an assumption), progressing and improving its demonstrated viability, to find its transformation as an innovative product or service.
- Our goal is to take stock of the assumptions built into our prototype, validate their fitness and utility, and accept or reject them in our final rendering. Every prototype is a testable model that will become more refined as more is learned about the aptness and workability of the concept. While prototypes are simple, they still must be concrete enough to spark conversation and interaction and to enable the collection of feedback to extract an improvement to the next instantiation of the concept in a new form.
- The willingness to pivot means that a company is open to reinventing itself based on new information or a disruptive innovation. If the validated and closely studied behavior discovered in the OpenXFORM:Explore phase tells us something new and important, then ignoring it because it doesn't fit

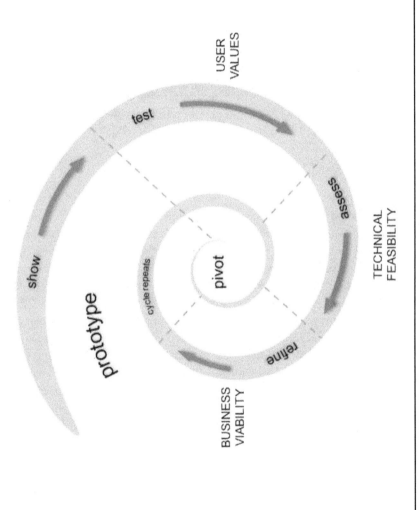

Figure 3 OpenXFORM: Explore challenges assumptions across the domains of user values.

the dominant storyline of the company means that growth opportunities (perhaps even risking corporate viability) will surely be missed. A pivot is a theoretical opportunity to consider these aspects of the refined prototype.

Chapter Ten: OpenXFORM:Transform

Achieving Readiness to Produce

Building on the concepts in the previous chapter describing OpenXFORM: Explore, this chapter discusses the phase of achieving development readiness through the process of *Transform*. These strategies reflect the challenges of the increased system uncertainties and increasingly rising decision stakes in the domain of advanced and future technology. Furthermore, we explore both the theoretical perspectives and the practical approaches to reducing risk.

Key Concepts

- OpenXFORM:Transform does not promote a specific production methodology; instead, it explores the issues related to vetting and specifying a refined and ready prototype that gives the development team its best chance of succeeding. This is accomplished through the production of artifacts that are sufficient to increase a high-quality outcome with a reasonably efficient process.
- Although prototypes are useful for the engineering team, managers, clients, and even venture capitalists, their value is too often overstretched by a misinterpretation of purpose. One of the reasons innovative projects fail is that prototypes are used as a proxy for requirements gathering.
- Corporations and companies must learn to abandon process fetishism, especially when that mentality impedes ideas and creativity from emerging under the pressure and force of proprietary rituals. Ironically, even the well-intended impulse to "loosen things up" can bring burdensome mandates, directives, and decrees meant to define what a more relaxed system ought to look like.
- Heavily systematized programs of innovation, often bolt-ons to existing organizational configurations, are described and compared to more innovative companies. Such firms tend to specifically attribute this readiness to a *non-systematized* sense of individual cross-pollination that is described as *interdisciplinary* design, and which is imbued with the idea that innovation is expansive and should be the constant focus of the work.

- The increasing rate of change in society creates massive uncertainty, often with very high stakes, and there is a marked loss of space and time to act with the kind of confidence that business, engineering, and science stakeholders often prefer. Furthermore, within the course of casting new rules, it is increasingly difficult to efficaciously resolve contradictory perspectives, especially with the impact of many viewpoints on the process. Even well-conceived innovative concepts may follow a winding path to market.
- Incremental production methodologies—properly implemented—provide a solid system of focused efficiencies. And while customer acceptance is considered a core tenet, when it comes to building a product, the time of addressing the question of "why" the product is right for the customer must be answered before production begins. This is true even when the development team finds that they must adapt and revise to bring the idea to life. In good practice, development methodologies prescribe "how" to build the product, represented by a concept prototype appropriate for all stakeholders involved.

Index